☆ LIFE SIGNS ☆

Julia and Derek Parker were both born in 1932 in the West Country of England. Derek Parker began his career as a journalist and in television, Julia as a design artist with a special talent for dance. In 1957 they were married, and two years later moved to London where they began to be interested in astrology. Julia took a diploma in Astrological Studies, while Derek wrote a book on the history of astrology. In 1971 they collaborated on *The Compleat Astrologer* which became a bestseller in several languages. Alongside her career as a teacher of art and ballet, Julia then became President of the Faculty of Astrological Studies, and took part in a series of television programmes for BBC South-West, called *Zodiac and Co.* Derek developed his talents in writing and introducing innumerable programmes on radio.

Both the Parkers make frequent appearances on radio and television on the subject of astrology, and lecture on various aspects of it world-wide. They are resident astrologers to *Woman* magazine and have written a large number of books, both individually and together.

LIFE SIGNS

An Astrological Guide To The Way You Live

Derek and Julia Parker

PIATKUS

For Cynthia and Brian

First published in Great Britain in 1986 by
Judy Piatkus (Publishers) Limited, London
This paperback edition first published in 1987
Reprinted 1989

British Library Cataloguing in Publication Data

Parker, Derek
Life signs: an astrological guide to
the way you live.
1. Astrology
I. Title II. Parker, Julia
133.5 BF1708.1

ISBN 0–86188–679–8

Designed by Paul Saunders
Illustrated by Rowan Clifford

Phototypeset in 11/12pt Linotron Sabon by
Phoenix Photosetting, Chatham
Printed and bound in Great Britain by
Mackays of Chatham PLC, Chatham, Kent

FOREWORD

This book takes a look at the Signs of the Zodiac. Everyone recognises their names—Aries, Taurus, Gemini, Cancer and the rest. Everyone knows whether they 'are' a Leo, a Virgoan, a Libran, a Scorpio, and so on, because their birthday is on a particular date: if you are born between November 23rd and December 21st, for instance, you are a Sagittarian. What this means is that when you were born, the Sun was passing through an area of the sky which, when astrology was born many thousands of years ago, was marked out by the constellation of Sagittarius.

However, astrology is more complicated than this. For instance, the Sun moves into and out of the signs at a slightly different time each year, and sometimes on different dates—which is why if you were born, say, on November 23rd, you may find yourself described in some sun-sign books as a Sagittarian, in others as a Scorpio. The only way to find out the truth is to look up a table of planetary positions—an 'ephemeris'—for the year of your birth.

But, you see, we are already in deep waters—on the edge of real, personal astrology, where what matters is not 'what sign you are', but a map showing the positions of all the planets in all the signs of the zodiac, not just for the day but for the very minute—and from the very place—of your birth. That is your real horoscope, which an astrologer will consult before giving you personal advice.

Among the people who criticise astrology, many ask, 'But how can you possibly divide the whole population of the world into twelve sections and say anything useful or truthful about them?' Of course, to some extent that is true—and yet, rather to the dismay of some professional astrologers, the statistical evidence which now appears to support some of the premises of astrology includes some which strongly suggests that the old sun-sign traditions are accurate. And it is these that we present in this book.

Many are extremely ancient, dating from even before the invention of writing, and the earliest horoscopes to come down to us enshrine some of them. The association between the signs and various parts of the body, for instance—from Aries, governing the head, to Pisces governing the feet—is first set down in a translation of an ancient Greek text, the *Liber Hermetis*, which appeared in Latin in the fifth century A.D. And the first attribution of certain gem-stones to the zodiacal signs is to be found in the Old Testament.

It was the great astronomer, geographer and astrologer Ptolemy who collected astrological lore together to form the earliest surviving textbook of astrology, his *Tetrabiblos*, which was written sometime between A.D. 161 and 139, and is still in print! In the course of it he attributed certain countries and cities to certain signs; recorded which signs were ascribed to which 'elements'; and made many other assertions which are still recognised today. Over the long period of history many other astrologers contributed other theories, from Thrasyllus (astrologer to the Emperor Tiberius) to Bardesanes (one of the earliest Christian astrologers) through to Queen Elizabeth I's astrologer John Dee, to William Lilly and his huge textbook *Christian Astrology* (1647) and the modern astrologers faced with the problem of bringing the more recently discovered planets within the discipline.

It is the age-old as well as the more modern astrological traditions on which we have relied in a book which we hope will be revealing and helpful, as well as fun—and astrology, now used so often as a tool by psychologists and counsellors, *should* be fun.

So look in the mirror, and see if you recognise yourselves—and your friends—in the astrological reflection we have placed there.

J.P D.P

★ ARIES ★

· MARCH 21 — APRIL 20 ·

☆ THE MYTH

The original winged Arien ram with its golden fleece was sent by Zeus to rescue the handsome Phrixus, about to be sacrificed to end a famine in Boeotia. Phrixus and his sister Helle flew away on the ram's back, but over the straits between Europe and Asia the girl lost her grip and fell into the sea (now the Hellespont). When they reached land, Phrixus sacrificed the ram to Zeus, and its much-sought golden fleece hung in the Temple at Colchis.

☆ THE SIGN

The *ruling planet* of Aries, with which it has a special relationship, is Mars; it is a *cardinal, masculine, fire* sign. *Positive traits* include passion and enthusiasm, optimism, decisivenes, enterprise, a straightforward approach, a love of freedom and a pioneering spirit; *negative traits* include selfishness, impulsiveness, impatience, aggression, argumentativeness, a quickness of temper, pugnaciousness.

Aries in a Nutshell There is a need to win, but an open mind and a straightforward approach to life based on living in the present.

☆ GENERAL CHARACTERISTICS

The very fact that theirs is the first sign of the zodiac seems to have infected Ariens with a deep-rooted psychological need to lead, to be a pioneer, and this will emerge, in one way or another, in all members of this lively, energetic and very positive zodiac group. Many Ariens will express it through sport, others will find inner satisfaction and a sense of achievement in their everyday lives through exploring new areas of work or relaxation. This can be a marvellously positive motivation, leading to feats of bravery and daring; but it needs careful control, for taken too far it can result not only in foolhardiness but also in ruthlessness and a tendency to put self before all else—which can be disastrous both in a career and in personal relationships. A tendency to be stubborn can be equally unfortunate, should it emerge. Determination is rarely lacking in an Arien, nor is the ability to make snap decisions (which are usually right). Superficial forgetfulness can be a plague.

Ariens like to be surrounded by plenty of action, and are not dismayed by a busy, noisy environment. Their high energy-level must find positive expression through physical activity and a rewarding sex-life. They can suffer from periods of restlessness, and this may become a serious problem if there is not sufficient activity to fill the day.

The Arien sense of humour is great fun, and often spiced with satire and a sense of the absurd; their laughter is infectious, and will cheer everyone within range.

Looking at *Ariens in Fiction*, an example of the straightforward, simple Arien performing daring feats for the sheer joy of them is Tarzan of the Apes; much more complicated is Shakespeare's Kate, from *The Taming of the Shrew*—matched by an equally Arien lover in Petruchio.

Almost naively straightforward, physically active, ready to brave any danger to rescue his girl from the clutches of villainy, Tarzan fits the Arien bill perfectly. He obviously controls his temper, channelling his energy into action. Shakespeare's Kate can be active, too, hitting out at her love; but it is her temper that makes her famous throughout Padua as 'Kate the Curst'. In Petruchio she meets a fellow-Arien, and which one subdues the other is probably a matter of supporting planets!

The Arien's *greatest asset* is an uncomplicated approach to life. Their *greatest need* is adventure, and *greatest problem* coping with frustration. The *greatest vulnerability* is in accepting others at their face value. *The Arien Motto*—first come, first served!

☆ Friendship, love and marriage

Friendship Enthusiasm will dominate in Arien friendship. Members of this zodiac group are always very eager for their friends to take an active interest in whatever interests *them*. Fortunately, their enthusiasm is infectious, and the other person will in no way be bored when Aries talks on and on about any pet subject. Ariens should realise, however, that they can be extremely selfish where their friends are concerned—for instance, making arrangements to meet, and then failing to keep the appointment because somebody or something more interesting has turned up. The Arien conscience will, however, be troublesome, and the offended party will probably receive a bunch of flowers or at the very least a handsome apology. Ariens do not find it difficult to make new friends, for they are extremely good at accepting

others at their face value. Acquaintances soon turn into firm friends, and the Arien will be forthcoming and welcoming, suggesting all sorts of interesting activities for mutual enjoyment. They are also always pleased to introduce their friends to each other, and are capable of spending freely when it comes to entertaining them—and incidentally themselves. When differences occur, it is as well for the Arien to speak out and make the situation quite clear, resolving the problem as quickly as possible. When dealing with others, it should be remembered that not everyone reacts as quickly and simply; so patience is a very necessary characteristic, and should be cultivated.

Love Ariens rank high in the zodiac when it comes to falling in love at first sight. This can be exciting, and may work out very well—decisiveness is often based on sound intuition—but there can also be disaster if the Arien leaps in too quickly, and is committed to a long-term relationship before all the factors have been worked out. That Ariens are passionate is well known, and their need for a positive, adventurous and fulfilled sex-life is certainly well above average. They do not find it difficult to win the heart of anyone to whom they are attracted, and make excellent, if demanding lovers. Those in a relationship with an Arien will experience a lively and enjoyable partnership, but will probably have to cope with a certain amount of selfishness. Provided the individual can be made aware of this tendency, it is not too difficult to control it, and it will certainly be outweighed by natural exuberance, fun and a positive outlook, and the desire for uninhibited pleasure and happiness. Young Ariens should consider their partners' creature comforts: sometimes in their enthusiasm for sex they fail to be very good at scene-setting. This may not seem very important to an individual Arien, but it certainly can be to his or her partner! Their own strong sex-drive should ideally be matched by an equal delight in sensuality, and indeed by a willingness to experiment so that the sexual side of the relationship is continually reinvigorated and doesn't become boring.

Marriage The major danger for any Arien in a long-term relationship—or for that matter, the danger for anyone married to an Arien—lies in his or her inherent selfishness. This can emerge in different ways: in putting their own hobbies or spare-time activities not only before those of their partner, but before their family life; in setting themselves so firmly on achieving success in their career that their partner feels neglected and left out—or indeed in their sexual life: the partner who turns over and goes to sleep leaving a lover unsatisfied

could just be an Arien! Restlessness is perhaps the next danger: a joint interest with the partner can help to counter it. On the positive side, Ariens are marvellously practical, so there will be no difficulty when home improvement is needed: knocking down walls, building a garage, mending kitchen equipment . . . this is all meat and drink to an Arien, ideal for using energy. Even if individual Ariens are wealthy and could well afford to employ others to do such work for them, they will probably prefer to do it themselves. It is vital for an Arien to remember that marriage is a partnership, and that there will be periods when we need to give extra support to our partners, matched by others when we need their strength to comfort and support us. Keeping the balance is essential, and when it is achieved, sharing one's life with someone of this zodiac sign can be a very fulfilling and rewarding experience.

☆ PARENT AND CHILD

Sun-sign Ariens make wonderfully enthusiastic parents; they want to get maximum pleasure from the company of their children, and will be very eager to watch them develop their own interests both at school and at home. It is good for both parents and children to have a very full schedule of activity during leisure hours; in that way the Arien enthusiasm and need to get as much as possible out of life will be passed on to the children, who, irrespective of their sun-sign, will profit by it.

The Arien parent must be aware of the possibility that because he or she gets completely involved in a particular activity or enthusiasm, the children are left to their own devices, and may end up just watching television. So activities should be shared as much as possible.

Ariens like to keep abreast of the times, so a generation gap will not usually be a problem. Shortness of temper and impatience, however, may make for trouble, especially in early years. Fortunately an Arien's anger is soon over, and there is little chance of resentment leading to a poisonous atmosphere.

It is always a good thing for Arien parents to become involved in parent-teacher organisations; they are good achievers themselves, and their enthusiasm for any project they undertake inspires other, less assertive types.

It would be silly for the parents of a small Arien to expect a great deal of peace and quiet while he or she is growing up. Arien children are full of energy, and will probably become mobile at an early age! Because the sign is slightly accident-prone, their attempts to do so may

lead to a good number of bruises, especially on the head. Tomboyishness and a need for adventure will emerge at an early age, and many parents will rightly feel some concern when young Ariens start climbing trees or exploring the neighbouring countryside in what seems a rather too adventurous spirit. Their lively enthusiasm and spirited approach to life should always be encouraged, and they must be allowed to express these wonderful qualities in their own individual way. Arien children hate to be bored, and at school will often be remarkably lazy during lessons which hold no interest for them. Parents should be on the look-out for this tendency; it can lead to a build-up of unexpressed nervous and intellectual energy and frustration.

While these children need plenty of freedom of expression, they also need discipline if they are to become pleasant and well-adjusted people. It is not difficult to correct them, for they have a strong desire to please, and verbal persuasion should be enough.

When there are other children in the family, parents should be on the look-out for Arien selfishness, and encourage the small Arien to take an active part in caring for younger brothers and sisters and helping them to develop; older siblings should be persuaded to include him or her in their games—the competitive, adventurous spirit deserves encouragement.

☆ CAREER AND SPARE-TIME

The strong, positive Arien characteristics need plenty of expression at work, and the need for challenge combined with the strong Arien pioneering spirit, properly controlled, can be enormously beneficial both to the working Arien and to colleagues and employers.

Whatever the chosen field of work, it is important that it should be interesting and demanding, and never boring—Ariens do not respond at all well to a predictable routine. Generally speaking, Ariens like working in a busy, noisy atmosphere surrounded by lively, competitive colleagues. It is equally vital that proper use is made of the high Arien energy-level, and there must be a good incentive to work and the opportunity for enthusiasm. It is important, too, that in one way or another the Arien is given the chance to 'win', which is done partly by the capacity to cope very well with difficult conditions—whether physical (the kind of pressure undergone by working in tough physical situations, perhaps in professional sport) or mental (in competitive selling, for instance). Aries likes to surmount difficulties, and will posi-

tively enjoy overcoming them. Battles are there to be won, and once victorious the Arien will feel fulfilled and satisfied, and ready to move on to the next field of endeavour.

Sun-sign Ariens are of course found in all professions, and it is difficult to generalise; but careers which seem particularly suitable to characteristic Ariens are to be found in engineering, in its various forms, and in any work involving metals (from foundry work to artistic metal-working). Fire-fighting and work on the railways also spring to mind, as does the manufacture of weapons and work for the trade unions. Motor mechanics and the motor industry would also provide rewarding opportunities. Many Ariens qualify as psychologists and psychiatrists, and the dental professions are often well represented. If a young Arien wishes to express his or her competitive spirit in professional sport, every encouragement should be given. Ariens need to push boundaries outwards, in whatever work they do—whether this means physical exploration or research within their own discipline. If the possibility of this kind of expansion of interest doesn't occur during working hours, it may be possible during leisure time—perhaps by seeking out an adventurous hobby.

Patience is something that does not come naturally to most Ariens, so it is important for them gradually to develop it. But at the same time they should not allow themselves to become frustrated or bored by their choice of spare-time interests: for instance, the creative Arien will want to get colourful, impressive and quick results from any hobby, and it will be as well if, for instance, they are interested in painting, for them to buy large tubes of paint and big brushes, and work in a broad, free style. The same can be said about most kinds of craft-work—fine, delicate sewing or lace-making is unlikely to appeal. When an Arien has musical talent, it will not usually be related to anything as discreet as the violin or the harpsichord!—don't be surprised if your Arien friend expresses a desire to play the drums or the trombone.

Ariens of both sexes can get a great deal of satisfaction and pleasure from car maintenance—and they don't usually mind getting their hands dirty. Any work involving metal will be fun for them. It is very important that they have some physically demanding hobby, perhaps related to sport—not only for health reasons, but for psychological ones too. The Arien will benefit perhaps more than most zodiac types from games which promote a team-spirit and camaraderie among participants. Football, hockey, wrestling and boxing are all good outlets for abundant Arien physical energy. This acts as a good counter to their possible selfish traits.

Speed is of considerable importance to characteristic Ariens: they

are often fast car drivers, and it will be as well for them to develop driving skills.

☆ FINANCE AND INVESTMENT

Ariens are enterprising people, there is no doubt about that. They enjoy making money, and equally enjoy spending it—and they like to see quick results from their efforts. Many of them have more than one source of income: for instance, spending the working day concentrating on their careers, and then developing a profitable hobby or interest.

This works very well in many cases, but there are one or two points to consider. In the first case, they will want a quick return for their skills, and sometimes will not give themselves enough time to develop their technique sufficiently highly to be really professionally competitive. This of course is likely to cause impatience. Then there is their tendency to get easily bored with their second-string business projects. If they can learn to persevere and to enjoy the steady growth of a project, while at the same time maintaining their enthusiasm, it is often the case that the original spare-time interest grows in profitability until they can give up their perhaps duller mainstream work, and turn all their attention to the more interesting and now financially viable project.

When it comes to the investment of capital, Ariens must be careful not to get too easily carried away by the prospect of quick returns. Fortunately, many sun-sign Ariens allow a naturally good business sense to govern their natural wish to make money quickly; every Arien should try to make this a rule, for it is by far the best way of achieving the financial stability which will permit a fulfilling and rewarding lifestyle.

Because of the natural sense of immediacy which is an integral part of the Arien personality, there is often a tendency to buy impulsively. This may not be as disastrous for Ariens as for members of some other signs, for by nature snap decisions are for them usually the right ones. Nevertheless, the temptation is always present, and is something which needs control, especially when it comes to buying things for the home, or when the Arien is visiting a favourite store or shopping centre at sale time.

Once started on a regular savings scheme, Arien enthusiasm will see to it that the process is continued: there will be great satisfaction in seeing the figures mount up in the periodical statements of account.

This is one way in which to begin to develop a keen business sense, and encourage the awareness of financial security. It is obviously a good thing to encourage the young Arien to open a savings account as early as possible.

As to the type of investment best for an Arien, engineering and motor industry shares will interest and should be profitable; so will shares in insurance and fire prevention, in mining or the steel industry. The symbol of Aries—the ram—suggests perhaps an interest in sheep-farming. But in all these fields, current financial and investment trends must be the first consideration.

☆ HEALTH AND EXERCISE

Exuberance and the inner need to expend a lot of physical energy are perhaps the bases for the good health of the typical Arien. Provided the individual maintains a balance in his or her physical life, there should be no ongoing problem. But when an Arien stagnates physically, or is prevented from moving about freely and energetically, things can go wrong.

The Arien body area is the head, and it is true to say that Ariens either suffer from continual and inexplicable headaches, or get none at all! If the former is the case, it is always as well to have the kidneys checked, for slight kidney disorders can be the source. Needless to say, a headache as the result of a night out is another matter! There is another kind of headache which can be the result of too much concentration on an apparently insoluble problem; this will only go away when decisions have been made and the problem itself has been solved. So here, too, are areas to be watched. Knocks, bruises and cuts to the head are common with Ariens, and not only in children, though perhaps it is they who suffer most. If they fall, from a wall or from trees (they love to climb) the chances are that their heads will suffer. Milk teeth are often lost at an early age as the result of this kind of accident.

The glands attributed to Aries are the subrenals, which in emergency or at times of anger pump adrenalin into the blood-stream. This tends to exacerbate Arien impetuosity.

Because the Arien is usually in a hurry, and sometimes rather careless, general accident-proneness is always a problem. Mars, the planet which rules the sign, can aggravate the situation, and our Arien friends are often seen with bandaged fingers because of some too-hasty careless encounter with a sharp knife or tool or a hot saucepan. It is very difficult for them to overcome this tendency to haste, and while in

theory they know they should (for instance) wear an oven-glove or protective clothing, in their enthusiasm for everything they do, they tend to forget to do so.

It cannot be too strongly stressed that if they are to remain healthy, Ariens need to maintain a balanced lifestyle. This is not always easy. They may happily embark on a really progressive series of physical exercises, or an admirable exercise regime, and then find that their enthusiasm for their work or for some spare-time activity gets in the way, so that there is no time left for exercise. Their hatred for a predictable routine is no help, either, for exercise generally needs a sustained pattern; regular exercise both of mind and body really is necessary for them, however, and they should make a strong effort to get it.

But what sort of exercise? Sport is important to Ariens. Ideally, it should be competitive sport, giving the Arien the opportunity to go out and win—something that both sexes are happy to set their heart on, and which gives psychological satisfaction as well as providing physical exercise. By nature, they are assertive and to some extent aggressive (not necessarily in an unpleasant way); many enjoy boxing, wrestling, and the eastern martial arts. Fencing, though perhaps rather too subtle and delicate an art for many Ariens, will also be worth consideration.

If an Arien joins a health club, he or she will certainly enjoy lively aerobics dance classes—some young Ariens will make good break-dancers. Working on sophisticated machines to build strength and muscle-power will be popular. This can be done at home, of course; but there will be a stronger motivation at a club, where there is competition from other members.

All this can be very expensive; anyone who finds heavy membership fees inconvenient can get a lot of pleasure from being inventive—much good exercise can be obtained with the help of a simple skipping-rope or broomstick, or a good book on isometrics; a steady run at the end of the day will also be beneficial—preferably with a group of like-minded friends to compete with.

In view of Arien enthusiasm, it should be stressed that those of this sign must use common sense and modify their exercise programme according to their age and degree of fitness: check with the doctor before starting any exercise regime, especially if you have not exercised for some years, or are starting a new and demanding programme.

☆ Home environment

Ariens are on the whole very physical by nature, and this informs their

attitude towards the home. They will be very happy to spend a lot of time on home improvements—re-planning the garden, the kitchen, the bedroom, and then Doing It Themselves. This is a real pleasure for them: it is not so much the end product that is of prime importance, nor are Ariens specially keen to steal a march on the neighbours or show off the results of their efforts. Fun and enthusiasm provide their motivations, and everyone eventually benefits—even if their partners have to encourage them to make a neat job of clearing away the mess, or even to finish off a project once the main bulk of the work has been done.

Few Ariens would want to look out of the window at a halcyon country scene in which the chief excitement is provided by a munching cow. They will much prefer a busy street, or at the least a view in which things are continually changing. They need to feel free to come and go as they please—they have no time to spare for gossipy neighbours, nor will they want to be hemmed in by heavy traffic jams right outside their garages. Most Arien homes have a warm, colourful glow, and it is quite common to find the Aries colour (red) a part of the decoration scheme. Interestingly, while Ariens love to be warm, they quickly feel any stuffiness in the atmosphere, and rush to open a window or get to some fresh air. Although they like to have new things, they do not bend over backwards to be fashionable where furnishing or decor are concerned, and the Arien living-room may be furnished with strong, perhaps fairly conventional styles of furniture. They dislike fussy design, and will often go for bold, plain areas of colour, or perhaps stripes, checks or plaids. Many Ariens will find shades of pale blue pleasing and relaxing when it comes to furniture. (This relates to their opposite or polar sign in the zodiac, Libra—pale blue is one Libran colour.) Wrought iron-work is often popular, either as a form of decoration indoors, or perhaps in the garden in the shape of furniture or barbecue equipment—for many Ariens, whatever climate they live in (hope springs eternal!) take great delight in owning or building a barbecue.

Sometimes we find a collection of weapons or swords in the Arien home—or perhaps prints of battle scenes or historic military uniforms—and the members of the sign can be nostalgic about old ships or steam engines! Ariens will be attracted to sensual paintings of nudes (perhaps by Rubens or Renoir), and the blazing colour of Van Gogh's sunflowers or the vitality of Toulouse-Lautrec's paintings of Paris café life may also find a place on an Arien's walls.

Ariens give special thought to their bedrooms: they are members of a highly-sexed sign, and like to make love in a conducive atmosphere.

A focal point of any Arien home will probably be their workshop. To the outsider it will look chaotic—a clutter of tools, pieces of material, or whatever. Aries will know where everything is, and will get great pleasure out of showing others the products of his or her labours.

Moving into the dining-room, we will find the same clear-cut use of colour in the china on the table—it might well be decorated with a simple flower such as a poppy, or with a simple, strong geometric design. The glass-ware is likely to be fairly thick and chunky, and the cutlery too will be functional, perhaps because Ariens tend to damage things rather easily because of their tendency to haste. The food we can expect to eat will probably be fairly traditional, and while many Ariens love highly-spiced and exotic food, this does not always agree with them, and they have probably learned the hard way to cut down on such extravagances! Main dishes such as roast lamb or a good beef casserole, perhaps followed by some fairly exotic sweet combining a hot sauce and a cold ice-cream could well be popular.

Many Ariens enjoy making beer at home, and their choice of wine veers towards the unpretentious rather than the 'fine'.

As the conversation gets going it may be necessary for the Arien host to turn down the level of the background music, which will probably be distinctive, rather brassy and perhaps a mite too powerful, whatever the individual musical taste.

☆ Image

Clothes The overall Arien image is a casual one—though within the individual's generation not particularly unconventional. As Ariens make material progress and find that more money is available for clothes, while they will always wear comfortable garments they have a happy knack of always looking extremely stylish and very becoming. Perhaps the most important thing is that once they have decided what to wear and have put it on, they can forget about it until they have to take it off again! It is essential that their ease of movement should be unimpaired: women, for instance, would probably hate wearing a tight skirt which has to be manoeuvred into the right position as they sit down. If they are well organised they will try to buy things that go well together, so that should they get up rather later than they ought, they will have no problem when it comes to quickly choosing a matching outfit. Although they are not particularly nostalgic, many Ariens have a favourite garment in their wardrobe with which they are loath

to part, and it has been known, when the time comes to throw out a much-loved item of dress, for them to go to a dressmaker or tailor and to get it copied as accurately as possible. Sometimes their friends tease them about this.

In general, Arien robustness and good health are reflected in their image—track-suits and bright sweaters, often in shades of red or blue, are extremely popular, as, rather surprisingly, is a slightly nautical look: many have a brass-buttoned blazer in their wardrobe. The overall appearance is clear and crisp; Ariens do not, generally speaking, like fussy details or frills, and there is nothing muzzy about the general impression of their image. Very often, irrespective of fashion, hats are popular; these are usually worn in a jokey kind of way—a cap or beret, for instance, worn at a jaunty angle—or if the Arien male wants to look mysterious or perhaps seductive, he may go for a Humphrey Bogart-type trilby, while the women of the sign in a similar mood can make a big impression with a 'vamp' look – but will probably have their tongues firmly in their cheeks when they wear it.

On formal occasions, the Aries male will look particularly dashing in evening dress, and might perhaps sport a cummerbund, although he will not risk breaking too many rules on such occasions. The women will be at their best in simple styles which, even on the most formal occasions, allow them freedom of movement, comfort and a relaxed elegance. Soft evening blouses in *crêpe-de-chine*, with perhaps a matching skirt, are likely to appeal, with a contrasting colour in the choice of accessories making for interest. Shoes must be comfortable, since no Arien wants to stagger around in agony for the sake of appearance; they should spend as much as they can on ensuring the comfort of their feet! Hairstyles will be uncomplicated and easy to manage.

Extenders Ariens love good quality belts and handbags; a shiny patent leather surface is sometimes popular, and when it comes into fashion they will seize the opportunity of investing, for instance, in red patent accessories. The women need fairly large handbags which will add to the generally bold impression of their image. They like quick results, and so will choose a camera which is easy to use and foolproof, and may well wear it around their necks ready for that unexpected interesting shot. Instamatics might also be popular. The traditional metal of the sign is iron—not an easy one to wear as jewellery; but as compensation many may invest in some heavy gold or silver chains, or perhaps, for a joke, in semi-military accessories. They fare very well when it comes to precious stones—the stone of the sign is the

diamond! Many young Ariens will be especially attracted to large junk-jewellery—vividly-coloured brooches of cut-glass, and a splash of diamante will do much for them during the winter season. As to choice of perfume, Ariens will definitely *not* want an over-sweet one, or one which is at all cloying or heavy. Something that will do much to enhance the sporty outdoor image will be preferred, and it is also important for them to use a perfume that will have an immediate impact on other people and one that they themselves can enjoy. Having said that, Ariens will be happy with a perfume that has sexy undertones: this will be fun for them, and should certainly have the desired effect on the opposite sex.

Cars The Arien car will be as sporty as the individual can afford or get away with within his or her lifestyle! Ariens will tend to hang on to an old banger, perhaps because they do not worry too much about the noise it makes! In any case many of them will get considerable pleasure from finding out where the noise comes from, and repairing the fault! Others will enjoy rushing about on a motor-cycle, but in prosperity will prefer the most expensive sports model.

☆ TRAVEL

Ariens' need for adventure and excitement will continually pull them towards extensive travel, if they can afford it. At a very early age they may try to persuade their parents that they are sensible enough, as well as independent enough, to make long journeys. They don't mind sleeping rough, and will happily go off to the ends of the earth with as few possessions as possible—a sleeping-bag, a change of clothes, and remarkably little money.

Many Ariens make their way around in the world in this way, and of course learn a great deal from the experience. Their tendency to take risks sometimes gets the better of them, and they can suffer in a somewhat above-average way as a result of carelessness. Wallets stuffed into the back pockets of jeans will get stolen; minor forgetfulness can be fatal when they leave their passports or valuable articles on the beach or in restaurants. The sooner they consciously develop special care, particularly when moving around the world, the better. They will not enjoy the frustration and annoyance of having to hang about in police-stations or consulates, or trying to contact credit card companies by phone—and in fact are temperamentally less able to cope with this kind of situation than people of most other signs. They have absolutely no fear of venturing into difficult or unknown territory, even into politically hostile countries.

The ideal holiday must have an element of excitement and adventure about it, and even the tired Aries career person, while obviously requiring some pure relaxation, will want to combine lying on the beach with something of stimulating interest. Many will want to follow up their much-loved hobbies and interests while travelling abroad, and will strive to find out what is going on locally. This will add a whole new dimension both to the holiday itself and, when the Arien returns home, to the Arien's attitude to his or her hobby.

The resort itself should have plenty of facilities for sport, so that the Arien can experiment with wind-surfing or para-gliding—or any of the more conventional sports such as golf or tennis. They are prepared to spend a lot of money on holiday, if they have it, but on the other hand lack of funds will not keep them from the travel experience. In every Arien there is an area of the personality that enjoys taking risks, and when on holiday they will particularly enjoy the occasional visit to the local casino. This may or may not be beneficial—but it will certainly be fun.

Many Ariens tan extremely well, and enjoy sunshine, but their native impetuosity can show itself in a desire to rush straight on to the beach and stay there until their skin turns crisp and falls off; they should take the advice on the back of every pack of sun-cream, and take their sunbathing gradually. If they are in a humid climate, they could suffer more than most people, for it will drain even their abundant energy. Somewhere hot, with minimal humidity, will be most acceptable. On the other hand very cold climates, where the air is crisp and clear, will be enjoyable; so the excitement of winter sports will prove yet another potentially happy adventure.

Ariens are not too concerned about how they actually travel: making their own way overland is an adventure they often enjoy—in fact the individual will make sure he or she does so; but in general it is fair to say that the sooner they arrive, the better!—air travel will probably appeal most strongly. Many young Ariens will enjoy adventure holidays: pony trekking, mountaineering, canoeing and sailing all have a specially strong appeal for them, and parents should not be too concerned when their youngsters set off on what may seem to them to be a perilous journey. Provided there is good organisation and supervision, the youngsters will develop strength of character, and mature as a result of the experience.

There is a tendency for older Ariens sometimes to overdo things when they go on holiday, partly because their enthusiasm gets the

better of them. This is something to watch. It is vital to take with them their favourite headache remedy—the rigours of the journey followed by the excitements of the holiday and perhaps unusual food, are very likely to bring on a flurry of typical Arien headaches!

☆ PRESENTS TO PLEASE

Because Ariens are generous and enthusiastic, they do not find it at all difficult to be enthusiastic and happy at the receipt of a present—especially if it is given at a time other than the birthday, anniversary or Christmas. They will be excited to receive any gift, and no matter how attractive the wrapping paper, it will be soon torn away to reveal whatever is inside. Here is the kind of person who finds it very difficult to put presents aside until Christmas morning, or even until after guests have gone, before opening them.

Giving an Arien a present, the first thing to consider is his or her special interest: a set of tools for a particular purpose, the latest book on a favourite handicraft or study, will certainly be well received, and immediately put to good use. Women appreciate colourful headscarves and hairdressing products. Men enjoy receiving a chunky sweater or colourful tee-shirt. If your special Arien has a collection of anything valuable, and you can afford to add to it, that will be popular; but if they have not yet got round to forming one, try to think of something that perhaps might lead to the start of one.

The Arien taste in books will involve novels with an element of high adventure—historical, contemporary, perhaps science fiction. Any book given to an Arien should be one which makes the reader desperately want to turn the page to discover what happens next. This is especially true for Ariens who because of individual circumstances are not leading the kind of adventurous life they would really like.

But what about presents for the Arien home? Some oven-mitts would be useful, remembering their tendency to burn their hands in the kitchen. A pure linen table-cloth in a plain, bright primary colour is also a good idea, and to round off a dinner-party a box of crystallised ginger might be just the thing.

The young Arien child will adore a toy fire-engine! For older ones, equal pleasure will come from a book of stories about mythological Greek heros and heroines. You might give the young Arien girl a boy-doll—a bit of a tomboy herself, she will like that. The Arien boy might appreciate a present connected with the home—perhaps a cookery book; this will give him the opportunity to think a little more than he

★ FAVOURITE TO ARIES ★

★ **ARIES COUNTRIES**—include Denmark, Germany, England, France, Poland and Syria.

★ **ARIES CITIES**—include Leicester and Birmingham (U.K.), Capua, Crakow, Florence, Marseilles, Naples, Verona, Utrecht, Brunswick.

★ **TREES**—Arien trees include the holly, some kinds of fir, and all thorn-bearing trees or bushes.

★ **FLOWERS AND HERBS**—Arien flowers and herbs include arnica, bayberry, briony, broom, cayenne pepper, furze, geranium, honeysuckle, hops, juniper, leeks, mustard, nettles, onions, peppermint, rhubarb, thistle, tobacco and witch-hazel.

★ **FOODSTUFFS**—Onions and leeks are the most prominent foods rules by Aries, though most strong-tasting foods fall under the sign. The hop, and therefore beer, is also ruled by the sign. Tomatoes contain a high quantity of potassium phosphate, the lack of which causes depression, somewhat an Arien trait.

★ **CELL SALTS**—Kali Phos. and Nat. Phos.

★ **STONE**—Diamond; it is sometimes suggested that the amythyst and bloodstone fall under the sign.

★ **COLOUR**—Red.

otherwise might about other members of the family, and what might give them pleasure.

Any sports equipment for young Ariens of any age will always be welcomed and well-used.

Remember that Ariens are almost invariably more romantic than they care to admit, and that any present which has colour and charm will be appreciated—especially if it is a little unusual.

★ TAURUS ★

· APRIL 21 — MAY 21 ·

☆ THE MYTH

Falling in love with the beautiful Europa, Zeus turned himself into a handsome snow-white bull, a single lock of black hair between his small, gem-like horns. Beguiled by his beauty, Europa played with the gentle beast, garlanded him with flowers, and finally climbed upon his shoulders—whereupon he leaped into the sea and swam to the island of Crete, where he became an eagle and ravished her. He later placed the image of a bull in the heavens to commemorate his adventure.

☆ THE SIGN

The *ruling planet* of Taurus, with which it has a special relationship, is Venus; it is a *fixed, feminine, earth* sign. *Positive traits* include reliability, patience, practicality, endurance, affection, trustworthiness, determination and strength of will; *negative traits* include possessiveness, inflexibility, stubborness, self-indulgence and the tendency to bore.

Taurus in a Nutshell Taureans have a need for security and a very practical approach to life, but their tendency to stick to routine can be unnecessarily restrictive.

☆ GENERAL CHARACTERISTICS

It is absolutely essential for every Taurean to feel secure both materially and emotionally. Taureans need to live their lives in the knowledge that a regular pay-cheque will be paid into their bank, and that there is a tender, loving partner who will respond well to their high level of warm affection and emotion. It is, however, all too often the case that a Taurean becomes very set in his or her ways, so that when unexpected or exciting developments occur they find it difficult to accept them or to adjust to a new routine or lifestyle.

Taureans are extremely stable, and their reliability, when running their day-to-day lives, but also in dealing with others, is well-known. They are the salt of the earth, in the very best sense of the words; but irrespective of other planetary influences working for them as individuals, we seldom find a sun-sign Taurean who does not have a possessive streak somewhere in his or her psychological make-up, and this can often mar their relationship with their partners. It also relates to their attitude to money, sometimes to the point that they have an entirely materialistic outlook.

Taurean patience is something to be envied—as is their charm. Some people find this zodiac group slightly dull and even boring, and the truth is that they can be slow to react in conversation—but what they say is almost always interesting, shrewd and incisive. They aren't usually in the foreground when it comes to taking risks.

Looking at *Taureans in Fiction*, we find Shakespeare's Falstaff at the top of the list—genial, with enormous charm, but lazy, stubborn and extremely possessive of his conquests. Billy Bunter, the plump English schoolboy, greedy and determined that nobody else should get their hands on his 'tuck', is another obvious Taurean, making the most even of his negligible personal charm! Sarah, the maid who became a star of music-hall in the TV series *Upstairs, Downstairs*, had a more genuine charm, and also the musical ability which often occurs in members of this sun-sign. Dickens' Mr Pickwick liked good living, was rather fond of routine, and was extremely possessive of his friends.

The Taureans' *greatest asset* is charm. Their *greatest need* is for money, and their *greatest problem* is not having enough of it! Their *greatest vulnerability* is self-indulgence. *The Taurean Motto*—What's yours is mine; what's mine's my own!

☆ Friendship, Love and Marriage

Friendship There is much to be said in favour of having a Taurean friend, partly because they instinctively know how to live—enjoyment comes naturally to them—and also because in times of stress they always provide a good, strong shoulder to cry on. A Taurean friend is a friend for life. You will immediately notice their legendary reliability—if they say they will meet you at a certain time and place, they will certainly be there. You will have many an enjoyable and luxurious outing with them: their *bonhomie* is infectious, and they will know all the best places for eating and enjoyment. But their possessiveness can emerge to strain even the firmest friendship. Break a regular routine with Taurus because you want to meet someone else, even of the same sex, and they will be most upset, sometimes to the point of expressing jealousy or perhaps resentfulness—they will see your action as a break of trust or confidence. Taureans are good listeners when one is in trouble—they are sympathetic and extremely

kind. Taurus' friends should gently coax them into developing new interests; they are often too fond of what is well-tried and familiar. They can get so bogged down in routine that life is drearier for them than they realise, and certainly drearier than it need be. When Taureans say 'I'm fed-up!'—as they do from time to time—they are in need of greater excitement. But in a strange way they are often reluctant to seek it: encourage them to do so.

Love When it comes to love, the Taurean has two things very much in his or her favour—one is incredible charm, and the other good looks (Taurus has the reputation of being the best-looking of all the twelve signs). These elements will obviously strike their potential lovers most vividly at the outset of a romance. The next thing in their favour is their ability to get a very great deal out of life, and their love of luxury, good food and wines—of everything that makes life agreeable and worth living. They will spend a great deal of hard-earned money on such pleasures, so generally speaking their lovers really have a wonderful time—both in and out of bed—for the Taurean expression of love and sex is as delightful and rewarding as their sensual and luxurious lifestyle. From all this it can be guessed that they make marvellous lovers—second to none, in many respects. But once a relationship has been established, Taurean possessiveness all too readily emerges, and in spite of all the fun, good sex and good living, this can come between lovers, and often creates a claustrophobic atmosphere which few partners will find it easy to tolerate. Should such circumstances occur, it is essential for the Taurus' lover to explain the difficulty quite clearly and forcibly, so that the couple can come to terms with the problem as soon as possible, and find their way around it.

Marriage Everything that has already been said about Taurus in love applies in marriage, and even more heavily emphasised. Many Taureans really blossom after the ceremony, however, for they have now achieved emotional security, which is as important to them as material security. Right from the start, however, it is advisable for the partner to make it quite clear that he or she needs a certain amount of personal freedom of expression—to continue, for instance, to take an interest in matters (perhaps hobbies) which occupied them before marriage. The partner should also be on the look-out for the Taurean tendency to become over-involved in making money (so that they can enjoy a good standard of living with and for the family), and try to see that this is not self-defeating, coming between them and the enjoyment of real companionship. Taurus is also a sign noted for its conventional

outlook, and it is very important that the balance within the partnership is quite clear—who is going to do what, for instance. Otherwise difficulties can arise, especially perhaps in the climate of women's rights, for the Taurean man can still cling to the opinion that the woman's place is in the home! A wife with a career, on the other hand, contributes to the family income, and this has its own appeal for a Taurean husband! Excellent taste and a love of quality inform the Taurean lifestyle, and will do much to impress friends and colleagues invited into the home of a half-Taurean couple!

☆ Parent and child

The Taurean parent will work extremely hard to ensure that the offspring are well provided for and able to take advantage of opportunities the parents may have lacked. Taurus' child will early be taught the difference between right and wrong and will behave beautifully at all times—or else! Taureans are sticklers for discipline, sometimes perhaps going a little too far in insisting on it. If a strict line seems necessary, they should make quite sure that they explain in detail the reasoning behind the discipline. Because they tend to be strong, silent types—men and women of few words—they tend occasionally to fail to do this. Rather differently, there is a tendency for them to over-indulge their children as they over-indulge themselves. Their children will be the first to be able to show off the latest bicycle, to have the most expensive music lessons, to sign on for elaborate school holidays. However, because Taureans are clever with money—there is nothing they like more than to see mounting figures on a bank statement—they will also encourage their children to save pocket-money for any luxuries they may want.

On the whole, Taureans make very good parents, but when their children reach the teens they may well seem stubbornly stick-in-the-mud, so that there can be a considerable generation gap, and all the problems that that brings.

The Taurean child will be patient and very good-natured. As babies, they are usually contented, and from a very early age we often find them smiling happily at us for no particular reason. They will positively gorge themselves on food from the breast to the hamburger; because of their healthy appetites they may tend to become rather chubby even as active toddlers. It is, alas, all too easy for the parents of child Taureans to win them over with a little discreet—or even indiscreet—bribery involving sweets and cookies.

Taurean children are well-organised and extremely methodical. Because they are so charming, they are usually extremely popular with their teachers. It is very important both for parents and teachers to remember that a Taurean child should never in any way be rushed. They must be allowed to take their time when it comes to practicalities such as getting up and making ready for school, and they must also be allowed to develop at their own pace, intellectually. Don't expect to be able to dragoon young Taurus into rising meteorically from the bottom to the top of the class—their minds don't work in that way. What can be expected is steady progress, from term to term. It is also essential that parents watch out for any possible laziness; their children's charm can easily be used to get them out of doing anything they think will involve too much hard work, or which is remotely distasteful to them.

☆ CAREER AND SPARE-TIME

It is already apparent that security is something which is of prime importance to the Taurean—so many of them will get great satisfaction at all levels of their personality when working for a large organisation—a bank or multi-national company, perhaps. They make excellent stock-brokers, and their natural flair for making money can be put to good use as a mainstream career, provided they have a sneaking regard for adventure and at least a marginal liking for risk-taking. They may have to acquire this.

They cope very well with careers which impose a predictable routine—they don't in the least mind facing a lifetime of catching the 7.23 every morning to the city, and the 5.49 every evening back to the suburbs. Once they know the structure of a business, and have discovered how to raise the necessary finance, they are very good at building up their own firm, though they are often at their best in partnership with someone whose temperament is more assertive, and who is willing to cope with marketing, or anything requiring a more outgoing personality.

Taureans make wonderful beauticians, and enjoy working in the luxury trades. Many Taurean women make their mark in the fashion industry; working in a big store is something they find really rewarding. Architecture, town and country planning and accountancy also attract many Taureans; so does farming and agriculture. There is plenty of scope for the creative Taurean, for their natural patience brings them naturally to craft-work, while this is also one of the most musical of the signs, and many become professional musicians—particularly, perhaps, singers.

Sometimes their need for security persuades Taureans to let good opportunities slip; this can be related to a certain fear of the unknown and the unfamiliar. They should be aware of this, for their tendency to cling to the routine they know and love, to dislike change, can cramp their style and indeed inhibit their material progress. Most Taureans find it difficult to be really adventurous. It would be silly to suggest that they should wind themselves up and take wild risks, but on the other hand they should try to keep an open mind when good opportunities present themselves, especially if they are working for a company and a rival firm comes up with a potentially excellent and exciting offer. They should have the self-confidence to explore every interesting possibility. Flexibility in their relationship with colleagues is something they really should develop; they tend to know they are right, to close their minds firmly, and to be bloodyminded enough to make difficulties for themselves; a gentler, more open-minded attitude is far more desirable and suitable, complementing their natural charm and keenness to work hard for their own good and that of their firm.

Because Taureans are extemely patient, they tend to enjoy hobbies which demand a great deal of that admirable quality: many will spend long, happy hours working meticulously on a piece of embroidery or craft-work, or perhaps making some intricate model requiring skill and delicacy of approach. Although the average Taurean is physically somewhat heavy, they so appreciate fine and delicate things that they will want to create them, and are often very dextrous in the use of their hands.

A wonderful spare-time occupation for Taureans is membership of a choir or perhaps an amateur operatic society. They make excellent potters, too, and sculptors, and any work that involves the use of natural materials will be almost a 'must', in one form or another. Here we also have the gardeners and horticulturists of the zodiac; they will adore growing beautiful flowers, since the aesthetic satisfaction plus the psychological rewards of working close to the earth are considerable. Many enjoy making wine, as well as drinking it, and if there is an interest in cooking, the average Taurean will be particularly good at cakes and rich desserts. This can of course make for additional difficulties as far as their figures are concerned!

Taureans involved in sport will get most pleasure out of heavy team games when they are young, and more relaxing contests, such as bowls, when they are more advanced in years.

☆ FINANCE AND INVESTMENT

The old proverb about teaching your grandmother to suck eggs has a relevance where Taurus is concerned; of all signs, Taureans know precisely where they are going and what to do when they get there, especially when it comes to financial affairs.

It is fair to say that even the most financially aware Taurean will agree they get the greatest satisfaction from a secure and steady growth of capital. They are unlikely to go for any get-rich-quick scheme, for loss of financial security would be psychologically damaging and a blow to their self-confidence, as well as their capital. The young Taurean investor will do well to find a savings scheme geared to a large insurance company or a building society, rather than buying a portfolio of varied stock, or even making a unit trust investment. The whole spectrum of savings and investment can in itself become an interesting hobby, and that is fine.

On the other hand, any extra cash that is made is there to be enjoyed, so perhaps when the individual gets to buying blocks of shares, he or she might like to consider investing in the hotel or restaurant business—at least partly because of the possibility of discounts when the respective establishments are patronised! Investments in agriculture, cereals and fertilizers should turn out well, and the acquisition of land and property is perhaps best of all for the astute Taurean who wants to enjoy a comfortable lifestyle together with increasing collateral.

As a general rule, the better-established the company or organisation, the more secure Taureans will feel about investing in it. Common sense will stand them in excellent stead, and their slow, careful approach to money matters will also help them to avoid silly and expensive mistakes.

Sometimes the Taurean attaches far too much importance to his or her possessions, which all goes back to an inherent need for security. Having said that, it is as well for them to be aware of the fact that these are not the only things in life, and that human relationships and self-expression are more important. If money is spent in great quantities on the home and its contents, it may be that other areas and considerations are getting a little weighed down by materialism. To counter this tendency, and to fulfil both needs, the Taurean might start a collection of truly beautiful objects such as small pieces of sculpture or perhaps paintings; in this way art and beauty can be combined with financial security and the individual will get aesthetic pleasure and some additional security as well.

☆ HEALTH AND EXERCISE

Because of their slow metabolism, most Taureans tend to move slowly and deliberately, and partly as a result of this have a considerable tendency to put on weight; it is often extremely difficult for them to slim. One heavy meal or even a single rich dessert, and the scales are once more unbalanced. When on a strict diet, they can be dissatisfied with the rate of their progress; but there are times when they must simply blame themselves—they cannot resist just one more piece of cake.

The Taurean body area is the neck and throat. If they start a cold, it almost invariably begins with a sore throat or perhaps loss of voice—a positive nightmare for Taurean singers. The Taurean gland is the thyroid, which controls the rate and consumption of the heart and body tissues as a whole; it is sometimes the case that its malfunction is the root cause of a weight problem, and if they begin to feel specially lazy and 'heavy' Taureans might begin to suspect this. However, they should not fall on it as an excuse not to watch their diet—after all, they are basically very disciplined people in other areas of their lives, so why can't they be as disciplined when it comes to cutting down on the calorie intake?

To live a really healthy life, the Taurean should keep a balanced diet and a steady exercise pattern; this may seem obvious, but it is something that many of them seem to find particularly difficult, and if this is the case they really should turn their minds to it if they are not to feel lethargic and unable to cope efficiently with life. One of the best things they can do for their general well-being is to try to increase their metabolism, for Taurean careers are often sedentary, and as they progress at work the time spent sitting behind an office desk is increased. (Incidentally, they also find themselves, on many week-days, enjoying extremely rich business lunches in the best restaurants.) Taurean women with their love of beauty and natural grace of movement have excellent potential for dancing, and the strict regime of a dance class should provide a satisfying way of achieving a slimmer figure. However, it is fair to say that if they have not danced before (and assuming they are fit enough to exercise regularly) it would be as well for them to start with a slow stretching dance class rather than suddenly frightening their system by leaping into something as dangerously energetic as aerobics. An appeal to the Taurean sense of beauty will generally succeed in getting them to start a work-out of some kind; our awareness of their good looks will appeal to their vanity, and if we add that they can easily lose these if they don't start taking care of their bodies when they are young, they will be on their

way to the gym before even reaching for a second helping of toast.

At the gym, they will probably get above-average benefit from the exercise machines available; this form of exercise will appeal to them because they can work at their own steady pace, and will be able to build up their muscular strength in just the right way and to just the right level for their body framework.

In order to avoid flab, exercise and a reasonable diet are paramount; but Taureans will get special pleasure from regular massage, which will add to their awareness of their physical condition. Saunas will be specially beneficial, for they help to expel toxicity from the system, and as Taureans are great gourmets and enthusiastic imbibers, this will help ease any negative results.

It is as well for them to acquire a taste for fresh fruit and vegetables. Most Taureans realise that their enjoyment of rich food is not kind to their liver or kidneys, and the acquisition of a palate for sweet eating-apples, honey and, of course, healthy fibre could prove particularly beneficial. These shouldn't be too hard to accept as alternatives to Black Forest *gâteau*.

A useful additive to the diet could well be brewers' yeast, which is extremely beneficial to the thyroid gland (which Taureans may find troublesome).

☆ HOME ENVIRONMENT

For the typical Taurean, the homes should be as big, beautiful and comfortable as possible! He or she will be making a very definite statement this way. Even if the owner is not especially well off, the home will ideally appear permanent and secure, giving the impression that its inhabitants are comfortably placed. The Taurean will certainly spend as much as can be afforded on the home, and the overall 'feel' will be solid, and attractive if quite conventional in furnishing and decoration.

Greatest satisfaction will come from a house with a garden, ideally in the country. But forced to live in town (and many Taureans follow professions which make this necessary) they will opt for living in a pleasantly leafy suburb, not too far from a railway station. If they have to live right in a city centre, they will at least aim to have a small back-yard or patio, a balcony crowded with plants, or even a set of window-boxes in which they can grow a few beautiful flowers.

The ideal Taurean house will be detached, in its own grounds, and steeped in tradition. The elegance of Georgian architecture springs to mind; or even the Tudor style of building—genuine or reproduction. But a garden will be very important, and the Taurean will spend many happy hours in it.

Indoors, Taurean colours—the colours of Venus—are likely to predominate: soft blues and pinks, with a certain amount of gentle green. It is almost certain that these colours will find their way into the individual's scheme of decoration. As the Taurean loves to grow beautiful flowers, so we find them in large arrangements in the house itself, and, needless to say, not only will the flowers be beautifully arranged, but they will also chime in very harmoniously with the overall scheme of decoration. Taureans love pretty, charming things, and this may lead to a certain winsomeness—but there will be no lack of attractive and comfortable cushions to soften even the most luxuriously upholstered sofa or armchair, and curtains and pelmets (perhaps of rich or floral fabrics) will often be decorated with deep frills.

A Taurean collection will have an eye to permanence, so if the individual is wealthy we could see some miniature bronzes or statues. Large floral paintings, perhaps of the Dutch school, will also be in evidence; but in contrast we may find reproductions of paintings from Picasso's pink and blue periods.

Generally speaking, Taureans enjoy a rich and fulfilling sex-life; couple this with the love of sensual enjoyment, and there is usually a spectacularly attractive and welcoming bedroom. Everything about it will be geared to relaxed love-making and deep, refreshing sleep. The lighting will be warm but not dim, and the bed-covers are sure to create a superbly seductive atmosphere. The Taurean woman's dressing-table will not lack lavish pots of beauty cream, quality skin-food and other cosmetics.

Taureans, with their love of good food, like to furnish their dining-rooms with real distinction. In many respects, this is the focal point of the home! The chairs will probably be heavy. The table-setting, while conventional, will be charming, and the china and glass even if a little on the solid side will nevertheless be elegant and traditional. We can expect to handle some fine cut-glass, and our Taurean host or hostess will probably have acquired some impressive glasses or goblets in which to serve the carefully-chosen wines. The china will probably have a floral design; don't be surprised if it involves roses! Expect the menu to be traditional: a large roast joint would be an obvious choice, as would *tournedos Rossini*. The dessert will more than likely be extremely rich, and probably contain a lot of chocolate and/or cream. Taureans are adept at matching wines to food, and because they enjoy entertaining they will no doubt spend quite a lot on them. Taureans,

being sympathetic to music, may dislike the idea of using it to provide a background for talk; but whatever their individual tastes, Taureans represent quality.

☆ IMAGE

Clothes On the whole, Taureans present a conventional image of themselves to the world—that is, according to their respective generation. They will spend a lot of money on their clothes, partly because of their psychological need for valuable possessions; so at one end of the scale we find the city gent with his impeccable three-piece suit from an up-market tailor, and at the other end the young man at a pop concert maybe dressed in jeans, but jeans with an extremely expensive label.

Tending to be conventional, Taureans sometimes fail to move with the times, with the result that if they are not careful their image can be slightly 'dated'. They look their best in well-cut but not too tightly-fitting clothes. Both sexes often sport the colours of their sign somewhere about them—the men, for instance, will enjoy wearing pastel-coloured shirts and ties, and when floral prints are in fashion, will take the opportunity of having at least two shirts or ties with such designs. Hard, primary colours are not always becoming to a Taurean; when the individual gets even remotely flustered or angry he or she tends to suffer from blotches of colour on the face and neck, which is accentuated if he or she is wearing bright red, for instance. However, once the Taurean has resolved the emotional problem, the blotches soon disappear. Irrespective of fashion, women will also wear floral prints, and perhaps the biggest fashion clue to a Taurean woman is a frilly blouse with a floppy bow-tie at the neck! Scarves and cravats are especially popular! Many women have a collection of expensive squares—but also enjoy wearing long scarves of fine, pure silk or perhaps georgette. All this may relate to a basic instinct to protect the vulnerable Taurean throat.

Sometimes a tendency to fussiness can mar the overall effect. Very bold designs such as plaids and large checks should also be avoided, unless the Taurean is especially slim and at least of average height—not always the case with this sun-sign. On the whole, soft fabrics are very popular; remembering the Taurean liking for comfort, it seems hard to believe that any member of this sign would be at his or her best in a harsh material which does not mould itself easily.

Taurean hair styles are usually abundant and lustrous, and very often, as with the bull symbolising their sign, we find it growing in attractive curls rather low on the forehead—equally true for men as for women. Here is another clue for sun-sign spotters.

When the Taurus woman has to wear a hat, she will probably spend a great deal of money on it, and it will be extremely pretty. But she should be a little careful, for she may tend to diminish the overall effect of her outfit by choosing an overwhelmingly large hat with one huge flower too many.

Extenders The accessories with which Taureans have most fun are handbags, briefcases and luggage. The woman's handbag must be of above average size to accommodate her abundant make-up kit, her wallet full of credit cards, and other necessities. The business person's briefcase will be impressively grand, and again fairly large. Like the handbag, it will be of good quality, and conventionally classical design.

When it comes to jewellery the women have a good opportunity to draw attention to their neck by choosing attractive choker necklaces—pearls especially spring to mind. Though these are not traditionally related to Taurus, they are popular (one thinks of the legend of Venus rising from the sea on an oyster-shell—Venus is Taurus' ruling planet!). Pearls with a pinkish hue will be especially attractive.

Both men and women enjoy scents, tending to wear those with strong floral fragrances. They should perhaps be a little careful that their choice is not too sickly-sweet, and should always ask friends and lovers for their reaction—which may be rather unexpected.

Shoes may be slightly on the heavy side, but perhaps this is necessary, as the Taurean tends to stomp around in a plodding sort of way. As far as choice of belts, sun-glasses and other accessories is concerned, quality and a certain prettiness dominate; at the same time, Taureans will not be any more experimental than in any other thing they wear.

Cars The young Taurean who has just passed the driving test will look for a very solid car, however old. They will feel secure behind the wheel if they know that their car is really well-built—they won't want grandeur at the expense of solidity. As they grow older, they will choose vehicles with a soft, comfortable ride, and will probably be disinclined to change their car annually—it will be not only a status symbol, but a family friend. We find the same need for reliability and solidity in other forms of transport too—especially motor-cycles.

☆ TRAVEL

While Taureans get a great deal of pleasure from time spent away from homes, they tolerate travel as a means to an end rather than enjoying it for its own sake. Many feel positively insecure in an aeroplane; they will have to psyche themselves up for the flight, probably making for the airport bar and the duty-free shop as soon as they have checked in. As they get older and more prosperous, they will probably consider flying Club or first-class, in the interests of easing the rigours and general discomfort of the journey by allowing themselves more seating space and a better in-flight menu!

Taureans will plan their trips well in advance, and budget almost obsessively for holidays. They tend to return annually to the same resort, as they know what to expect there; the uncertainty of arriving in unfamiliar places is not for them, if it can be avoided. When young Taureans plan an extended journey abroad, they too will be methodical about it, making firm financial arrangements, and carefully plotting their itinerary—arranging for instance to have the facility to pick up money at points along the way rather than carrying bundles of travellers' cheques. They will be especially considerate about giving the older generation some idea of where they will be at any particular time.

Taureans may be unadventurous in their travelling habits, but when booking an hotel will make quite sure that it has plenty to offer, especially where good, comfortable bars and restaurants are concerned. If they are staying for a week or two at one resort, they will do well to enquire about other facilities, too—is there a good golf-course, for instance? Or maybe a salmon stream? Most important for the women, is there a beauty salon on the premises? Especially in a foreign country where language is a barrier, Taureans may not be too keen to venture out into the town to find a hairdresser and explain exactly what is wanted.

The Taurean will be keen to look at beautiful scenery and architecture, but will probably do so from the comfort of a luxurious air-conditioned tourist bus, taking excursions rather than risking the vagaries of local transport. Many will enjoy hiring cars, but should make quite sure that they have excellent and very detailed maps of the area they wish to explore.

The ideal Taurean holiday will be spent somewhere where there are more than adequate facilities for relaxation, away from the rigours of career and day-to-day work; but it will also be important that the chosen resort has beautiful places of interest to visit. Taureans will expect to spend money on all this, but at the same time they will see to it that they get good value. As to temperature, a hot, humid climate may not be very easy for them to cope with, for they tend to get easily over-heated, and humidity could make them feel more languid than usual.

Holidaying Taurean children will be very keen to try local ice-creams and confectionery; they will also want to collect souvenirs of their visit, and should be encouraged to do so, for in that way parents can try to mould individual good taste. Here is a chance for young Taurus to learn the difference between trash and beautiful things of good design and quality, often available from local craftspeople—and as inexpensive as the rubbish. Certainly young Taureans will start the holiday with a good supply of local currency; they will be keen to go to the bank and change their pocket money into dollars, pesetas, or whatever, keenly assessing the rate of exchange and examining the new notes and coins with real interest.

If there is some useful advice for travelling Taureans, it is that they should watch carefully the amount of luggage they take. They will want to take a lot of things while travelling, and should perhaps be prepared to cope with a very full car boot, or the expense of excess baggage! They may care to invest in very lightweight travel-irons and hair-dryers, and perhaps syphon off small quantities of favourite beauty products into convenient plastic containers.

☆ PRESENTS TO PLEASE

Taurean charm will certainly blossom when we present them with even a small gift—whether it is a tiny spray of flowers or an endowment policy which will give them security in their old age. Smiles and abundant thanks will be the immediate response.

However, we should nevertheless be careful in our choice of gift: far better to give a Taurean something small but of real quality than something flashy which may fall to pieces within the first week. A piece of hand-made pottery, easy on the eye and not too unconventional in design, will be a lasting source of pleasure, and if it is large enough to be filled with beautiful flowers, so much the better. It is worth considering, too, the Taurean taste for music: a record or tape would be extremely popular, even if the individual already has that particular piece, recorded by someone else—studying the difference between the two will be fascinating for them. Needless to say, if your Taurean is a

★ FAVOURITE TO TAURUS ★

★ **TAURUS COUNTRIES**—include Ireland, Cyprus, Iran, Switzerland, the Greek islands, Parma, Capri, Ischia.

★ **TAUREAN CITIES**—include Eastbourne, Hastings, Lucerne, Leipzig, Mantua, Palermo, Dublin, St Louis.

★ **TREES**—Taurean trees include ash, cyprus, the vine, almond, fig, apple and pear.

★ **FLOWERS AND HERBS**—Taurean flowers and herbs include alder, artichoke, asparagus, beans, brambles, cloves, columbine, daisy, elder, foxglove, marshmallow, mint, poppy, primula, rose, sorrel, violet.

★ **FOODSTUFFS**—Cereals, particularly wheat, are ruled by Taurus; so are berries, apples, pears and grapes; spices generally also fall under the sign.

★ **CELL SALTS**—Nat. Sulph, and Calc. Sulph.

★ **STONE**—Emerald, moss-agate.

★ **COLOUR**—Pale blue, pink and green.

singer, some music would be highly acceptable, to suit the individual's taste.

If you are thinking of a bunch of flowers, choose some which are either rather large and long-lasting (crysanthemums, for instance), or sweet-smelling (such as garden roses or carnations). A bottle of choice wine or a box of hand-made chocolates will be rapturously received.

As to reading, the male Taurean will probably enjoy adventures in the world of big business and high finance; the women tend to spend many a long, happy hour in the company of a romance. Both will also like their reading to have a reasonable level of spicy, sexy action.

A present for a Taurean moving into a new home would ideally be something for the garden—a blossoming cherry tree, for instance, or some other long-lasting, slow-growing shrub. Spring-flowering bulbs, too, will be welcome. If there is no garden consider something of copper—a little jug or saucepan, or something decorative for the table.

If you want to give your Taurean nephew or niece a practical present, a brightly-coloured muffler in soft wool will be welcome—young children do not usually like pastel shades. Some kind of toy which will encourage them to build—bricks, or a Lego set, will be fine. They will probably already have a moneybox—but Monopoly will set them on the right Taurean path to financial dexterity!

In general, veer towards convention and practical design when choosing presents for Taureans of any age, always making sure that your gift is pleasant to handle and easy to look at.

★ GEMINI ★

· MAY 22 — JUNE 21 ·

☆ THE MYTH

The original Geminian twins were the Olympic champions Castor and Pollux, the first a soldier and horse-trainer, the second the best boxer of his day. When Castor was killed, Pollux prayed to Zeus that he should not outlive his brother, and indeed declined immortality for himself unless they could share it. As a reward for brotherly love, Zeus allowed them to spend their days alternately in the upper air, and in the underworld, and set their images among the stars as the Dioscuri, or Heavenly Twins.

☆ THE SIGN

The *ruling planet* of Gemini, with which it has a special relationship, is Mercury; it is a *mutable, masculine, air* sign. *Positive traits* include adaptability, versatility, spontaneity, wit and logic, scepticism, continual activity, duality and communicativeness; *negative traits* are superficiality, restlessness, inquisitiveness, changeability, a tendency to gossip, inconsistency, cunning.

Gemini in a Nutshell There is a need for a pacey lifestyle including great variety and stimulating continual mental activity.

☆ GENERAL CHARACTERISTICS

Geminian duality will be expressed in most spheres of the individual's life. There is a need for involvement in many, varied activities, and even on the rare occasions when we find a Geminian specialist, he or she will continually explore the possibility of branching out and seizing new opportunities within the narrower sphere of interests. Many Geminians will have more than one job, and will often make an important change or two within a career. On a day-to-day level it is usual for this zodiac type to read more than one book at a time, or to cope simultaneously with at least two or three household tasks. The main reason for this, consciously or not, is to ward off the possibility of boredom, which is a real Geminian nightmare.

Geminians enjoy an extremely lively lifestyle; but they have a tendency to live on their nerves, which can sometimes lead to a build-up of strain and tension. It is important that they are aware that this can happen to them. They have excellent minds, and are very positive and logical in outlook. If they do not get enough intellectual stimulation there is a tendency for this excellent potential to work negatively, and such traits as cunning, deceit and even fraud can emerge.

There is a great measure of scepticism in every member of this lively zodiac group. Generally speaking, this is a very healthy element, but sometimes it can lead to mistrust. Restlessness too can get out of hand.

Looking at *Geminis in Fiction*, we find Mercutio in Shakespeare's *Romeo and Juliet* witty, quickwitted and never still: 'a gentleman that loves to hear himself talk, and will speak more in a minute than he will stand to in a month.' Notice, by the way, that the name alludes to the sign's ruling planet. In Dickens' *Oliver Twist* Fagin seizes on the Geminian talents of the Artful Dodger, whose sleight of hand and quickness are turned to crime; and Christopher Isherwood in *Goodbye to Berlin* (filmed as *Cabaret*) depicts Sally Bowles as sharp, full of native wit, promiscuous if not amoral, resilient and talkative.

The Geminian's *greatest asset* is the ability to communicate. Their *greatest need* is variety, and *greatest problem* a fear of boredom. The *greatest vulnerability* is in their superficiality. The *Geminian Motto*—variety is the spice of life.

☆ FRIENDSHIP, LOVE AND MARRIAGE

Friendship Those of us fortunate enough to have Geminian friends will never be bored in their company: they are full of surprises, enjoy entertaining, and are always eager for new experiences. They will want to see every new film, go to the latest restaurant in town, meet each unfamiliar and interesting person who comes within hearing. We must however recognise the fact that the Geminian fear of boredom will influence the way in which our friendship develops, for they need continual intellectual stimulation and if we do not keep up with their lively minds and speedy lifestyle, sure as eggs they will drop us and move on to more stimulating company. Geminians will certainly help to keep you young both in mind and body; do everything possible to encourage their lively enthusiasm, and remember to question their every statement, and make an effort to be as sceptical as they are when they put some new idea or opinion to you. The typical Geminian likes to get as good as he gives, and will even invent an argument to stimulate discussion. Very often these zodiac types can exhaust their friends, but it is up to others to make them aware that they can become

so high-key and highly-strung at times that this can lead to considerable mental and nervous exhaustion. The rest of us should be observant, constantly watching out for danger signals, and when we see them, making our individual Gemini consciously aware that there may be rocks ahead.

Love No Geminian will be backward in coming forward when it comes to love! The Geminian ability to communicate will be at its most endearing and amusing when the individual falls for someone. The lover will receive a continual stream of telephone calls, letters, and compliments designed to encourage the development of the affair, which will get off to a deliciously exciting, entertaining and frothy start. It may well be the case that the 'getting to know you' period will be of above-average length, because it is vitally important to Gemini to have a lively intellectual rapport with lovers as well as good sexual harmony. When it comes to sex, the expression should be as lively as in all other spheres of Geminian life: they like plenty of variety in love-making, and have a great deal of energy with which to express themselves. The well-known, even notorious, Geminian duality will often make its presence felt, and sometimes we find an individual involved in more than one relationship at a time, ingeniously arranging their lives to accommodate both partners. This situation often arises as a result of the inherent fear of boredom shared by all Geminians; they will go to extremes to avoid it. But this can lead to disaster: life can get very complicated, such negative traits as cunning and deceitfulness appearing. Quick thinking and quick talking will often, however, extricate them from the Geminian's trickiest situation.

Marriage Marriage to a Geminian may tend to be like a ride at the fun-fair—all ups and downs, sudden changes of direction, and sharp corners, with the partner hanging on doggedly, never quite knowing what's coming next. Anyone whose main consideration is security, routine and an entirely predictable life should think twice before commiting themselves in partnership with a lively, stimulating, versatile Geminian. Sometimes the expression of deep emotion is difficult for this type: many Geminians are afraid to express their feelings really freely—perhaps because of their tendency to be apprehensive of the result of 'letting go' in this way, or of any commitment which may follow. In spite of this, there is usually good communication between Gemini and his or her partner, and the phrase 'I love you!' is often on their lips. Highly-charged emotional scenes are less likely than with many other zodiac people; these will be replaced by quick verbal

battles during which the Gemini will fence enthusiastically for a winning position. It takes a strong, quick mind to win such a battle, but you can always appeal to inherent logic, even if surprising stubbornness emerges. A high level of friendship and shared common interests is vital in marriage with a Geminian; any tendency to jealousy should be kept under control if possible, and the almost inevitable flirtations should be coolly and logically discussed. The partner should ideally be youthful in outlook and of a bouncy, optimistic disposition.

☆ Parent and Child

The generation gap should not be too much of a problem for the Geminian parent; indeed it is quite often the case that their ability to grasp new ideas and changing opinions keeps them more in touch with current trends than their children are. It is sometimes necessary for them to control a tendency to bombard young people with new ideas and interests. It is difficult to over-stimulate a child's mind, but a Gemini parent should realise that the child may in fact be less capable of a quick grasp of ideas or concepts than he or she, and should make allowances accordingly. Try not to be too impatient or over-critical of your child.

The young Geminian mother looking after a baby or a toddler will be fascinated by the dawning intelligence, and much stimulated by the child's progress, but unfortunately could get easily bored by childish chatter. To counter this, it is essential for her to have a few hours every week somewhere totally away from the home environment—at a discussion group or serving on a committee, or perhaps keeping in touch with her career in a part-time capacity. As a result she will be a lively and positive parent, coping in the best possible way with the challenges of motherhood. The Geminian father should set time aside at weekends to read or watch TV with his children, take them to museums or art galleries, and put them in touch with the ideas he himself finds stimulating.

The Geminian house is usually buzzing with ideas and things to stimulate children—books, records, radio, television, computers—but all these things need to be used as a source of ideas rather than simply things to be read or looked at for themselves.

The bright-eyed Gemini child is so friendly and approachable that it is important to warn him or her, without being frightening, about possible danger from the approaches of strangers. These children make an ideal brother or sister. They can be extremely argumentative, but their

vivacious energy will do much to keep the rest of the family on its toes and continually stimulated. Parents must, however, watch out for superficiality, and should try, in particular, to encourage consistency of effort, for a Gemini child will tend to jump from one task, one game, one hobby to another (probably because boredom so easily catches up with them). *Never* say 'One thing at a time!'—they actually benefit from playing more than one game, performing more than one task, at a time. The important thing is to make sure that each game, each task, is carried through to its natural conclusion.

It is important too to encourage children of this sun-sign, very early on, to express their own opinions. They will tend to say, 'What do *you* think, mummy?' If this happens, turn the tables on them, question them until they are forced to form their own opinions! The only circumstances under which young Geminians will accept discipline are when they are carefully shown the reasons for any restrictions imposed on them.

☆ CAREER AND SPARE-TIME

A job with a predictable routine and no variety is definitely not a good choice for those with this sun-sign. Should circumstances force them into such a job, there are two things they should do: aim to get out of it as quickly as possible, and in the meantime counter boredom by thinking of their spare-time interests as the real channel for their self-expression.

Any work involving communication is first-class for Geminians: a profession in which travel is involved will also be excellent, since Geminians like to move around. So they do well in the travel industry (as couriers) or in business as salesmen or travelling representatives. Communication is really a key-word with the sign, and work in telecommunications should suit any Geminian. Most notably, we find an above average number of Geminians in the media, working as newspaper or TV and radio journalists, news-readers or presenters, disc-jockeys, interviewers. Those Geminians looking for part-time work will find they very much enjoy interviewing for public opinion polls. Bookselling, the stationery or newsagent trades, also offer satisfying careers; women will also enjoy working in a beauty salon or the busy environment of a lively up-to-date large department store.

Geminians who decide to follow the teaching profession could find the atmosphere of school or college very stimulating, and their ability to keep well ahead of the younger generation will stand them in

excellent stead. They might get bored with a repetitive examination syllabus, however, and should find ways of enlivening it, not only for themselves but also for their pupils, whose minds they will continually seek to stimulate. They should perhaps concentrate on working with older children or university students; as they could find teaching infants rather trying, because Geminians generally lack the necessary patience.

It may be that many will be attracted to the medical profession, making excellent G.P.s—their ability to communicate with their patients, and to cope with all types of people will be a great asset. They may want to specialise in fringe medicine. Because of their manual dexterity, they make splendid masseurs. Artistic Geminians will do well to consider going in for book-design and layout, book-binding or illustration. They are often extremely successful in the competitive world of advertising, which offers scope for constant variety and change, and the opportunity for individuals to do verbal battle! But once more, repetitious, boring work, or work slow to show positive results, is definitely not for them.

The tendency to be easily bored means that individual Geminians should plan very carefully the use of their spare-time—and moreover should try to anticipate occasions when because of a light workload, unemployment, or even holidays they will have more spare-time than usual. Their hobbies—and there will certainly be more than one—should be as contrasting as possible. They need intellectual as well as physical exercise (for the latter, see *Health and Exercise* on page 45). In Victorian times, young university students often had 'reading parties', in which a group of them would have a holiday devoted to reading and talking about their reading. Heaven for any Geminian! But these days discussion groups, debating societies, language classes will all be enthusiastically attended. Many Gemini women like to be ultra-fashionable, and enjoy the end-product of dressmaking: they will not wish to spend a great deal of time on their creations, and their motto in this field will be 'Make it tonight, wear it tomorrow.'

Many Geminians take great pride in their driving, and their quick-thinking (if not their impatience!) generally makes them good at it. Developing their driving skills to the full will profit them as well as other road-users—many hold certificates for Advanced Driving.

The most important thing for members of this sign to remember is that they should persevere with their hobbies: if something proves unsuitable after a fair period of time, that's fine; but don't give up after only a few hours' study—you may be missing out on something absorbing and rewarding.

☆ FINANCE AND INVESTMENT

Although many Geminians are sharp *entrepreneurs*, an equal number find it very tedious to cope with the financial side of a business, and when they have made money they also find it boring and, sometimes, confusing to have to cope with tax affairs and investments.

Their general propensity for quickness and their lack of patience means that they can sometimes fall heavily for get-rich-quick schemes. They are clever and shrewd, but this does not mean that such schemes cannot be as disastrous for them as for anyone else. Geminian financial good sense emerges, at its best, in the development of sufficient insight to spread their financial eggs among a wide variety of baskets. Apart from being a good way of minimising risk, this is also an antidote to boredom, since the individual will feel very much a part of each company in which he or she invests. Overall, Geminians are not too much concerned about money, and often spend rather too freely. This results in over-loaded credit cards and rude letters from bank managers. The Geminian bank account will tend to go up and down like a yo-yo. However, where money is concerned hope springs eternal with this zodiac type, and they usually manage to get by.

If a Geminian has the opportunity to start a business, it will be as well for him or her to be very much the front-person—becoming involved with possible clients is excellent for them. But it might be as well for them to work with a slower, more financially-orientated partner–the Gemini will be excellent at the hard sell, but the slower (possibly Taurean or Capricornian?) partner will find it easier to handle the accounts. Working as a freelance, in a variety of chosen fields, is probably ideal, since the Geminian, more than most zodiac types, can cope with the uncertainty of the lack of a regular guaranteed income.

Traditional areas of investment, interesting and rewarding for them, are the motor industry, department-stores, newspapers and magazines, the printing and publishing industry in general (indeed all areas of the printed word) and telecommunications. Travel firms and the hotel industry also have their attractions.

It is important to Geminians to keep up-to-date—not only from the point of view of fashion, but to buy the latest book, the latest recordings made by their favourite performers and composers, and the latest sound-and-vision equipment. These areas will be a major expense, and a surprising amount of money will disappear into them. It is very difficult for Geminians to restrain themselves in this respect, and when times are hard and perhaps the individual is out of work, they could suffer considerably just because they are not able to keep up with their favourite interests. They should fall back on their natural ingenuity: as far as clothes are concerned, for instance, they could remake existing garments, and can always do battle at their local library to get hold of copies of the latest and most expensive books published on their interests.

☆ HEALTH AND EXERCISE

The energy level in most sun-sign Geminians is high, and having a very high metabolism they burn up a very great deal. Their nervous energy is high, too, and needs plenty of expression in everyday life. Sometimes individuals can burn themselves out, and become exhausted through physical or mental over-work. In order to keep their systems in balance, they should always give some time to relaxation, preferably involving steady physical exercise.

The Gemini body areas are the shoulders, arms and hands, which are often vulnerable to accidents—we find many have suffered broken collar-bones, arms or wrists at one time or another. Both sexes should take special care of their hands, for they often tend to use them rather more than other people—the professional pianist, the busy journalist, the radio officer can be in serious trouble when coping with a finger swathed in band-aid. Almost unconsciously Geminians have an awareness of their hands, and lots of women of the sign will have a good assortment of hand-creams, and will take special care of their nails; both sexes usually have several pairs of gloves to protect them against rough weather.

Gemini also rules the lungs, and indeed perhaps the greatest vulnerability of this sign is a weakness in this body area. They need to be very careful, after a common cold, that it does not hang on for too long as a racking cough, or turn to bronchitis. Those who smoke heavily should think even more seriously than others about giving it up.

Mercury is the ruling planet of Gemini and of the nervous system, and because of this emphasis there is an above-average tendency for members of this sign to become tense, and sometimes nervously apprehensive. It is important that any negative symptoms are recognised as they build up; if they are ignored—as can happen—Geminians can get caught up in a frenzy of activity, finding themselves totally unable to relax and unwind, and this can lead to quite serious problems, sometimes even to the point of breakdown. It is very good for Geminians to have some interest which will enable them entirely to cut out from

their much-loved mainstream occupation; this can be listening to music, or reading, but they should also aim to develop some relaxation techniques. Sometimes deep breathing will do the trick; but attending a regular yoga class will be most beneficial, especially if the instructor encourages an interest in the philosophical and meditation areas of this discipline.

A little preventative medicine: the vitamin B complex is very important to the nervous system (it has been successful in treating hyperactive children), and brewer's yeast as well as unrefined grains, nuts and seeds should form a very valuable part of a Geminian diet.

Because of their busy lifestyle, Geminians may not be terribly good at noticing when tension is building up, and, while we do not wish to be alarmist and encourage hypochondria, care and forethought are better than cure.

It is good for everyone to be involved in some kind of sporting activity or regular exercise, and when making suggestions for Gemini the most important consideration is their hatred of boredom—and let's face it exercise can be very boring indeed! The very best way for Geminians to take exercise is to join a large gymnasium or sports centre, where they can ring the changes—perhaps enjoying a fast game of squash one day, then moving over to the exercise machines or the trampoline. Dexterity of movement is something that they do not lack, and all kinds of dance exercise and aerobics are excellent for them, as are tennis and badminton. The list of possibilities is a long one, but it needs to be, for the more Gemini can experiment with different forms of exercise, the better. Gemini has the reputation of being the most youthful of the signs, and can often continue exercising into old age; this does not mean they should not be careful to modify exercise programmes so as not to overstrain their systems.

☆ Home environment

Enter a Geminian home and it will be found to reflect the busy, varied lifestyle of its owner. There will be a great many books and magazines scattered about, covering a great number of subjects; the overall appearance will be colourful and lively, if not particularly relaxing!

Whenever the age of the house, it will be fully adapted to modern needs—functional to the *n*th degree, the rooms used practically: for instance if there is a guest room, the chances are that it will also provide space in which the Gemini can work at his or her spare-time interest. Because Geminians are adaptable, they can, generally speaking, cope well with living in the smallest village or the largest, throbbing capital city. Perhaps, however, a large, lonely house in the middle of a desolate moor would *not* be the best home, even if it had telephone and telex machines in every room!

The interior decoration may rather lack the unity of an overall theme: we can expect to find each room rather differently decorated—one perhaps in a Laura Ashley style, another dedicated to art deco, a third very modern—but the overall effect, though slightly 'bitty', will be interesting and pleasing, and certainly very cheerful! The use of colour will probably embrace yellow and fairly strong pastel shades. Patterns will tend to be small and a trifle 'busy'; the recent trend for mixing stripes and spots, flowers and abstract patterns, will appeal.

The furniture will be light in appearance—in no way over-solid—cane and chromium for chairs and tables, for instance, and light-coloured wood. Curtains will be drawn back as far as possible, letting in the maximum amount of light, and the home as a whole will have quite a stylish air. We often find Geminians buying ornaments in pairs—an expression of their duality. They will, for instance, have two matching pictures or two similar vases. There may be an air of untidiness, partly because there is never enough shelf-space for all the books in the house. Gemini will enjoy lively, sunny pictures such as Dufy's views of the south of France; the work of Paul Klee will amuse; David Hockney's landscapes of the American west coast will also appeal.

The kitchen will be stocked with every available gadget, and each visit to a department-store will supply at least one more. In theory this should make for an ultra-efficient kitchen—if a rather cluttered one. The urge to be up-to-date in every aspect of life will certainly be indicated elsewhere in the Gemini home by the presence of expensive labour-saving devices.

The theme of wide general interests and liveliness will be extended to the bedroom, and even there we will find plenty of conversation stimulators—perhaps the prints on the walls will be erotic—as well as sources for amusement, echoing the Geminian tendency to enjoy love and sex in the lighthearted way. There will probably be a pile of books or magazines by the bed, and certainly a radio, casette recorder or portable TV.

In the dining-room, we can expect the table-setting to include some interesting small ornaments, to stimulate conversation. The china and glass will be pretty and colourful, the plates decorated with a border of fruit, flowers and nuts. Modern glass will be preferred, with elegant and lightweight cutlery, either all-metal or with wooden handles. Don't expect an over-rich, heavy meal when dining with a Geminian: sauces containing a lot of butter or cream do not agree with them. A chilled soup might be served—*gazpacho* or cucumber is often popular—and the main course could include dual flavours (sweet-and-sour pork, for instance, or chicken with almonds). There will almost certainly be a delicious salad, and the dessert might be a *soufflé*, a platter of fruits, or maybe *zabaglione*. The Gemini will probably choose a wine to complement the lightness of the menu: the fruitier German or Austrian white wines are popular, as are very dry, white French wines.

There will be no lack of background music when you spend an evening with a Geminian, and the chances are that they will be keen for you to hear the latest additions to their disc or tape library, playing you one band and then changing rapidly to something entirely different, so that you may start off with a Mozart aria, go on to traditional jazz and end up with number one in the current charts.

☆ Image

Clothes It is quite important for most members of this versatile and busy sun-sign to keep right up-to-date with fashion. Sometimes, however, this leads to unwise investment—especially when the Geminians are young. There is a tendency for them to buy too many 'separates', and if they are not very careful the overall appearance becomes extremely 'bitty'. When they are a little more experienced, they can develop a clever knack of combining their separates in an ingenious and interesting way; but it is good for them to have a collection of classically-designed basic garments as a starter. They can then go on to combine them with much-loved blouses and shirts, ties and scarves, and perhaps the odd jokey cap or hat. Achieving an overall look is not easy, and can be particularly difficult just because the Gemini gets bores while assembling it!

Geminians of both sexes are, however, very good at mixing colours and textures; indeed, texture is very important, for the Gemini will either like or loathe the feel of velvet, will respond well to wool and tweed, and so on . . . They will take risks, and can be quite daring in their choice of clothes, probably finding that many more conservative types will say, 'Oh, well, *you* can wear that because *you* can get away with it!'

The Geminian colour is yellow—but it doesn't end there, for a

quirky zodiac tradition says that most colours come under the rulership of this sign. Geminians, as a result, look good in a greater variety of colours than most people! Perhaps mix-and-match should be their motto. They will experiment with hair-colour and styles, somtimes disastrously but sometimes with great effect. They use cut and colour to complement to really dazzling effect the natural brightness of their expression, and their characteristically quick head- and eye-movements in conversation enhance this too.

The Gemini metal is mercury—'quick-silver'—not a very useful one when it comes to jewellery! Gemini might be interested however to go in search of pretty pieces of enamel or titanium jewellery, the changing colours of which reflect the whole Gemini image. Jewellery will, like so much connected with this sign, often be a good conversation-starter. An interesting ring, for instance, of unusual design; they may have found this in their local boutique for very little money—or perhaps, if they are wealthy, it will have been custom-made by an inventive young designer. The same can be said of pendants and earrings.

Gemini women love high fashion shoes, but also walk very quickly, and this does not do the shoes a great deal of good. A compromise must be found. Youngsters will particularly enjoy wearing colourful training shoes, and older Geminians will no doubt find fashion shoes which are simultaneously elegant and comfortable.

Extenders Any Gemini image will be supported by a great variety of accessories which add even more interest to the basic impression. This sign loves to own a sizeable collection of belts, gloves, ties, socks and handbags. They often add even more variety with belts that are reversible, watch-straps that are interchangeable, and handbags as numerous as income will allow.

People of this sign like to be able to take photographs very quickly, so it is necessary that they own a camera which can spring into action at a moment's notice, with no fuss or bother, no necessity to set shutter-speeds and apertures. Polaroid cameras are often popular, for these allow the individual to present friends with prints as soon as the picture is taken; but the Geminian's dream will probably be the most modern electronic camera which does everything accurately and instantly.

When Gemini travels, it is necessary for him or her to cram as many clothes as possible into a small space; so those large, silky travelling bags which can be folded into a tiny space when not in use will be very popular.

The choice of fragrances is particularly interesting: Geminians enjoy light, spicy scents with a hint of floral undertone (lily-of-the-valley, for instance). Heavy, seductive essences which perhaps include rose, or some of the more sensual essential oils, are unpopular.

Cars The Gemini will hang on to a sports two-seater for as long as possible, and it will be a sad day when the time comes to exchange it for something larger—but there will be the challenge of finding a substitute which will be quick away from the traffic lights, but roomy enough for children, luggage and pets. Very young Geminians will be keen to own a bicycle, being anxious to explore the neighbourhood, and will want to have driving lessons as soon as the law permits.

☆ Travel

The need to be able to go anywhere at a moment's notice and with as little fuss as possible is paramount when Gemini travels, and on the whole they enjoy the process. Any form of travel except a very slow one will do: Concorde will appeal to almost all of them—a rural tour in a gypsy caravan behind an ambling horse will appeal to very few.

Many Geminians will particularly enjoy driving their own cars (though they can tend to be a little careless in maintaining them): they often love maps and working out ingenious routes to avoid boring traffic jams. A long row of maps, atlases and motoring books will find a place on their shelves—and they will enjoy being their own travel agents, writing innumerable letters to hotels, ferry booking-offices and emigration authorities.

The ideal Gemini holiday will not involve going to sleep on the most delightful beach; they will sit in the sun surrounded by a pile of carefully-chosen holiday reading, and, when not involved in that will be arranging excursions for the afternoon, or working out the way to their second holiday centre, the following week. They won't want to be alone much, preferring to go away with family or friends, or perhaps to make new friends in new places—they will do this, anyway. They also want plenty to do, new places to explore.

A holiday with a specific purpose or theme will appeal, whether it's centred on the temples of the Nile valley, the Chateaux of the Loire or a big international football match or athletic meeting.

Geminians will very much enjoy the prospect of sampling foreign food and drink; but the reality is not always as enjoyable, because their digestions can be less adaptable than they think, and a sudden change of diet may result in stomach upsets. They shouldn't let impatience

force them into sampling every variety of local wine on the first evening. It is impatience, too, that can give them trouble with sunburn, for they will want a really impressive all-over tan by midday on the second day. They must learn to go slow. Another frustration is not being able to communicate with local people; before leaving home it will be really very worthwhile for them to learn at least a few basic phrases in Italian or Greek or whatever. Fortunately, the idea will appeal to these verbal creatures, and the fact that they don't have to swallow an entire dictionary will encourage them.

If they are not careful, Geminians return from their holidays with enormous quantities of souvenirs, ranging from postcards and local pieces of kitsch too ugly to be resisted, to perhaps a beautiful piece of pottery, a painting, or a carving. The only warning is against undue haste: something which looks fine in Portofino can look horrid in the sitting-room at home.

The Gemini child on holiday will mirror the frustrations of a Gemini adult, but more so. They won't be driving, so will get easily bored by long car journeys (they're not great scenery-samplers), and reading can promote car-sickness. Prepare a few good verbal games to keep their interest going. On arrival, they should have plenty of challenges to prevent the boredom of just sitting on the beach: they can collect postcards and ephemera; encourage them to keep a diary, and to try to talk to the locals.

In spite of all their love of travel, excitement and variety can strain the vulnerable Geminian nervous system. Going on holiday *is* a strain, and they may worry rather more than they realise—about the safety of the home or the well-being of pets while they're away, about the journey, about hotel arrangements. They should learn to relax into the holiday—what else is it for? The Geminian may relax into a holiday love affair, and there's not a great deal wrong with that: but they should keep it in mind that other people may take this more seriously than they do, and should try to make sure that no-one is hurt by what for them is just another enjoyable little adventure.

☆ Presents to Please

Almost any present you care to give a Gemini will please them, provided it stimulates their imagination or natural curiosity in some way. If you think of their individual taste in music or books, do make a point of finding out the latest book written by a favourite author, or the latest album cut by a much-loved performer. You will also do well

★ FAVOURITE TO GEMINI ★

★ **GEMINI COUNTRIES**—include the U.S.A., Belgium, Lower Egypt, Sardinia, Wales and Armenia.

★ **GEMINI CITIES**—include London and New York, Plymouth, Melbourne, Metz, Cardiff, Nuremburg, Bruges, Cordoba, Versailles, San Francisco.

★ **TREES**—All nut-bearing trees.

★ **FLOWERS AND HERBS**—Aniseed, azalea, balm, bittersweet, bryony, caraway, elfwort, fern, haresfoot, lavender, lily-of-the-valley, maidenhair, myrtle.

★ **FOODSTUFFS**—Most nuts, especially hazel and walnut; most vegetables (except cabbage).

★ **CELL SALTS**—Kali Mur., Silica.

★ **STONE**—Agate.

★ **COLOUR**—Bright yellow; but most colours appeal.

to discover when the book or record was released, because if it has been around for more than five minutes, the chances are that Gemini will have it! More personal presents might include a bracelet or ring.

For the Geminian home, if you're thinking in terms of a wall-decoration, a poster from the past, perhaps advertising a car or a cruise line, will be enthusiastically received; so will an antique map, or an interesting lithograph by an up-and-coming young artist. For a birthday or Christmas, your Gemini friend will be sure to appreciate a subscription to a magazine devoted to a current hobby or interest. Remembering the Geminian need to keep up-to-date with the news, a subscription to a good news magazine will also be popular.

Anything for the car—from a map-reading light to a pair of driving gloves—will probably go down well. A good fountain-pen or the latest pocket calculator (perhaps one that becomes a portable reference system) will be welcomed. The Geminian who has everything will be intrigued by one of those silly 'executive toys' such as Newton's balls—or perhaps an unusual make-it-yourself clock, demanding Geminian dexterity, and perhaps developing the attribute of patience! Advanced models of ships, cars, planes, will have the same effect. For women, a pack containing everything you need to make a brilliantly-coloured hand-knitted sweater will be popular—provided it uses thick wool, so it will be quickly knitted! If you are dining with a Gemini, a handsome box of mixed nuts or sugared almonds will be appreciated. Beauty products such as hand cream will be popular, as will a particularly elegently-designed manicure set. If in doubt, a gift voucher for a favourite department store or a record or book-token will be excellent.

It is never too early to give a Geminian child a book, or indeed a typewriter—these days, perhaps a word-processor (they will be very attracted to computers, in any case). They will want their own walkman radio and tape recorder, too. A small child will enjoy something like a post office set. The current range of toys which start out as a fire engine and can be reassembled as something quite different, will be fascinating. Very often toy animals are preferred to dolls, and all kind of board games (Scrabble particularly) will be popular. The girl teenager will appreciate junk jewellery, especially a cluster of brightly-coloured plastic bracelets, a string of beads, or flashy, amusing earrings.

★ CANCER ★

· JUNE 22 — JULY 22 ·

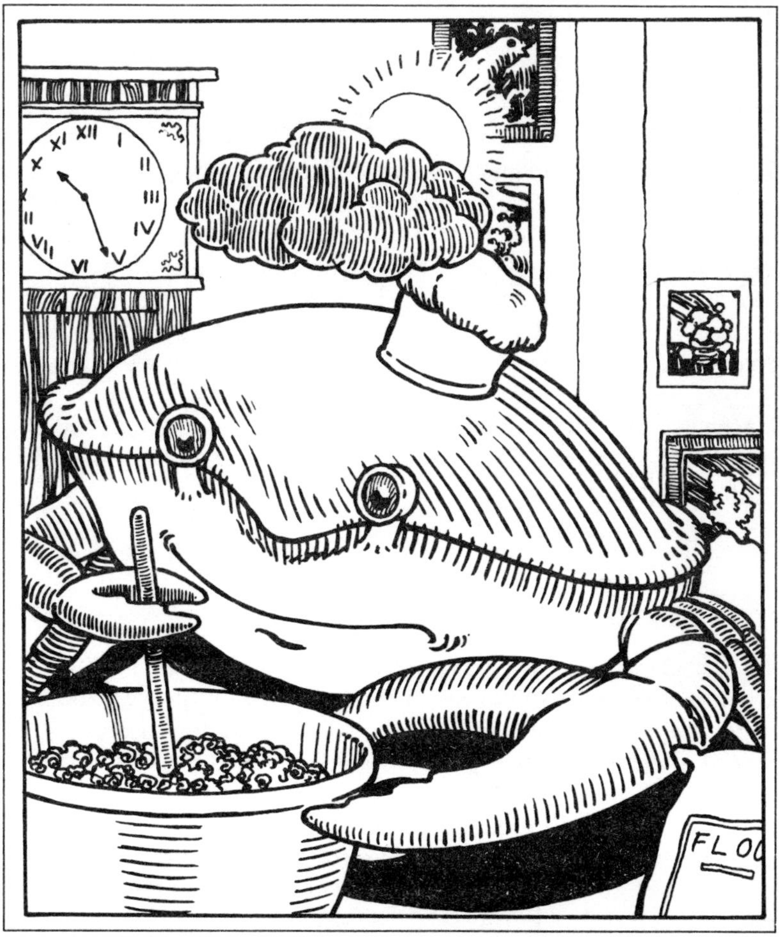

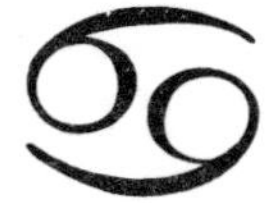

☆ THE MYTH

The crab which is the symbol of Cancer came to the aid of the Hydra, the dog with ten thousand snaky heads which Heracles had to destroy as his second Labour. After it had nipped his foot, the hero crushed the shell of the enormous crab and killed it; but as a reward for its help, the jealous Hera, always Heracles' enemy, set the creature among the zodiac signs in the sky.

☆ THE SIGN

The *ruling planet* of Cancer, with which it has a special relationship, is the *Moon*; it is a *cardinal*, *feminine*, *water* sign. *Positive traits* include kindness, sensitivity, tenacity, a powerful imagination, strong protective paternal or maternal instincts, excellent intuition, thrift and shrewdness; *negative traits* include moodiness, changeability, hypersensitivity, a snappy temper, a hard exterior hiding a weak character, untidiness.

Cancer in a nutshell Beneath the defensive Cancerian shell is great kindness, sympathy and understanding, and an intense love of home and family life.

☆ GENERAL CHARACTERISTICS

The Cancerian character is interesting but difficult to understand. When we first meet members of this somewhat complex zodiac sign, we get the impression that they are rather hard and aggressive. Challenge them, and at once psychological barriers appear, designed to protect them, their opinions, and those who mean much to them. Once we break through that barrier, which is as brittle as an egg-shell, and get to know the Cancerian better, we find someone who is tremendously aware of the problems and difficulties of others, and will use great intuition and kindness to help them. People of this sign are notoriously moody, and if we spend any amount of time with Cancerians we become aware of this: at one moment they will be talkative, kind, attentive, amusing and gentle, at the next a cloud will sweep over them, a deep frown appear between their eyebrows, and for no apparent reason we will become victims of bad temper and harsh words. Once the cloud passes, which it will do as quickly as it appeared, the Cancerian will be eager to put matters right, perhaps by cooking some special dish or making some kind of practical apology.

The Cancerian imagination is quite beautiful, and at its best can produce wonderful effects. Sometimes, alas, it is expressed in irrational worry about imaginary evils. Always encourage a Cancerian to use imagination positively and creatively.

Looking at *Cancerians in Fiction*, our eye might fall first on Peggoty in Dickens' *David Copperfield*—motherly, affectionate, almost stupidly protective; then on Captain Hornblower—who actually *was* a Cancerian, for C. S. Forrester tells us that his birthday was July 4th, 1776. Tenacious and short-tempered, very much enclosed in his Cancerian shell, he was also loving and caring. The heroine of Puccini's opera *Madame Butterfly*, so carefully preserving her home for the lover who never returned, is another obvious Cancerian.

The Cancerian's *greatest asset* is a sensitive caring quality; the *greatest problem* is often irrational worry; the *greatest vulnerability* an over-inventive imagination. *The Cancerian Motto*: Home is where the heart is.

☆ FRIENDSHIP, LOVE AND MARRIAGE

Friendship Form a friendship with a Cancerian and, like as not, you have a friend for life. Their superb memory will make it easy for them not to forget you for long, even if they have a busy social life and a wide circle of friends. Do them a good turn, and they will remember it, returning your kindness in their own individual way. This often means that you are treated to wonderful meals, unexpected and unusual presents, and some interesting meetings with other people. On the negative side, a thoughtless, casual remark or perhaps criticism of someone else they love will immediately put you in the Cancerian's bad books. They will spring to the protection of the third party, and you will be thoroughly put in your place! Their superb intuition will add an interesting perspective to your friendship: if you are not well, for instance, the telephone will ring and there will be words of comfort out of the blue—Cancer will have intuitively felt that you need support. It is particularly good to share a common interest—they are first-rate stimulators of one's imagination, and help one to take a really deep interest in a joint enthusiasm. The tendency to worry about their friends can become embarrassing or even something of a bore—it

is always as well not to be late when meeting a Cancerian, for their imagination will immediately involve you in a fatal accident, and when you eventually arrive you will find a flustered, frantic person trying to telephone your family to discover where your body has been taken!

Love The emotional forces of a Cancerian find new and wonderfully positive expression in love, and life will take on a totally different meaning—even more than for someone of another sign. There is a tendency to be over-protective and caring, and this can sometimes mean problems if the lover is independent and repelled by the claustrophobic air which a relationship with a Cancerian can sometimes involve. The Cancerian expression of sex is enhanced by a marvellous sensuality, and their lovers will experience great joy in this area of the relationship, though over-emotionalism sometimes provokes dramatic scenes, and makes life just a little uncomfortable. But in a Cancerian one finds a lover who will not lack a feeling for true romance, and will use imagination in a wonderfully imaginative and unusual way to express true emotion, warmth and consideration. It is often difficult to end a relationship with a Cancerian, so the bad news must be given with great tact and care. Cancerians must try to learn to take a philosophical attitude when love dies, recognising the fact that they can all too easily be over-clinging. Much better to use their self-defensive system and put a brave face on the situation. But it will never be easy for them to come to terms with this kind of situation, and the lesson will be learned the hard way. Rather than always looking backwards, it is best for them to look forward to a possibly happier future.

Marriage Once committed to a permanent relationship, it is very easy for a Cancerian woman to become so bogged down in running the home that she will tend to neglect her own individual needs and interests. Her partner should be aware that this can happen, and always encourage her to use her ample tenacity to keep in touch with interests that in point of fact mean a very great deal to her. Both men and women make wonderfully caring partners, and there is a great deal of true meaningful love to be expressed within marriage. For them, the seal of permanance cannot too soon be set on a relationship, and they will work very hard to make it permanent—especially if the couple run into emotional problems. Sometimes there can be a tendency to live too much in the present, and to be reluctant to make change: many Cancerians will not want to move house, even when the family has grown up and left home. Their roots strike deep, and although their moods can change very quickly they can feel very insecure if they do not feel thoroughly at home in their environment, or if their lifestyle is threatened. Anyone forming a permanent relationship with a Cancerian must be prepared to accept the fact that their partner will hoard—Cancerians are so reluctant to throw away anything that living-space can be seriously over-crowded! This can be true psychologically, too—they rarely forget past actions, pleasant or unpleasant.

☆ PARENT AND CHILD

Cancerians will become psychologically whole, and life will be especially rewarding for them, when they start a family. The sign is top of the list when it comes to a positive expression of maternal and paternal love; and Cancerians certainly make excellent parents. However, it is also all too easy for them to become over-protective of their children, and over-concerned about their welfare and safety. It is often difficult for them to take a logical and rational approach to their children's needs. For instance, when it is necessary for them to go to school, or later on to leave home, this can seem a crisis far greater than any other that could possibly ever occur. Awareness that such exaggerated responses can take place is essential. Above all else, the Cancerian feels a deep need to preserve the family unit; when it is broken up, the individual must go through an important period of readjustment.

Looking at this from the view of the child (of any sign), the relationship with such a parent can be difficult simply because of Cancerian possessiveness, and a reluctance to allow sufficient independence. It is marvellous if this sensitive, caring group of people can use their imaginations creatively when bringing up their children—they are at their best telling original, perhaps slightly weird bedtime stories, and encouraging their children to be deeply interested in a great variety of out-of-school occupations.

From a very early age, the Cancerian child will assume the role of mother or father of the family, at least where brothers and sisters are concerned. Sometimes a very young Cancerian boy will be tremendously protective of a sister very much his senior. The young Cancerian girl will adore her dolls, but parents must be aware that it is all too easy for her to become ultra-feminine and perhaps less assertive than the future will demand. To counter this tendency, the development of her Cancerian courageousness should be encouraged. In both sexes it is excellent for these youngsters to have a young animal to care for;

this gives them early responsibility, which is an excellent practical expression of so much that is basic to the personality.

At school they will be very good at remembering facts, especially when it comes to historical dates; history is often a favourite subject. It is important that the imagination is stimulated through art lessons, the writing of short stories and plays, and also through creative movement. When the children are worried it may not be to easy to persuade them to talk about the reasons. If boarding school is a possibility, parents should think carefully about inflicting it on Cancerian children, who could suffer much more than most as the result of being sent away from home.

☆ CAREER AND SPARE-TIME

Any career that encourages the expression of the Cancerian ability to protect and care for others will be excellent for this zodiac type. The nursing profession springs to mind, as does working in a nursery school—there are very few who are not devoted to young children. Cancer has the reputation of being the best cook in the zodiac, and catering can certainly be a very rewarding profession. Interestingly, many cooks seem to be rather bad-tempered by nature, something not unknown among Cancerians!

The antiques trade is extremely popular; we find many Cancerians owning small stalls in an antique market, perhaps as a second source of income. But many specialists in antique silver are also members of this sign. The preservation and repair of antiques is a worthwhile occupation, as is working in a museum or art gallery. The shrewd business sense of this group must not be ignored, and many make wonderful business-people—they are often extremely clever with money, and their intuition gives them a 'feel' for investment. Any small business will be fortunate to have a careful Cancerian connected with it, and will be almost sure to grow slowly and steadily. Obviously it will be excellent for a Cancerian to start such a business, if possible.

Not surprisingly (this is a *water* sign) the sea has a great attraction for Cancerians, which fact coupled with a love of caring, may lead many Cancerians to a career working on liners, perhaps as pursers or stewards. This provides challenge, even a certain amount of excitement and danger, yet there is also the somewhat confined security of a fairly luxurious 'home'. We find other Cancerians are keen boat-builders. They also do well as estate-agents, and any Cancerian about to retire might consider running a small boarding-

house, or perhaps starting a market garden. Cancerian moodiness can sometimes make them rather difficult colleagues: when one joins a firm, it will certainly take a while for him or her to be fully understood. When the Cancerian frown appears, it will be as well to let them severely alone: they will simply be working with more concentration than usual. If the job is physically demanding, the Cancerian will work off anger and aggression on it, and the results will probably be excellent. If intellectual demands are made at a time when the Cancerian is worried, the end product could be less good, because of a tendency to 'flap', and get into a muddle as a result.

Because members of this sign are very faithful and constant, they are unlikely to take up an interest and as suddenly drop it. But we must allow for the need for variety. If a Cancerian doesn't want to do something, he or she will certainly *not* do it. At such times entirely different occupations must be found. Perhaps the best possible spare-time occupation for a Cancerian is the formation of a collection of some kind. From a psychological point of view, this will turn an almost overwhelming tendency to hoard into an ability to be a discriminating and enthusiastic collector, forming a collection which should be not only interesting but profitable. Not only will Cancer enjoy the actual process of searching for and acquiring things for the collection, but an equal amount of satisfaction and fun will be gleaned from the in-depth study of whatever objects are engrossing them. Much has been said about the Cancerian interest in cooking, and this can be an engrossing hobby as well as a possible career.

No creative Cancerian will find it difficult to develop ideas for spare-time work; but they should have the courage of their convictions, and be really bold in their chosen form of self-expression. Many women of the sign are superb at all kinds of sewing and craft-work; silver-work too is often favoured, and as something quiet and contemplative, fishing can also be popular. A lot of people sometimes feel they want to write a novel; any Cancerian who tries this should set it in a favourite historical period.

☆ FINANCE AND INVESTMENT

Two things dominate the Cancerian attitude to money: both have a deep-rooted psychological basis. One is their tendency to hoard, and the other their disinclination to take risks.

From an early age, we find the young Cancerian deeply interested in and very much aware of how much he or she has in the bank—or the money-box. At the earliest age, they will keep a little supply of money in a private place unknown even to parents, and having collected a store of cash, they will not be at all eager to entrust it to anyone else for safe-keeping, or—later—to any investment scheme which does not have a long tradition of respectable and steady growth. The richest or poorest Cancerians will think carefully before investing, trusting their own judgement rather than risking their precious cash to the manipulative hands of others.

Many Cancerians are rather 'careful' with their money, and even when they become comparatively well-off, they will think that they are much less prosperous than they really are. Having cash ready to hand gives them a particular sense of security, and, more important, the feeling that they are masters of their own destiny where this sphere of their lives are concerned.

We must not forget that nearly all members of this zodiac group are extremely shrewd, and if they decide that they wish to start their own business, they will spend a great deal of time planning the detailed financial arrangements. Because they are shrewd and careful to a degree, they can sometimes err on the side of caution; perhaps it is good for them to work with somewhat more adventurous partners—though when it comes to taking risks, another interesting facet of their personality comes into play, and while they are not particularly daring they are very brave, and will make an audacious financial move with conviction, once they have done all the background work, and intuition tells them that the time is right.

Areas of investment which will be profitable for them, as well as holding their interest, are fisheries, baby care products, the dairy industry, the hotel trade (and perhaps shipping cruise lines), the restaurant industry, builders specialising in private housing. Many Cancerians have a love and knowledge of antiques. For most, this will be expressed in an enthusiasm for collecting; but if Cancerians wish to become professional dealers, they will find it a fascinating business and will do well to specialise in one particular period or area—silver is often extremely popular. Any Cancerian could also get a great deal of satisfaction from opening a convalescent home or perhaps a nursery school. If a young mother wants to make a little extra money, she will find running a small play-group will give her satisfaction, and that she will have a natural aptitude for it. Breeding ornamental tropical fish might also offer an opportunity for money-making.

☆ HEALTH AND EXERCISE

The Cancerian system is tough and resilient, but it is likely to suffer when the individual is worried. This sign is perhaps the one most inclined to worry, and almost before individuals realise that they are concerned about something, their system will let them know it—their food will begin to disagree with them, and they will become 'moody' for no apparent reason. All such situations have a very direct effect on any Cancerian's health, and in some circumstances worry can lead to breakdown or stomach ulcers; sometimes, too, skin problems occur as a result.

It must be remembered that in trying to help them it is no good to say 'Pull yourself together and stop worrying!' That simply does not work. What can be done is to try to get them to accept the fact that they are this way inclined, and to remind them that they are superbly intuitive. It is very often the case that if they listen to their intuition and follow it up, they can resolve their problems.

The Cancerian body area is the chest, and the breasts are also emphasised where there is a Cancerian sun-sign. There is absolutely no association between this sign and the disease cancer; but because of the association with the breasts, it would be wise for Cancerian women to be at least as careful in regularly checking this area as women of any other sign. The ruling planet of Cancer is the Moon, and thus there is also an association with the alimentary or food system, the oesophagus, stomach, gall-bladder, bile ducts, pancreas and intestines.

There is a certain toughness about members of this sign: they will battle bravely on under difficult conditions, sometimes long after the rest of us would have given up. The natural tenacity of Cancer will help to carry them through periods of strain, tension and illness in their life, and those who sadly contract incurable illnesses are extremely brave, and will continue with a rewarding lifestyle, coping wonderfully with the limitations imposed upon them.

Many Cancerian women are at their best, and look their most beautiful, when pregnant: we find a great number who enjoy the state, being psychologically at one with themselves and with the child growing within them. Here is their greatest expression of fulfilment.

The Cancerian complexion is usually pale, irrespective of ethnic group, and it is very often the case that the sun treats it badly. Caucasian types will often turn an unpleasant shade of pink when exposed to it, while darker pigmentation is particularly sensitive to the slightest cut or injury, and scars can remain prominent. All Cancerians should

therefore take very great care of their skin, using a sun lotion with a very high protective factor for much longer than those of other signs. Here, of course, is an important warning for mothers of Cancerian children: their prams should be kept in the shade, and a lightweight, long-sleeved, cover-up garment should be taken to the beach, or be ready whenever they are in the sun.

Exercise for Cancerians should either be tough or extremely rhythmical, and preferably both—so swimming must be at the top of any list. They might especially enjoy working with a group of friends in a synchronised swimming team. Cancerian dancers like working in a group, for intuition makes them naturally aware of the general mood, and what the others are feeling and doing. Here again, however, Cancerian tenacity can be expressed: we find Cancerian boxers training feverishly for their matches, Cancerian runners spending hours of precious time readying themselves for that all-important marathon. Patience, the desire to overcome almost unsurmountable obstacles, leads to success; but this zodiac group is not over-concerned with *winning*. Their basic motivation is the achievement of their objective, which may only amount to finishing the course; their demonstration of determination is another important factor. This means that they will often be valuable members of a team, for they will be eager to show that they can keep up with the toughest, fastest, most determined companion. Any sporting interest developed in youth will last for life, even if participation has to be modified with the advancing years.

☆ HOME ENVIRONMENT

It is important for Cancerians to be able to look out from their home on to a tranquil, quiet scene. There may not, of course, be such a view from every room in their house or flat; but if they have to live in the middle of a throbbing city, it is advisable for them to have, if possible, one aspect at least which will be quiet and calming, even if it only consists of a tiny balcony or area, or a small window-box filled with sweet-smelling flowers and herbs.

Ideally, the Cancerian home should be near water: a nice, lazy river or lake, or of course the sea. If this is impossible, then it is a good thing for them to acquire seascape pictures or at least landscapes including a view of a river or stream. The home itself will probably be an old one, and perhaps over the years the Cancerian will have added extra rooms and living-areas to accommodate a growing family. Any Cancerian will like to be part of an on-going tradition, and many will be eager to discover as much as possible about their house and its previous owners.

Entering a Cancerian home can often make us blink: it is usually over-full of furniture and ornaments—there will hardly be any wall-space left, especially if the individual is getting on in years, or has been married for a long time. We have already mentioned their tendency to collect and indeed hoard, and this will certainly be very evident to visitors. The individual collection will have pride of place, and sometimes will be beautifully displayed and interestingly lit—though this is not always the case, for, while the items themselves will be of enormous sentimental value to the collector, Cancerians are not always good at showing their things off as tastefully or effectively as they could. Untidiness is often apparant, so that even in the best-run Cancerian home we find piles of books and magazines, pictures hanging at a slant, and toys that the children have not got round to putting away.

When a Cancerian has come to terms with the tendency to hoard, and has given thought to interior decoration and the use of colour, we find they have superb taste. If they can discipline themselves to be tidy and at least reasonably selective where their possessions are concerned, the Cancerian home will become extremely comfortable, relaxing to visit, and a joy to the eye. This, however, takes time!

Cancerians are the number one cooks of the zodiac, so the kitchen will be the focal point of the house. Many love a large, farmhouse-style kitchen which can also serve as dining-room. In this way, Cancerians can continue to put the finishing touches to their elaborate dishes and continue a stimulating conversation while they do so. They should, however, bear in mind the fact that some of their friends may be very tidy, so it will be as well for them to arrange the seating in such a way that the fussy types have their backs to the vast number of used dishes, knives and so on which are bound to have accumulated during the preparation of the meal. Favourite dishes may include a white soup, fish as a starter or main course, and some delicious pudding swimming in cream. Wines will tend to be unobtrusive. The china will be plain white, perhaps with a delicate silver border; the glassware old—perhaps glasses will have been individually collected rather than bought as a set.

A Cancerian will tend to buy bits and pieces of furniture when they appeal, rather than buying a suite; so their living-room is likely to lack a comprehensive overall 'look' where furniture is concerned. Comfort will certainly be stressed, and we will feel that we are in a lived-in

room; but don't be surprised if sinking into a tempting-looking sofa you are attacked by a loose spring! Soft velvets and silky textures will be in evidence, and the colours will probably include a certain amount of pink or perhaps silver-grey. This will also be true of the bedroom, which will have a rather cluttered appearance, though we will be impressed by the size of the bed, and the temptingly comfortable duvet.

Spending an evening with a Cancerian host and you may find Debussy or Smetana on the sound system—or, in a lighter vein, perhaps sentimental ballads, or selections from romantic musicals. Hard rock will not be favoured—rather contemporary pop with a social message.

☆ IMAGE

Clothes Cancerians perhaps need to take more care of their appearance than members of any other sign, if they are not to look a mess. They must take really sound advice when choosing clothes—and even more important, ask their partners to give them a critical look-over just before they leave home: it is all to easy for them to step out with one major or minor slip in their image, which can spoil the whole effect. The men, for instance, will often look superbly smart in a well-cut suit, with just the right tie and other accessories—but with totally unsuitable socks or shoes. The women often love décolleté necklines, but the sensual effect will be ruined by a stray shoulder-strap; a hemline may be uneven, or perhaps it will have been torn the last time it was worn, and not repaired. All such things are, unfortunately, very common indeed among Cancerians, spoiling a look which aims to be elegant, soft and romantic.

Hair can often be a problem, too. There is sometimes a reluctance to cut it, and many women of this sign have extremely long hair: they will braid this, and pile it up. But untidiness can again mar the effect, for hairpins or clips will be shed in a positive shower, so that stray strands of hair slip out of place at the least provocation. A shorter, more interesting cut will often make them look younger and improve the overall effect.

The Cancerian sense of colour is very good, and usually extremely subtle: texture, too, is often used to great advantage, and there are few Cancerian women who do not sport a bit of shimmery glitter during the winter party season. Most are unlikely to allow this tendency to get out of hand. Pearls are much connected with the sign, and we find them used on embroidered items or of course in necklaces or rings.

Women of this sign should wear very simple outfits with as little clutter as possible: they can then dramatise them in a stunning way by wearing some interesting and perhaps quite large piece of antique jewellery, which may have cost them a fortune, but which can just as easily be something they have found in a junk-shop and lovingly cleaned, restored and repaired. So much the better if it is made of silver, the wonderful metal traditionally associated with the sign.

The craze for finding and wearing antique clothes is manna from heaven for our enthusiastic Cancerian friends; they will dig out great-grandmother's calico petticoat from the old box in the attic, and wear it as a summer skirt—or adapt a family wedding veil as a beautiful lacy blouse. This will be great fun, and could open up a whole new area of interest for them. While they will usually dress their children in the best of modern clothes, wanting them to be free to move about, they will enjoy making a Kate Greenaway dress for a party, for it will appeal to their sentimental streak to see children looking charmingly old-fashioned.

Extenders It is very necessary for the businessman or woman to carry a nice, large briefcase or handbag—Cancerians do seem to need to carry more things than usual about with them. They can all too easily burden themselves with toys for their children or more than enough books for reading on train journeys—the phrase 'everything but the kitchen sink' can almost literally be applied to the Cancerian's 'essential' kit!

Cancerian women often have considerable flair when it comes to choosing make-up: they will love iridescent eye-shadows and softly-coloured lipsticks, but sometimes do not spend long enough applying them. It is good for them to set extra time aside in order to ensure that the overall effect is not spoiled.

A small camera is a 'must'; Cancer is very keen to record every conceivable incident for the family archive.

There are several fragrances on the market with a great appeal to Cancerians: they should consider choosing one with quite a strong floral tone, but which also has a lingering, musky base. This will enhance the Cancerian sensuality, and interesting, gentle but powerful sex-appeal.

On the whole, Cancerians seem to be cat rather than dog people, and many Cancerian homes will be decorated by a huge and gloriously fluffy cat and her off-spring. They will, of course, be very much members of the family, and sometimes inhibit the humans from taking holidays abroad.

Cars Think of the typical Cancerian family and as far as choice of car is concerned a large station-wagon or estate car seems inevitable. This is because the Cancerian wants to move around *en famille* as much as possible; so extra space for children, for baby's necessities, pets and their needs, and perhaps for camping gear, is essential. A mobile home will not be unusual.

☆ Travel

Many Cancerians are somewhat apprehensive about travelling: involved in a profession requiring rather a lot of it, they will put on a brave face and pretend it doesn't bother them when in reality they may well be suffering from all kinds of irrational fears and worries. As a result their digestion can all too often play them up.

It is almost too obvious to say that most Cancerians will enjoy travelling by sea—but, interestingly, this is the truth. They will often work out all kinds of elaborate routes which include water-transport, even if this is not strictly necessary. They will use cargo boats, luxury liners, small vessels of any kind, as well as the ordinary car ferries. If time is at a premium they will tolerate flying one way, but if at all possible returning by a much-preferred water route. Caravans and camping vehicles are also enjoyable for them, especially if this means that the whole family can travel together.

The ideal Cancerian holiday should undoubtedly take them somewhere near water—either to the sea, the lakes, or a river: travelling in a long-boat on the canals will provide a fascinating and unusual break, and the family will be able to remain together, also very important. 'Messing about in boats' is always a delight to them, and sailing holidays often attract them. In fact many Cancerians' idea of heaven is to own their own boat, whether it's a small sailing boat, or something larger. Many are natural sailors, in total harmony with the sea and its many changes of mood. Developing sailing skills is worth consideration—even if the individual cannot afford to buy a boat, hiring one for the annual summer holiday may not be out of the question.

Rather than large, elaborate and expensive luxury hotels, those are run on 'family' lines will be most favoured. The food should certainly be good, and ideally there should be extensive grounds. When choosing a hotel, attention should also be paid to the facilities for swimming—an indoor pool, perhaps, in case of rain? Young Cancerians could be encouraged to go snorkelling.

Many Cancerians will enjoy a holiday with a purpose—perhaps one which links them to some historic event in which they have an interest such as a pilgrimage following an historic trail. So much the better if they know they are sharing an experience with their ancestors. Places which stimulate the imagination will always intrigue people of this sign, and the children in particular should be encouraged along these lines. Rather than Disneyland, or some similar pleasure park, take them instead to some caves or ruins on which their imagination can play, inventing their own fantastic stories rather than relying on the tall tales of a guide. They will also enjoy hunting for local souvenirs, and can be quite clever at finding unusual and original momentos. But at the same time they will be very reluctant to part with innumerable shells and dried pieces of seaweed encountered on the beach at low tide.

Cancerians can cope well with dry heat, but humidity is not good for them—they seem to get dehydrated very easily; and sunburn can be a difficulty. They will enjoy experimenting with food—though this will probably amount to their trying new recipes in their own kitchen rather than actually sampling what the local restaurants have to offer. And this is, in fact, very sensible, for Cancerians can have slightly delicate digestive systems which may suffer badly from a sudden change of climate and diet. Self-catering holidays are often enjoyed, though this is no special holiday for the cook!

☆ PRESENTS TO PLEASE

Give a Cancerian even the smallest present, and not only will it be treasured for many years, but your kindness and thoughtfulness will be long remembered, and a casual remark made much later, long after you have forgotten the incident, will remind you of it.

If it is at all possible try to find out what your Cancerian friend enjoys collecting—obviously, if it is Georgian silver, you are in trouble! But spending an evening or dining with them, you might be able to find a small book on the subject which will interest them. The association with the sea is always a hint to remember, and if you come across a beautiful old print of a sailing ship, or one of those sailors' embroideries, or—a real triumph!—a ship in a bottle, such a gift will really be a hit. Cancerians also adore all kinds of curios—little pieces of Victorian china or souvenirs from the seaside, and the latest kitchen gadget will undoubtedly go down very well. You cannot go wrong if you give them anything that is old, promotes feelings of nostalgia, and stimulates their lovely creative imagination.

★ FAVOURITE TO CANCER ★

★ **CANCERIAN COUNTRIES**—include Scotland, North and West Africa, Holland, New Zealand, Paraguay, Algeria.

★ **CANCERIAN CITIES**—include New York, Manchester, York, Amsterdam, Istanbul, Stockholm, Milan, Venice, Genoa, Cadiz, Magdeburg, Berne, Tunis, Algiers.

★ **TREES**—Cancer is traditionally associated with all trees, but particularly with those richest in sap.

★ **FLOWERS AND HERBS**—Acanthus, convolvulus, geranium, honeysuckle, lilies, saxifrage, water-lily, the white rose and white poppy.

★ **FOODSTUFFS**—Fruit and vegetable with a high water content: melon, cucumber, pumpkin; mushroom, cabbage, turnip, lettuce.

★ **CELL SALTS**—Calc. Fluor., Calc. Phos.

★ **STONE**—Pearl.

★ **COLOUR**—Smoky grey, pale blue, silver.

Think of the Cancerian need to protect their skin: a pretty sunshade or umbrella will be enthusiastically received, and so will a gentle skin food or perhaps hand-cream. Really luxurious soap is something to remember, too. A bunch of white roses sent round the day after your visit will be a most attractive way of saying thank you for what was probably a really splendid dinner!

The Cancerian taste in books is often for romantic family sagas, and you could consider a nice chunky novel set in the past. Books on interior decoration may be too much an obvious hint! But any Cancerian will love a book of family portraits, or paintings of children, and cookery books of course will be very welcome, although the kitchen library will already be extensive. Perhaps a book specialising in exotic desserts and confectionery will be new to them.

A Cancerian child will love stories of the past, so any romantic tales of adventure in the ancient world, or Arthurian Britain, will be snapped up. Smaller children will love a nurse's or doctor's outfit, and every small Cancerian should be encouraged to come into the kitchen as early as you can stand it. Boys as well as girls should be encouraged to cook.

Older children might enjoy making working models, particularly of steam-engines and vintage cars. Fishing gear will delight most Cancerian boys, and possibly girls; anything for a seaside holiday, from snorkelling equipment to good swimwear or large fluffy beach-towels will go down well, and not only with children!

Choosing a present for a Cancerian, remember their love of the past: but remember too that they love caring for others, and any evidence that others also care for them will give them pleasure, whatever it is.

★ LEO ★

· JULY 23 — AUGUST 23 ·

♌

☆ THE MYTH

The first of Heracles' twelve Labours was to kill the original Leo, the Nemean Lion, whose skin was impervious to weapons of iron, bronze and stone. First, he shot at it with arrows, which bounced off it; then bent his sword on its broad back; finally shattered his club by hitting it on the muzzle. Eventually, he wrestled with it, and though it bit off his finger, choked it to death, flaying it and wearing its skin as armour and its head as a helmet.

☆ THE SIGN

The *ruling planet* of Leo, with which it has a special relationship, is the Sun; it is a *fixed*, *masculine*, *fire* sign. *Positive traits* include magnanimity, organisational ability, broadness of mind, powers of leadership, creativity, generosity, a sense of drama and showmanship, an optimistic and enthusiastic outlook; *negative traits* include intolerance, dogmatism, snobbishness, pomposity, fixed opinions, stubbornness, vanity.

Leo in a nutshell The creative force should find positive expression, and the lifestyle should be rich and rewarding.

☆ GENERAL CHARACTERISTICS

Every sun-sign Leo will, in one way or another, rule over a kingdom. It may be a massive business empire or a tiny cottage garden but the individual will take great pride in every colourful flower that grows. The Leo outlook on life is very positive and enthusiastic, and when things go wrong or Leos are unhappy they will, like the lion, retire to some private place and quietly lick their wounds. There is a great zest for life, and a feeling that every day should be lived to the full. Leos will soon become enthusiastic and excited about any idea that is put to them, and in turn they will not find it difficult to ignite enthusiasm in others. Their organisational abilities are excellent, and in many respects they need to take centre-stage; on the other hand they will become willing and devoted slaves to someone whose personality and abilities they truly respect.

The individual Leo must be very careful not to become dogmatic or over-bossy; this can easily happen, especially if they are dealing with

irritating people whose breath of vision is narrow and who have a negative approach to life. Showiness is something that must also be controlled, and it is generally the case that as the individual increases in age so any tendency to too much glitter is more and more subservient to good taste and the appreciation of quality and beautiful things.

It is important for members of this sign not only to enjoy life themselves but to see to it that others do the same.

Any list of *fictional Leos* must surely include Lady Bracknell from Oscar Wilde's *The Importance of Being Earnest*—the perfect snob, determined to manipulate everyone she meets. *Tosca*, the heroine of Puccini's opera, is the true Leo who 'lives for art', but also has real dramatic quality; Dolly Levi, the heroine of Thornton Wilder's *The Merchant of Yonkers*, later the musical *Dolly*, is a quintessential Leo, happily organising the lives of everyone around her ('Some people knit, some sew—I meddle!'). Escamillo, the bullfighter in *Carmen*, is perhaps the ultimate Leo show-off!

The Leo's *greatest asset* is enthusiasm; the *greatest need* is for praise; the *greatest problem* over-enthusiasm. The *greatest vulnerability* is in being too trusting. The *Leo Motto*—'Live each day as if thy last.'

☆ FRIENDSHIP, LOVE AND MARRIAGE

Friendship There is something of a childish quality in the Leo attitude to friendship. Leos will want their friends to be as enthusiastic about their interests as themselves, so every time they arrange to meet the Leo will be excited at the prospect, and will do everything possible to make even the smallest, simplest occasion specially enjoyable and worthwhile. Leos do not make friends terribly quickly, although they are almost too ready to accept people at their face value; they will however very soon decide in their own minds whether the individual is to be a mere acquaintance or a real friend. It will be the other who must prove him or herself in the eyes of the Leo before being encouraged to graduate to the more meaningful bond of friendship. Leos must avoid sweeping their friends off their feet, especially when it comes to suggesting joint activities. They should make a conscious effort to take notice of their friends' suggestions, and from time to time be prepared to have less fun because the friend wishes to spend time on some activity which may be less exciting and rewarding to the Leo. If you

share a friendship with a Leo there will be times when their expression is clouded, and they are not their usual exuberant selves. If this happens, try to find out what is wrong, for there will inevitably be *something* wrong, and perhaps quite seriously so. It takes a lot to eclipse the Leo Sun; talking the problem through will probably restore the sunshine.

Love When Leos fall in love they fall good and hard. The Leo heart will be broken many times, and also takes longer to mend than the hearts of many other zodiac types; but once Leo is in love and that love is reciprocated, the individual will be at his or her best. Generosity of feeling will be considerable, and Leos will do everything in their power to make their loved ones happy. Sometimes they will over-spend both money and emotion, and this can lead to disaster. Sometimes, too, the partner cannot cope with their wealth of feeling—it simply overwhelms them, and to less positive and assertive types it can even be embarrassing. Leos are very faithful, and their warm hearts and natural passion need full expression. Sometimes, however, they may expect too much from their partners. As a result, relationships can go wrong; so we must always bear in mind the fact that because they have so much to give they need very responsive partners both from the point of view of companionship and affection, and where their sexual needs are concerned. They should be very careful not to be too dominating, and recognise as soon as possible that the very word 'partnership' means *sharing*. Certainly Leos will contribute much to a love affair where pleasure and happiness are concerned, and their natural sense of drama will be fully expressed, as will their ability to be enthusiastic and happy.

Marriage It is essential that the Leo partner is aware of a tendency to take the lead in marriage. If the Leo is attached to a weaker partner, this may of course be a necessary role; but even so there should be a development of tact and a gentle approach so that the partner can grow in strength rather than crumbling under the exuberant pressure of Leo decisiveness and flamboyance. It is important, too, that at times of decision-making Leo does not simply storm ahead and take the whole situation and its solution into his or her own hands. The negative tendency to be stubborn, dogmatic and 'bossy' should also consciously be curbed. Having said that, the marriage can certainly be great fun, and so lively that the partner is unlikely to be bored, or feel that nothing exciting is ever going to happen—Leo will see to it that it *will*! However little money there is, there will always be enough for the

occasional celebration, even if that means a mere cup of coffee—at the best hotel in town. Leos must be able to look up to and admire their mates: if for some reason they are not able to do this, they will do everything they possibly can to encourage the fullest development of their partners' potential, and when those partners achieve a success, no matter how small, the Leo sense of pride will blossom, and the partnership will progress.

☆ PARENT AND CHILD

Leo is traditionally the sign of fatherhood, and generally speaking Leos are enthusiastic parents: they will arrange an extremely busy schedule for their children, encouraging them in every possible way to make the most of their natural talents. But they can expect too much from their children. This may be no bad thing in some respects—they have, after all, the ability to encourage them to make even greater efforts—but they should be careful that they do not load their own wishes and desires too forcibly on their children.

Most Leos have an almost uncanny knack of remembering what it was like to be a child, and should always tune in to this when dealing with their own children, putting themselves in the child's position. They should also be careful to make allowances for any child who is shy and perhaps lacking in self-confidence, for they might tend to swamp him or her rather than gently encourage.

They will spend a very great deal of money not just on the children's school education, but on expensive and educational holidays and visits to museums, or to the theatre. The Leo type is straightforward and honest, and these qualities will be strongly emphasised in their treatment and upbringing of their children. The Leo parent will also see to it that the children enjoy a childhood exploration of the beauties of the planet, making them fully aware of its wonders.

The Leo child will be exuberant to a fault—indeed some effort should be made to control all that energy, if the child is not to be totally exhausted at the end of every day! He or she will organise brothers and sisters, no matter whether they are older or younger. We find them playing games in which Leo can be leader, producing little plays, playing at schools (with themselves, of course, as teacher) and generally making sure that the others follow their lead.

It is vitally important for parents to praise the Leo child's efforts. In this way the child will work even harder, and produce even more tangible results. Criticism must be handed out with great tact, and

with a sense of humour, for if young Leo feels deflated the natural self-confidence will crash, and his or her instinctive creative ability be thwarted. This can have very negative effects in later life, and perhaps lead to feelings of discontent and lack of fulfilment—and an unfulfilled Leo is a very sad and unhappy animal indeed.

The child's tendency to show off must, of course, be controlled, and this is best done by making them aware of the fact that they should give other people a chance, and not expect to be the centre of attention the whole time. To bring out the best qualities, encourage your young Leo to help less fortunate people, perhaps adopting an elderly person or making sure that toys with which they have finished are passed on to charities.

☆ CAREER AND SPARE-TIME

Perhaps the most important factor when considering suitable careers for Leos is that in one way or another there must be scope for the individual to express organisational ability and showmanship. Even if a Leo's job is not particularly exciting, there should be the opportunity for flair and enthusiasm. The young Leo teenager taking a first job in a large department-store, for instance, will want—and need—to be able to show off the products on sale and give the customer the impression that they are the very best available in the area.

Leos are generally ambitious, and will certainly want to reach the top of their chosen profession, whatever that is. But they are in no way ruthless, and will not step on others in the progress. They have the capacity to work extremely hard, and when they are in charge of others they will expect an equally high standard of effort and performance. They need emotional involvement in their work, and will see to it that this is the case; they have the happy knack of making something special out of the most menial job. Whether they are cleaning the house or preparing to make the most important political speech of their career, they will use every ounce of effort to make the result as good as it can possibly be. High standards and perfect quality are their constant objective (this can sometimes cause difficulty when they are working with less discriminating colleagues).

Of course Leos are found in all professions, but bearing in mind their enormously powerful creative urge, the fine arts are well represented—particularly perhaps the theatre, in all its forms; we also find Leo fashion designers, jewellers, painters and craftspeople of all kinds. But creativity of course takes many forms, and Leo chefs are in

command in many a highly-regarded restaurant. Leos also demonstrate their powers of leadership at all levels of the armed services, and many make the grade in professional sport.

The Leo attracted to teaching generally speaking works best with rather older children and university students; this sign finds the work rewarding because they can pass their enthusiasm on to their pupils, stimulating creativity in others. If a Leo is inclined to science, it is important that the chosen area should allow scope for creative thought and imagination rather than be solely concerned with, say, the checking of work done by others. There is really no occupation to which Leos are unsuited, provided there is scope for the exercise of their best qualities, and provided they do not have to cope with a small-minded boss or a restricted position.

One British astrologer claims that Leos do not have hobbies or spare-time interests: they only have additional careers. There is much in this, for the Leo needs to take every occupation really seriously, and to develop the highest possible standard in whatever is being done. If Leos wish to learn a new skill, they will want to employ the best teacher in town, and buy the most expensive instruments or machines available. They will work desperately hard trying to develop a high standard of technique as soon as possible. However high the standard they reach, they usually remain unsatisfied, and, even while showing their work off to friends and relatives, they will be quite conscious of the fact that it could be better.

It is difficult to suggest specific interests that Leos might like to follow up; but as a guideline, we can say that anything that will help to develop their artistic and creative potential will be thoroughly worthwhile. If individuals wish to extend their circle of friends and combine that with a hobby, they could consider joining an amateur theatre company. Very different but equally rewarding, they might consider taking a serious in-depth course in astrology—many of the world's finest astrologers have the sign Leo strongly emphasised in their full birthchart. They also make very good members of committees, which stretches their organisational ability. Very soon they will find themselves being elected to the role of chairman or president. Leos often welcome retirement, if only for the reason that it gives them the chance to develop a new career—or several of them!

☆ FINANCE AND INVESTMENT

Although Leos are not averse to excitement, where investment is

concerned, they tend to be cautious and somewhat conventional. Unless truly impressed by a new business project or some big money-making scheme which originates with themselves, they will be inclined to put their financial resources to work in well-tried areas: they will, for instance, be attracted to the glamour of large chains of department stores and any industry in which the products are of a very high quality.

They usually think two or three times before taking financial risks, or speculating with income or savings, for many work surprisingly hard for much less than other people might imagine—so when money is either salted away or put to work, the individual Leo would rather opt for a slightly lower level of return than for a get-rich-quick scheme. Leos like the best of everything, and will strive hard to increase their income as the years go by; even the youngest members of the sign soon realise that they would rather spend a lot of cash on, for instance, the occasional drink or coffee in the best place in town than on a whole series of meals in junk-food restaurants.

The natural choice for investment is gilt-edged securities, and it is as well for Leos to stick to investing in large enterprises—small 'flutters' don't usually pay off as well as anticipated. Leos attracted to the theatre will enjoy playing the role of an 'angel'—investing in shows. If it pays off, this is perhaps one of the most exciting investments a Leo could make, but we would advise caution: you must be able to afford the possible loss.

One thing in which many Leos enjoy investing is jewellery: when they are very young they will buy cheap fashion jewellery (see *Image* on page 84); but it is a good rule to encourage them to graduate from that to small pieces or real gold and gemstones. In that way they will enjoy their money, and can show off a little at the same time, and be in a good position to be able to raise instant cash if necessary. There are, however, one or two important considerations if they choose to take this particular path. Remember that the selling price is almost always below what you originally paid, and that valuable jewellery should be insured, which in itself is very expensive. If a Leo can accept these restrictions, then a lot of pleasure will be gained from a collection of jewellery.

Thinking of Leos' liking for their own individual 'kingdom', most of them will want to go in for house purchase as soon as possible. Although this is by no means unique to one particular zodiac type, very often we find Leos spending rather more than they can actually afford on buying and keeping up a handsome property. This is because they like to develop a luxurious and comfortable lifestyle which they

can share with family and friends, whilst ruling the roost at the same time.

☆ Health and exercise

The Leo constitution is usually good, but they should always be very much aware of the fact that in cold weather (or indeed even when it is reasonably warm,) their circulation can suffer. While many cope well with hot climates, there are very few who positively enjoy the cold.

The spine is the Leo area of the body, and it is absolutely essential for Leos to be aware of this—they can all too easily suffer from backache. Their inherent sense of pride usually encourages them to walk extremely well; indeed, sometimes they are accused of looking down their noses at others. This is usually nothing to do with snobbery, it's just their natural, perhaps unconscious, awareness that they should be physically upright in order to preserve their general well-being.

The heart is the Leo organ, and it is essential for our Leo friends even more than for others to take regular, steady exercise all their lives. This not only encourages good circulation, but keeps the heart muscles and veins in superb condition, so that the Leo may continue to live a necessarily full and rewarding life. Perhaps the most pleasant form of exercise for this zodiac group is dancing, not only because it is exercise, but because it is also a form of creative expression—another important aspect of Leonine life.

When they are involved in team-games, Leos' powers of leadership will soon emerge, and because they wish to be best at everything they do, they need to be careful that they do not strain their physique in the quest for perfection. We often find the young apprentice footballer or student dancer staying on the field or in the studio long after everyone else has gone home, trying to come to terms with some specific complex movement.

Because loyalty is part of the nature of Leos, once they have decided on a form of exercise they will stick to it for many, many years. In a way this is a good thing, for they get to know just what they can demand of their bodies, and where, if at all, inherent weaknesses lie. Because of their tendency to show off, however, it is sometimes as difficult for them to modify their exercise programme as anything else in their lives. Care should be shown here, for undue strain on the system may easily lead to strain on the Leo heart. One of the best Leo forms of relaxation is a total change of occupation and scene—from something which makes demands on the creative intellect to some-

thing more mechanical or physically orientated, and vice versa. But they should always try to ease slowly out of their many interests as bedtime approaches, especially if they are involved in creative work, otherwise it is almost impossible for their minds to switch off once they get into bed.

The gland associated with the Sun (which rules Leo) is the thymus, an endocrine gland behind the upper end of the sternum that is important during the early years of childhood and puberty. It seems to be connected with the immunisation of the body against bacteria. Leos should perhaps take more than average care to seek out every possible innoculation before travelling, and indeed preventative medicine is probably more important to them than to any other sun-sign group.

Leos will be more likely than people of other zodiac signs to feel unwell or out of sorts when for some reason their style is cramped—perhaps by unsympathetic partners, parents or colleagues. They will not be able to stand up straight and face the world as they want, and this can have a physical effect—clinging coughs and colds, for instance—and their own psychological sun will stay resolutely behind grey clouds. Although they are naturally resilient, when depressed Leos show remarkably persistent physical symptoms. Generally speaking, they have a high energy level and achieve much, but without realising it they can easily over-tax their energies and burn themselves out. Needless to say it is very important for them to be aware of this, and to develop truly relaxing interests as well as excitingly demanding and creative ones.

☆ HOME ENVIRONMENT

Rich or poor, the Leo will own a palace. Whether it is a vast castle, a villa in the South of France or a tiny terraced house in an industrial city, the individual will strive to make it something special, spending a great deal of money—as much as can be afforded—on improvements and beautiful things. If there is a garden, the chances are that it will be filled with as many colourful flowers as possible, and if the Leo is inclined to grow fruit and vegetables, they will be succulent and (where the climate permits) exotic.

The home itself will have an air of luxury, and will be colourful and warm. The furniture will be stylish and elegant, and the choice of patterns will probably reflect Leo's exuberance and enthusiasm for life—no small, wishy-washy meandering designs. We will rather find the boldness of William Morris' designs, of rugs with interesting thick

textures or perhaps the extravagance of a Chinese silk carpet—again with a strong, bold pattern.

Unless they live in a very hot country, Leos will like a living-room that gets its fair share of sunshine, and if the beauties of the sunrise or sunset can be seen from their windows, so much the better. Indeed, the Leo will positively blossom in the rosy colours of dawn or dusk. Although most Leos hate housework—there are far more interesting things to do than *that*!—they will endeavour to keep their homes looking splendid because their sense of pride would be hurt if the place wasn't always looking its best. Many who can afford cleaning ladies will do without them simply because they know they can do the job better themselves—and besides, it is a very good way of working off aggression!

So when we enter a Leo home, we can expect to find it looking beautifully polished, clean and tidy and easy on the eye, with every ornament, picture or piece of furniture placed in such a way as to show it off to its best advantage. Leos must be careful, however, to control showiness in their decoration schemes, as in other spheres of their lives. It is, for instance, a little too easy for them to display a grand picture which is perhaps a mite too large for the wall, two or three opulent candlesticks where one would be more effective, and so on. When this tendency is controlled, the true elegance and love of quality of this sign will be fully present.

Spending an evening with Leo you should be entertained well; a classic dish will be served, accompanied by a good quality wine (claret, perhaps, or if there is any kind of celebration there is a good chance of champagne). The dining-table will be impeccably set with white linen and china with maybe a touch of gold in the decoration; everything, in fact, will sparkle and give off an air of luxury.

Richness of colour, in interior decoration, will be second only to richness of fabric. There will be no lack of lush velvet or maybe high quality leather furniture. The lighting will be specially interesting, and a clever use of spotlights to enhance either a favourite possession (perhaps a minor work of art) is common. But the lighting will in no way be strong or intrusive, but as warm as the general colour scheme, and the Leo's ability to make everyone feel totally relaxed and comfortable—if perhaps also a little in awe!

There will be a warm glow of colour—red and warm brown, for instance; golden yellows are very popular, and indeed we may find a hint of gilt here and there. In contrast, Leos often use pale shades of turquoise or perhaps green to cool the hot colours which are their favourites.

The paintings on their walls will be happy and optimistic and full of sun-worship—the exuberance of Van Gogh's sunflowers, for instance; they may also enjoy Victorian *genre* paintings such as Frith's 'Derby Day'; paintings of the theatre by Manet, Degas or Sickert will be popular, and if the person is interested in collecting paintings perhaps some contemporary costume or set-designs may not be beyond the pocket. Others may be attracted to reproductions of the Lascaux cave-paintings or paintings of noble jungle beasts.

☆ Image

Clothes There is no doubt about it, Leos like to make an impact, so their clothes will in one way or another have an element of the spectacular about them. The young members of the sign enjoy wearing a lot of glitter and an array of very bright colours. This is fine for them, because from these early experiments a more tasteful and quality-conscious image usually grows. They are keen to keep up with changing fashions, but on the other hand are often attracted to more expensive ranges than they can afford, so have to come to terms with both these possibilities in their own way. Many Leos will go for quality and a slighty conservative look, while others, because they are eager to make an impact, may be tempted into buying a spectacular outfit which can only be worn once or twice, and they have to learn their mistakes the hard way.

It is quite important for Leos to have an extensive wardrobe and very often they will rest satisfied only when they know they have something suitable to wear on any occasion. They are proud enough to want to own some outfits with a well-known designer's name on the label, and even if they hang on to one of these for years they will be inventive enough to make them appear different by adding some spectacular accessory such as a pure silk scarf or interesting piece of jewellery. It is amusing to discover that most members of this zodiac sign are very aware of their appearance from behind; they will like clothes with a back interest, and will often ask friends and partners 'How does it look from the back?' Traditionally, Leos are attracted to expensive furs; these days, happily, no self-respecting lioness would seriously consider killing other animals for their skins. Fake furs have a greater appeal, and are more fun.

As we have already mentioned, jewellery can be quite important to Leos as an investment, and parents of young Leos should bear this in

mind and encourage them from an early age to collect small but valuable pieces as presents. Other than that it will not be too difficult for them, as circumstances allow, to convert pieces of fashion junk-jewellery into the real stuff.

The Leo mane is a source of considerable amusement among astrologers: indeed, its presence will often be a key factor in recognising this sun-sign type. Whether short or long, fine or coarse, and irrespective of colour, it will form an important part of the general image—Leos will like to make the most of it, perhaps adapting a slightly exaggerated style in order to do so. Usually it is vigorous in growth and not always easy to tame, but it does most certainly have something of the lion about it.

The overall Leo image has panache, elegance and a sense of drama, and provided that individuals can control their liking for glitter and showiness they can look extremely smart.

Extenders As Leos spend a lot of money on their main outfits, so with growing prosperity they will enjoy choosing and using beautiful handbags, umbrellas, sun-glasses and so on. It is almost impossible to describe the pleasure they will get from snapping shut an expensive handbag or briefcase, and they will be tempted to buy beautiful suitcases.

Despite all this, Leos are not very keen on being burdened down by bags and parcels, or any clutter, and it is surprising how easy it is for them to find a minion to carry even the smallest parcel—especially if it does not happen to have come from Harrods! Sun-glasses are an essential part of the Leo kit, for although they love the sun they hate its glare, and we often find them wearing interesting and unusual glasses.

The choice of scents often has a passionate but surprisingly light level, with undertones of almond. Leo make-up will bring out the tawny, healthy, sun-tanned qualities of the wearer, so that even in winter they will sport a look which suggests that they have been spending time in sunnier climes. Leo women are not terribly good at playing a *femme fatale* role, partly because this can involve their appearing pale and interesting rather than healthy and positive! Needless to say, the Leo choice in cameras will be of the highest quality, protected by a well-made and handsome case.

Cars It seems too easy to say that every Leo aspires to a Rolls Royce or Cadillac, but many Leos will find the staid, formal appearance and image of such cars displeasing, in spite of the quality. It is more

realistic to suggest that havng made a choice of car, Leo goes for the very best in the range, and equips it with as many extras as possible.

☆ Travel

Most Leos enjoy travelling, providing they don't have to sacrifice too many comforts. When they are young, they will cope with the rigours of camping or roughing it in some other way; but they will very soon come round to the idea that it is, after all, nice to be as comfortable abroad as one is in one's own home. And having reached that conclusion many will, of necessity, suffer considerable conflict when they want to chase off to see opera in Italy, ballet in Leningrad or the paintings in the Prado, but realise that they cannot afford to do so and at the same time enjoy the creature comforts of a five-star hotel. Needless to say, a compromise will have to be found, but hopefully not for too long!

Leos seem to cope with most means of travel—but again, with an eye to comfort. The Orient Express, Concorde or the QE2 will be ideal; but provided they can sit in reasonable comfort and enjoy reasonable food, they will put up with something less luxurious.

In view of their liking for the Sun, unless they live in a particularly warm climate, Leos will probably want to spend holidays in warm latitudes rather than chilly ones. They usually tan rather well, and are sensible about looking after their skins while abroad, but we would advise them to take strong sun lotions with them, and not to be too impatient, especially if they want the tan to last a good, long time.

Leos are also advised to take some extra vitamins with them when they travel, especially if the trip has a busy schedule—very often in their enthusiasm to get everything done they may overdo things and lower their vitality.

The more exclusive the holiday resort the better, but in spite of enjoying relaxing days on the beach or by the pool, Leos really do need some kind of cultural feast too, whatever their particular interest. If they can combine a relaxing holiday with concerts, open-air performances or perhaps the garish glitter of carnival time, this will be far more rewarding for them. They are often at their best in capital cities, and learning the first names of head waiters in the best hotels and restaurants can be an amusing and prestigious hobby. Many Leos become tremendously excited at extending their collection of countries, seas and oceans, and will be keen to find out what each place they visit has to

offer in the way of beautiful cathedrals and art galleries, flower festivals, carnivals or theatres.

Leos are reluctant to make fools of themselves, and for that very reason can appear somewhat pompous and aloof. If they go on holiday to a resort which is well-known for a sporting activity in which they have no experience, they should make quite sure that they can afford to spend quite a lot of money on the best tuition available. They will be eager to reach as high a standard as possible, and will take this kind of pleasure very seriously indeed. This doesn't necessarily mean, of course, that they lack the capacity to enjoy whatever they have chosen to do; but they will endeavour not to fall into the sea when wind-surfing, tumble from their skis or their ponies, more than is absolutely necessary.

Leo children on holiday will at once organise all the other children around in their age-group into some kind of game, and don't be surprised if it's follow-my-leader! Their imaginations will be enhanced and stimulated by visits to palaces and castles, or indeed to any beautiful building or city. They should always be encouraged to take a small artist's kit with them, and to draw and paint their surroundings as much as possible. Encourage them, too, to buy a few quality souvenirs which are really typical of the country, and watch the amount of time they spend in the sun—they may over-do the outdoor life.

Travelling with Leo children offers excellent opportunities to help them develop their organisational ability: why not make them totally responsible for one particular piece of luggage, thus increasing their confidence? Teaching them a few sentences of the local language will also be a very good idea, and will appeal, allowing young Leo to show off just a little in the hotel restaurant.

☆ Presents to please

Leo enthusiasm will readily surface when you give them a present. Even if this is something they don't specially want, their eyes will sparkle and they will be extremely expressive in their thanks, which means that the giver gets a great deal of pleasure, too.

You will not go far wrong if you give a very young Leo something colourful and perhaps glamorous; if your Leo friend is older and has 'arrived' remember that it is in no way important to spend a fortune on the present. He or she would not want you to. It will be much better to choose something you can afford, no matter how tiny that may be: a small cake of quality soap, a minute box of hand-made chocolates,

★ FAVOURITE TO LEO ★

★ **LEO COUNTRIES**—include Italy, Sicily, the South of France, the Alps, Romania, Czechoslovakia, Southern Iraq, the Lebanon.

★ **LEO CITIES**—include Bath, Bristol, Portsmouth, Chicago, Philadelphia, Los Angeles, Rome, Prague, Madrid, Syracuse, Damascus, Bombay.

★ **TREES**—Leo trees include the palm, the bay, the walnut, the olive, and citrus trees.

★ **FLOWERS AND HERBS**—Almond, celandine, helianthus, juniper, laurel, marigold, mistletoe, passion flower, peppermint, pimpernel, rosemary, rue, saffron, sunflower.

★ **FOODSTUFFS**—Meat; vegetables with a high iron content.

★ **CELL SALTS**—Mag. Phos., Nat. Mur.

★ **STONE**—Ruby.

★ **COLOUR**—The colours of the sun, from dawn to dusk.

will be far more acceptable than a vast bottle of cheap toilet water or an equally showy box of mass-produced chocolates, however prettily packed.

Presents that encourage Leo creativity are also certain winners; find out your friends' particular interest and help them to develop it. Likewise, if you know a budding, young ballerina, give her a new pair of first-rate satin ballet shoes and you will have a friend for life. Rather differently, if you can take a Leo to the theatre or cinema or arrange any kind of special evening out, this will be very popular. If you have cause to say thank you to a Leo, some tiny well thought-out and long-lasting gift will be very much appreciated—perhaps a small ornament or luxury item that they can use, for instance some special notepaper, or a particularly attractive fountain-pen. Such things always give lasting pleasure to our quality-conscious Leo friends.

If you are buying a Leo a present for the home, you might well consider choosing something from a craft gallery—a piece of pottery, for instance, or perhaps a small original drawing or painting. Leos also love beautiful glass and mirrors, so this is usually a safe bet. They like fairly adventurous reading—novels that move quickly and have an escapist element. They are not terribly keen on stories that concentrate on small areas of life, but will identify with heroes and heroines who make the most of their potential and are assertive without being ruthless. Biographies of royalty and theatre personalities are also extremely popular.

Perhaps the most fun thing you can give an imaginative Leo child will be a collection of dressing-up clothes and a box of cast-off beads and jewels; books of traditional fairy-tales with gorgeous illustrations will also be cherished for years to come. Always remember, or course, to encourage their creativity and latch on to any hint they may drop about wanting to learn to play an instrument, skate or go to drama classes.

· AUGUST 24 — SEPTEMBER 22 ·

☆ THE MYTH

Two thousand years ago the symbol of Virgo was a pretty girl of fifteen, an angel with wings representing Astraea, the heavenly goddess of Justice who lived on earth during the Golden Age. But Virgo was then an air sign; when Ptolemy made it an earth sign, the pretty girl became a cold, sharp-tongued old maid! The qualities of the sign lie somewhere between the two: but no goddess of mythology really symbolises the sign's modern qualities.

☆ THE SIGN

The *ruling planet* of Virgo, with which it has a special relationship, is Mercury; it is a *mutable*, *feminine*, *earth* sign. *Positive traits* include discrimination, keen analysis, modesty, cleanliness, tidiness; *negative traits* fussiness, a strong tendency to worry and nag, hypercriticism, over-fastidiousness, abnormal conventionality, inhibition, underestimation of the self.

Virgo in a nutshell The need to serve is paramount, often to the detriment of self-advancement.

☆ GENERAL CHARACTERISTICS

It is often the case that Virgoan modesty will prevent the full blossoming of many fine characteristics; a tendency to under-estimate the self, and a fear of not being able to cope, will prevent development. There is often an over-careful attitude to life, which must be corrected at an early age if the individual's personality is to blossom.

Here we have a very practical person, one who will plan every move with care, paying great attention to detail. It is important for this zodiac group consciously to develop breadth of vision in order not to get bogged down in the minute details of every aspect of life. The Virgo mind is usually extremely good, and will often be capable of excellent literary work. There is an incisive quality which usually blossoms in an interesting, lively way in argument and debate, though sometimes opinions can be given and facts presented rather harshly and over-critically.

This is an extremely hard-working zodiac type, always ready to help anyone in need, and often making great personal sacrifices for the

family, to the extent sometimes that careers are given up, and the individual becomes the slave of domesticity and routine. There is a very high level of nervous energy, which must be positively used if tension is not to build up leading to nervous strain or migraine.

Mrs Ogmore-Pritchard, in Dylan Thomas' *Under Milk Wood* is the absolutely archetypal Virgo: 'Put your pyjamas in the drawer marked pyjamas . . . and before you let the Sun in, mind it wipes its shoes.' Looking at other *Virgos in Fiction*, the heroine of Alice in Wonderland comes immediately to mind, with her hypercritical attitudes, precision and talkativeness; Maria in Shakespeare's *Twelfth Night* is a typical serving Virgoan, continually busy, and not without a sense of fun; Don Giovanni's servant Leporello is another example, with his meticulous list of his master's conquests, and his willingness to engage in all kinds of machinations in his service.

The Virgoan's *greatest asset* is practicality. Their *greatest need* is to be kept busy, and their *greatest problem* the tendency to worry. Their *greatest vulnerability* is lack of self-confidence. *The Virgoan motto*: Cleanliness is next to godliness.

☆ FRIENDSHIP, LOVE AND MARRIAGE

Friendship Our Virgoan friends keep us active and will do every odd job that may go with friendship; they will be the ones to offer to book the tickets, reserve the tables, and so on, but it is very important for us to make sure that they fully understand what we want, how much we wish to pay, and so on, since it is not easy for Virgoans to make decisions involving other people. Expect your Virgo friends to criticise you quite harshly at times; but don't take what they say sitting down—get a good debate going, and you'll be doing them a favour, for you will be exercising the Virgoan mind and speeding up the lively rapport between you. Virgoans are very practical people, and when we need help will be quick to spring to our aid; we can safely call upon them to do so, for they are extremely reliable. It is good to share a common interest or hobby with a Virgoan; on the whole friendship with one needs this kind of boost as it won't be like those friendships with some other zodiac types which drift on in an easy, motiveless way. Virgoans are very good at motivating us into all kinds of enthusiastic action. But their boundless nervous energy can also be a trifle wearing as it is almost impossible to encourage them to sit still and relax over a drink or a cup of coffee.

Love When Virgo falls in love, the natural reaction is all too often 'But he/she will never see anything in *me*.' It is at this point that Virgo modesty is at its strongest and least helpful. At its best, it can be a great asset, for when it is genuine (as it is with this group) modesty has a charm of its own. Unfortunately, it can become too dominant a factor, and as a result Virgoans often lose confidence in their powers of attraction, and tend not to express themselves as fully or rewardingly as they might. This can cramp their style, and from a sexual point of view considerable inhibition can sometimes occur. Many have a very romantic nature crying out for expression; it is up to the partner to encourage it, and also to encourage a total relaxation into the pleasures of love. Virgoans will work very hard, perhaps too hard, for their lovers; once again, this is a tendency which is a kind of cover-up for inhibition. There is sometimes a puritanical attitude to sex, to the point that the individual may even feel there is something 'dirty' about it. But here we have very faithful lovers, and if we can ease them gently into sharing, encouraging them to relax into a relationship, not to spend all their time worrying about where they live, what to eat next, whether the home is clean enough, we have a wonderful partnership, from which a great deal of genuine warmth and enthusiasm will grow.

Marriage Once settled into a permanent relationship, it is extremely important for a Virgoan to realise that the critical tendency in their nature is often too forcibly expressed towards the partner. The loved one's irritating individual habits and mannerisms can get totally out of perspective, and if Virgoans find this happening they should turn their critical qualities on to themselves, asking some pretty soul-searching questions, for they may well be using the partner's weaknesses (as they see them) as an excuse for their own inhibitions and shortcomings. It is in this area that they are most vulnerable to problems. If they become seriously worried about any aspect of their relationship, they must also realise that in no way will they be short of words to describe what is wrong, and they should certainly do so—their powers of communication are excellent (we must not lose sight of the fact that Mercury, the planet of communication, rules their sign). Those of us married to someone of this zodiac type are, however, unlikely to be bored!—there will always be something interesting to talk about, some new hobby to be started, or some household or garden task to be shared. Members of this sign will work hard within a marriage; there is a constancy and faithfulness which will develop provided the partner does not lack energy, and is prepared to spend it on rather practical, non-flippant hobbies and recreations.

☆ PARENT AND CHILD

Virgoan parents will be very keen to fill their children's lives with a great many interesting and varied activities. The sort of toys they purchase will have a good, firm educational aspect, and because they take such an active interest in their children's intellectual development they will try to get them talking and reading at a very early age. Of course this is splendid for the children, who will start school with a very considerable advantage.

But the Virgoan tendency to criticism will sometimes have a negative effect, especially if the individual child would thrive on an enthusiastic, warm response from parents, and actually needs a great deal of positive encouragement and praise. Virgo parents really should think very seriously about this particular aspect of their role, for sometimes what may seem to them to be a reasonable critical attitude seems a positive put-down from the child's point of view.

There is an element of the teacher in many Virgoans; this is a terrific asset, since it is easy for them to inspire their children, and as a result we find the youngsters always involved in some interesting occupation —they are not allowed to do nothing, or just slump in front of a television screen.

Virgoans like to live an orderly life, and there will be a certain amount of discipline at home; but we would suggest that when they become parents, they should delegate some household chores to their children as they grow up, otherwise the Virgoan mother will be cleaning the bedrooms and the shoes of teenagers or twenty-year-olds who have not yet left home, and are not likely to do so while life is so easy!

If you have a Virgoan child in the family, keep him or her busy. You may have to encourage consistency of effort, but do not discourage duality: this, too, can be an asset—Virgoans are usually pretty versatile. You will instinctively know if your young Virgoan is worried, for they will complain of tummy-ache and will immediately go off their food. Take this as a danger-signal, and encourage them to tell you what is wrong—the chances are that someone has upset them at school, or that they think they have not done as well as they should with some study project. Very often, however, these children become teachers' pets; they are usually neat and tidy (dirt seems to run away from them!) and their exercise-books and handwriting usually look good. They are also willing to do all kinds of classroom chores, and enjoy it; but like their elders they can assume too servile a role. This is a mixed blessing, for in many cases powers of leadership and good

organisational ability are present, and these should be encouraged and developed from an early age. The children will often do extremely well at literary and allied subjects, and should be encouraged to write.

☆ CAREER AND SPARE-TIME

While Virgoans need an above-average level of security, and are able to cope with a predictable routine, they should, ideally, search out a career which stretches them intellectually and gives them a certain amount of variety.

Most astrologers agree that here we have the perfect secretary and personal assistant, but while this is true Virgoans ought not to get too stuck in this kind of subservient role; with the development of self-confidence and with the reassurance of their partners and families that they are extremely practical and capable, they can go much further.

To help them along the way, they should always be consciously aware of the fact that they may tend to criticise their colleagues too harshly; it is easy for them to give offence and provoke hostility towards themselves. Many Virgoans make excellent teachers, and if they are interested in this profession they should certainly take it up. But their critical attributes are perhaps most positively expressed in investigative journalism, critical writing and market research. They will often use words extremely cleverly and economically, and will, for instance, develop an admirable interviewing technique. We find many Virgoans making the grade in politics and as trade unionists; many have the capacity to sell, and a good business sense is very often a tremendous asset.

The outdoors is usually important to Virgoans, so agriculture, horticulture and allied occupations are strongly recommended.

This sign is much connected with health and hygiene, so here too there are career possibilities, with a strong accent on alternative medicine and health-foods.

It is very important that Virgoans recognise the fact that there will be times when they will worry unduly about their jobs (as, indeed, about everything else!). This is likely to affect their health; so it is as important for them to talk over work programmes with their partners as it is for parents of Virgoan children to get them to talk over difficulties at school. When they are unemployed, it is advisable for Virgoans to work out a careful schedule for the day, and to stick to it. It should be divided up into time for writing letters applying for positions, for going to the local library to check the newspaper advertisements, and

most importantly for physical exercise. If this is not done, restlessness and discontent will add to their worries, and they will suffer even more than necessary. They should look upon periods of enforced inactivity as a challenge in themselves, and seize the opportunity to extend their existing knowledge within the fields of their career or profession, or perhaps to start learning a new skill.

Of all signs of the zodiac, Virgo has the reputation of being the most hobby-orientated; it is good for them to have a wide variety of spare-time interests. These should vary from the physically active to the intellectually stimulating, not forgetting that there should be at least one occupation which is practical but soothing to the often over-active Virgoan mind. Best of all in this category is gardening; or if the individual does not have a garden, rearing and caring for potted plants is an excellent substitute. But here is an interesting enigma: Virgoans either have very green fingers, or are instant death to plants—so that their homes are either full of beautifully thriving, lush foliage, or absolutely bare of it.

Generally speaking, Virgoans are good at any hobby which involves the dextrous use of the hands; they love to sew, to do patchwork, crochet and knitting; but in spite of their reputation for neatness, they are often in a hurry to get a project finished, and sometimes tend to cut corners, so that loose ends are far too apparent. Another golden rule is that they will enjoy and be good at working with such natural materials as wool, wood and clay, and make wonderful weavers, woodcarvers and potters. Others should encourage their development along these lines. They will also love reading, and book-binding might be fun, and profitable.

☆ FINANCE AND INVESTMENT

When Virgoans have a hard-earned sum to invest, they will be unlikely to take risks with it. With their usual meticulous care, they will collect together as many details as possible about the area to which they are thinking of committing their money, and consider every possible aspect. Because this is an *earth* sign, it is probably as well for them to go for steady growth, though sometimes they will be a little impatient and seek out more excitement. If this is the case, they should rely on their natural business sense and unique ability to question brokers and bank managers about the advantages and disadvantages of any investment opportunity on offer. On the whole, they are pretty careful with money, and often give the impression that they are less well-off than

they really are, perhaps because so many of them cannot stand showiness or the ostentatiousness natural to, say, a Leo.

Interesting and possibly lucrative areas of investment could be agriculture, insurance, the media and department-stores. But because Virgoans are hard-working, they might consider turning one of their interesting hobbies into a small business project, which could become surprisingly profitable just because they are so willing to put real energy into it.

When Virgoans receive an inheritance or in some other way get possession of a large sum, their immediate reaction is 'It won't change my life: I have everything I need.' Certainly their needs are often as modest as their personality. But even if they do not desire to change their life-style, they should develop their natural business sense, for there is potential there which it would be a pity to waste, and through it they may find a rewarding new means of self-expression. They may also be inclined to give large sums to charity. If this is so, splendid; but possibly they should become *actively* involved in a charity. For giving time and energy will be as rewarding for them as giving money, and they will certainly benefit psychologically.

Another area in which business acumen could find expression is in the growth industry of whole-foods. Opening a health food shop or perhaps taking a course in some form of alternative medicine is ideal for Virgos. Women whose children are at school or have left home would do well to think very seriously along these lines; they have talent in such areas. Specialising in some particular aspect of the antique trade would also exercise their ability to consider and check minute detail.

Virgoans will gather that they are the specialists of the zodiac. If they wish to start any business, they should concentrate on one specific area or aspect of it, which could exercise their particular psychological strength. They are in an excellent position to make a great deal of money from the accumulation of knowledge and the development and presentation of unique skills.

☆ HEALTH AND EXERCISE

It is absolutely essential for all sun-sign Virgoans to recognise the fact that they have an extremely high level of nervous and physical energy which must be positively used. If they don't have enough to do, or enough ways of occupying their lively minds, their systems will

stagnate, and they will be more likely than most people to become physically unwell.

The stomach is the Virgoan body area, and almost inevitably, when something goes wrong with their lives, they will go off their food and perhaps get serious stomach aches. They are also extremely vulnerable to tension—when they are worried they become tense and fidgety, and this, alas, leads to bad headaches and sometimes to migraine. Then they start to worry about the headaches or the migraine, and this sets up a vicious circle which will be very difficult to break, and cause their whole nervous system to suffer. The side-effects can include skin disorders and even stomach ulcers.

On the positive side, however, Virgoans are very good at self-analysis, and if they take time out to sit down and quietly assess their problems, they can usually detach themselves and be objective, and it is often in this way that they are able to resolve the difficulties. Once they do that, their physical well-being improves very considerably, and health is restored.

Diet is of prime importance. They certainly need a lot of roughage, in order to keep their rather susceptible bowel system in good working order. Virgoans respond well to whole-foods, physically as well as in terms of enterprise. Many indeed are attracted to vegetarianism, which can suit them very well, though the women of this sign should be somewhat careful: sometimes a purely vegetarian diet tends to give them a slightly unhealthy pallor, perhaps because it does not include enough protein.

Virgoans love the great outdoors, and strenuous use of the muscular system through long walks, or perhaps cycling, is fully recommended—it positively burns up both nervous and physical energy, and as a result eases the all too prevalent tendency to nervous tension.

Like their sister-sign, Gemini, Virgoans will also benefit from preventative medicine, and a dose of vitamin B complex will be excellent for their nervous system.

Mercury, which rules Virgo, is associated with the nervous system as a whole, and in particular the way in which the different parts of the body relate to each other; so it is not surprising that Virgoans can sometimes suffer from general tension. It is also very difficult indeed for a Virgoan to relax completely, so (as with some other signs) we particularly recommend the development of relaxation techniques, whether through yoga or some other system (maybe a physical one which involves controlled movement).

Some kind of physical exercise is important to everyone, but

because Virgoans in particular love being out of doors they should try to find some form of exercise which can be taken in the fresh air. Long country walks are ideal, for this will also satisfy their love of nature. Cycling, golf, and (for the young) heavy team-games are all very suitable. Virgoans who no longer have a career will get excellent exercise from gardening—they will attack each task with enormous energy and vigour. They should also aim to vary their exercise, for they hate to be bored, and although they are disciplined it will be best for them to express themselves in a variety of ways.

Virgo is another sign which favours such fast games as tennis, badminton or squash, which will be accepted as an exciting challenge both by the young and not-so-young. Because they are disciplined, people born when the sun is in Virgo should not find it difficult to work away at a very demanding sport. Young Virgoans, if they are of wiry build, could for instance make excellent gymnasts or athletes. Those who are artistic and creative make good dancers, and can be very brilliant at intricate balletic movements.

☆ HOME ENVIRONMENT

The Virgoan home will have a pretty and neat appearance. Virgoans love small patterns of a traditional nature, and so we often find pretty spots and floral designs, checks, and pine furniture in the house. Colours will be bright and cheerful, and the rooms will definitely be interesting in detail, if sometimes slightly cluttered, because our Virgoan friends have a great many varied interests. The overall appearance and atmosphere is tidy, however.

There will be a busy look; sometimes this sign tends to use a combination of patterns. We might, for instance, see a variety of attractively-embroidered or patchwork cushions set against a sofa, the cover of which is already chinzy. Generally speaking, the look of the home and the lifestyle of the individual will be 'country' rather than sophisticated 'town': frills, the use of natural materials, wood floors covered with woollen rugs will be much in evidence. There will be plenty of books and magazines (no doubt including famous works of literature, but a high proportion will be textbooks relating to the individual Virgoan's hobbies). Flower prints or paintings and drawings of the countryside will be popular. Some Virgoans will much admire the abstract paintings of Ben Nicholson, with clear, bright colours. Primitive paintings (like those of the Douanier Rousseau or Grandma Moses) will also have a strong appeal. If the individual Virgo has green

fingers the chances are that the house will be full of interesting and exuberant plants.

Ideally, Virgoans like to live in the country; but many of them find themselves tied to a city career, and unless they can come to terms with long hours of commuter travel they will necessarily be fish out of water. When choosing a house, they should try if possible to be near a park or green open space of some kind, and certainly this should include a few trees.

Fairly heavy pottery and china in warm earthy colours will probably be found on the dining-table, which itself might well be made of natural wood; the chances are that our host or hostess will use table-mats in order to show off the natural beauty of the table itself. Other than that, we may find a very plain classical appearance to the dining-table, with white linen and simple, classic china. But more usually Virgoans enjoy an ethnic look.

There is no doubt that a great deal of time, thought and energy will have gone into the preparation of Virgoan food. It will certainly be wholesome, if a touch unsophisticated. Don't be surprised if you have an entirely vegetarian meal. Approach it with a hearty appetite and an open mind: it may be far less dreary than you imagine! You may be presented with home-made wines or beers, and cider, too, is often popular. Honey or natural brown sugar will probably sweeten the dessert. In the background, classical, perhaps eighteenth-century music will be heard—probably recorded on authentic instruments. But country and western music might also be popular.

The overall country style will be extended to the kitchen, where traditional equipment—pestle and mortar, a set of wooden spoons, Victorian scales, weights and measures—will find their place. Surprisingly, it may not be as tidy as one would expect; very often the Virgoan tendency to 'flap', especially in the last few minutes before guests arrive, may cause them to abandon their usual sense of order and neatness.

You may have cause to smile when you enter the Virgoan bedroom or bathroom; the same modesty will also be present here. The lighting in the bedroom will be less subdued and relaxing than that of many zodiac types, and you may find twin beds with a reasonable distance between them! In the bathroom a splendid array of shower-gels, soaps and other toiletries, possibly scented with lavender and traditional fragrances, will be on display; these may well be traditionally made and come from back-to-nature ranges. There may be fewer mirrors than you might expect, and the extra roll of lavatory paper will be discreetly hidden nearby.

☆ IMAGE

Clothes The Virgo image is neatness personified. The characteristic modesty of the sign is also reflected in clothes and accessories. Many Virgoan women are typical Laura Ashley types, who choose the Victorian look, wearing simple clothes often in country styles, made in natural fabrics with patterns of spots or small flowers. City types of both sexes often look very smart and elegant in navy blue and white, and the men who sport this particular look will often wear an attractive tie with a flower design, contrasting with the severity of their suit.

Virgoans will go for quality and for clothes with a good, long life ahead of them. Over-fashionable, flashy garments are not generally popular—though they are usually quite good at teaming up separates in a variety of ways, in order to offset boredom with the contents of their wardrobe, or predictability in their appearance to their friends. We often find the women wearing white collars and cuffs, and it is surprising just how easily they seem to keep them clean! At the end of a long day in a busy department store or office, Virgoans will look as fresh as at the moment when they arrived in the morning. There is usually little flamboyance in the overall Virgoan appearance, especially on big occasions, whether they sport the simple, elegant city look, or the modest, pretty appearance with echoes of the past.

Colours attributed to the sign are those of the earth—rich greens and browns; sometimes we find an attraction to bright red, perhaps teamed up with the favourite navy blue, and dark grey is sometimes also popular. It is advisable for Virgoans to wear natural materials, and there is room for them to experiment with the different textures of wool and cotton, since this could add a little excitement and variety; they might consider wearing some of the lovely new mohair sweaters which are available—indeed, they may care to do some knitting themselves. They could also get considerable pleasure from cotton satins, velveteens and linens.

Because they lead busy lives, Virgoans will want to have a hairstyle which is very easy to manage: the sort of cut that they can wash easily in the shower every morning, and one where the use of rollers and gels is unnecessary. The chances are that it will either be cut very short or that they will enjoy long, flat styles which only need vigorous brushing and combing to make them look good. They will do well to buy hypo-allergenic cosmetics which have not been tested on animals, and are free of artificial ingredients. Indeed, a rewarding hobby for many of this sign is the making of beauty products at home from fruit and vege-

tables. We would advise Virgoans always to have a warm, lightweight track-suit in their wardrobe, so they can enjoy the fresh air in winter without being too cluttered by heavy clothing.

Extenders Virgoans are not terribly well-organised, but because they like, and need, to be neat, they should consider investing in the kind of handbag or briefcase which has plenty of sections for neatly tucking away pens, pencils, credit-cards, make-up and so on. They will then be able to put their hand immediately on what they want, avoiding minutes of searching when buying something or arriving at a ticket-barrier.

They will probably enjoy wearing very good quality leather gloves and smart belts (perhaps reversible ones). Many Virgoans are heard to say 'I think a nice belt *makes* an outfit!' If they wear a hat, it will be for a practical reason—a beret to keep their hair out of their eyes, for instance, or a hood to keep their ears warm. If they have to wear one on a formal occasion it will probably be as small as they can contrive, for it is something they will not be keen to spend a great deal of money on, even if they are well off.

The Virgoans love of and regard for nature may be reflected in their choice of jewellery, which will embrace beads made of wood, shells, beads, perhaps charmingly carved and coloured. Investing in something of greater value, they may look to amber, malachite, cat's-eye. Small, mounted fossils—a leaf, an insect, a fly—will be very appealing, too. Perfumes should be fresh, un-cloying, with overtones of the open air—perhaps of flowers and herbs.

Cars The Virgoan needs to be mobile, for they all love rushing about on their own and other people's business. The invention of the Mini might have been directed straight at the Virgoan, who will buzz busily around in one—usually a black one. Before that, they probably owned a bicycle, with an enormous basket attached to it to contain shopping, and all sorts of items carefully collected for the church jumble sale.

☆ TRAVEL

Although some Virgoans may feel rather insecure away from their homes and familiar surroundings, they are so inquisitive and eager to discover for themselves what other people, countries and landscapes are like, they will not be reluctant to travel as soon as they have the opportunity.

Perhaps the worst part of any journey for Virgoans is anticipation: will they catch the train, lose the tickets—what if the hotel reservations are faulty? But once they are nicely settled in their resort, their worries will turn homewards: Are the pets all right? Did they switch the electricity off at the mains? Will the neighbours notice the stranger hanging around in the garden? Partners and friends must do everything they can to reassure the Virgoan that all is well. It won't be easy: the best line to take is that as Mr. or Ms. Virgo is such a careful, practical person, there is every confidence that everything has indeed been done, and done well.

It is important for Virgoans to consider their diet when they are away from home. Vegetarians, of course, will try to book at a vegetarian hotel, or at least one which caters for them; a change of water, or diet, can easily upset the Virgoan stomach. A good supply of their favourite cure-alls should accompany every journey. Perhaps it is best to travel overland, if there is time—that way Virgos can see more of the passing countryside and gradually get used to the changing environment and climate. However, if this is not possible maybe they should consider a holiday which will cover at least two resorts, so they do not get bored or restless as a result of too many days in one place.

We can safely say that they will enjoy most kinds of landscape, but forests, mountain scenery and rich, fertile pasture-lands are likely to be favourites. The Swiss and Austrian countrysides, the fertile farming lands of France or the English Lake District could be ideal. Any scorched, parched landscape will be less attractive.

We feel that a temporate climate will also suit Virgos best: if it is too hot they will not be able to take the long country walks most of them find agreeable—besides, when it is very hot they will suffer even more than usual from stomach upsets. Many may also enjoy winter holidays, since these are invigorating, and there is usually plenty to do at sports resorts. Holidays which encourage a specific interest or study are enjoyable, as are visits to particularly attractive stretches of coast or countryside, especially if such places are related to a famous work of literature or art, or even a favourite film.

Virgoan children on holiday will have plenty of energy for sightseeing, and will ask even more questions than usual. They will demand detailed answers, too, and it will be up to parents either to provide the answers themselves, or to give the children extra pocket-money so that they can buy guide-books or maps which will answer the queries for them.

Though often shy, most Virgoans will enjoy visiting local markets, *souks*, etc., and will be readily prepared to drive a hard bargain with

the local stallholders when appropriate. This is because although they are keen to buy interesting souvenirs, they are not at all anxious to part with a single *dinar*, *sou* or *peseta* more than necessary. We suggest they consider buying local wood carvings, pottery or hand-made jewellery and clothing. They should also make quite sure that there is plenty to do in the way of sport and exercise; even when visiting a hot climate in summer, there is usually some local beauty spot (rather than the hotel pool) where the swimming is invigorating but safe.

We must not forget the fact that even in the sunniest climes the weather can become unfriendly; it is a very good idea for travelling Virgoans to take pocket chess, Scrabble, or at least a pack of cards with them, just in case they are forced to stay indoors for several hours. This should also form an essential part of the Virgoan travel kit, whether the journey is for business or pleasure.

☆ Presents to Please

There is a very large scope for choosing a present to please a Virgoan friend or lover. If you have read the previous sections, you will have realised that they are very attracted to natural fabrics, so you could start by deciding whether your gift should be made of wool, wood or perhaps clay!

A piece of hand-made pottery will certainly please, even if it only costs a little. Should you want to give something a little more elaborate, your Virgoan friend would be delighted to own a beautiful wooden salad-bowl. Likewise, if you are thinking in terms of something more personal, a sweater, woollen scarf or perhaps a more glamorous stole in pure silk with a small, perhaps traditional Paisley, or spotted design will also be received with great pleasure.

Presents for the bathroom might include skin products, beautiful soap or perhaps a lightly-perfumed talc or toilet-water. Thinking of the Virgoan liking for natural foods, a pot of your local honey or a selection of herbs and spices are possibilities, and if you happen to know that your Virgoan friend lacks one of Jane Austen's or Henry James's novels, or perhaps one by Barbara Pym, you could do no better than buy it for them. Because they like to keep up-to-date with current affairs and with what is going on in their own individual field of interest, a subscription to a favourite magazine would be popular, as would books on gardening, indoor plants and alternative medicine.

Virgoans will never lack for tea-cloths, pretty aprons, oven-mitts or gardening gloves given to them as presents. All these items spring

★ FAVOURITE TO VIRGO ★

★ **VIRGOAN COUNTRIES**—include Greece, Crete, Yugoslavia, Mesopotamia, Iraq, Syria, Lower Silesia, Brazil, Turkey, the West Indies.

★ **VIRGOAN CITIES**—include Paris, Lyons, Heidelberg, Jerusalem, Corinth, Athens, Boston, Reading, most spas and health resorts.

★ **TREES**—Virgo trees include nut-growing trees (not merely edible nuts).

★ **FLOWERS AND HERBS**—Virgo flowers and herbs are similar to those of Gemini, but particularly include those with bright yellow or blue colourings.

★ **FOODSTUFFS**—Those also ruled by Gemini (see page 52).

★ **CELL SALTS**—Kali Sulph. and Ferr. Phos.

★ **STONE**—Sardonyx.

★ **COLOUR**—Navy blue, dark greys and browns.

instinctively to mind for this sign, and you can actually keep one step ahead by avoiding such presents—the chances are that Virgo has already a cupboard full of them!

Most Virgoan children enjoy games and puzzles, so you can present them with table games and jigsaws on any occasion. It is quite a good idea to throw them a challenge, however, so why not give them some basic materials for a craft or art-form, and leave it to them to use their imaginations? Any kind of stationery makes a wonderful present for grown-up and child Virgoans alike—and if you give a young Virgoan a large exercise-book and some attractive pens and pencils, you could well find that in due course they will present you with the results of their efforts; you might perceive a good story-teller in the making. Because physical activity is important, by arranging for them to have special coaching you could give them a good start in a sport they've not previously tried.

· SEPTEMBER 23 — OCTOBER 23 ·

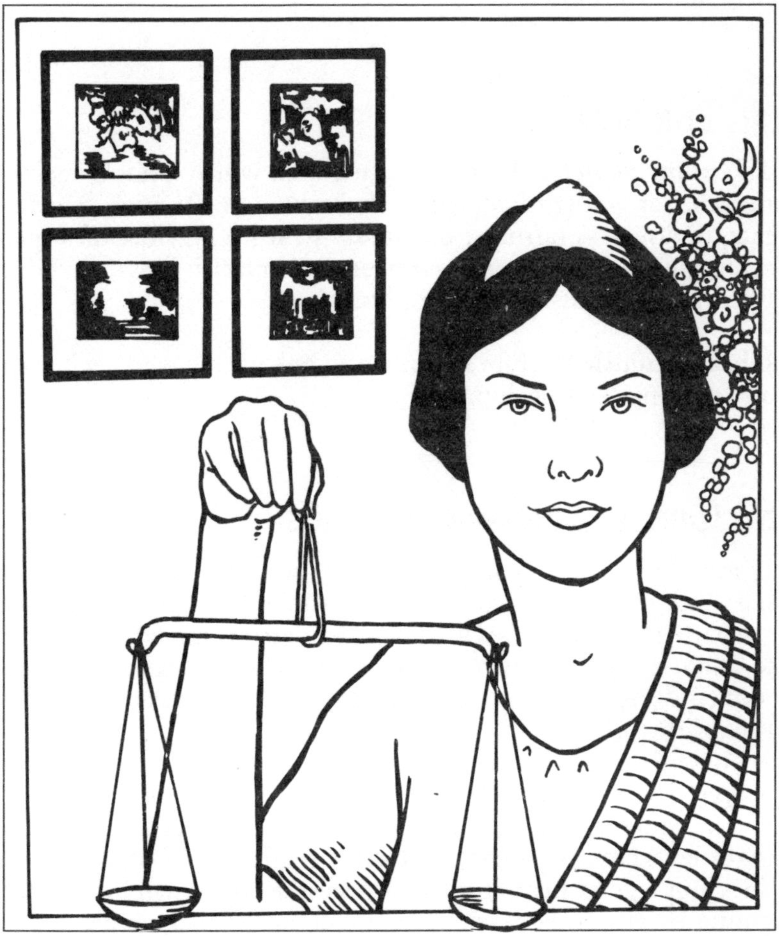

☆ The myth

There is no authoritative myth associated with Libra, but Zibanitu, the Scales, is a Babylonian constellation connected with the myth of the Last Judgement and the weighing of souls by Osiris, and in Egypt the goddess connected with the sign was she who held the Ear of Spring Corn celebrated at harvest-time. Hence a virgin holds the scales, rather than an earth-mother.

☆ The sign

The *ruling planet* of Libra is Venus, with which it has a special relationship. It is a *cardinal*, *masculine*, *air* sign. *Positive traits* include tact, diplomacy, fairness, the ability to see both sides of a question, sympathy; *negative traits* resentfulness, indecisiveness, a tendency to rock the boat, fulsomeness, gullibility.

Libra in a nutshell Libra is only psychologically whole when sharing a rewarding relationship.

☆ General characteristics

Libran characteristics are only seen at their best when the individual is harmoniously relating to another person. Librans have a great need, it seems, to share their lives with another person, and while their attitude to relationships will be fully discussed elsewhere, because it is so vital to their development as people it has to be at the head of any description of them.

Loneliness is something very difficult for individual Librans to accept. Their ability to be kind and tactful are strong points in their favour, and they are willing and ready to help others. But it is essential that they know that what they do is really appreciated—if a Libran does you a good turn, it really is necessary to shown him or her with gratitude, otherwise resentfulness will inevitably emerge.

One of the most distressing natural tendencies with which this zodiac type must come to terms is indecision. We must often wait around for ages while Librans make up their minds, and it is not uncommon for those of this sign to ignore totally the necessity to reach a decision, so that the event or opportunity overtakes them, and the necessity for action no longer arises. This is something of which they should all strive to be aware, and which they should combat, for it is not only detrimental to them and their progress in life, but overwhelmingly infuriating for those close to them.

Librans in fiction would certainly include Shakespeare's Desdemona, in *Othello*—loving and faithful, gentle and unfailingly devoted. Flaubert's *Madame Bovary* shows what happens when a Libra really falls in love with love, and Dora, Dickens' vacuous, silly wife of *David Copperfield* shows another aspect of the infuriating side of a thoroughly Libran character. Many astrologers consider Hamlet to be a Libran—the man who could not make up his mind.

The Libran's *greatest asset* is tact and diplomacy. Their *greatest need* is to be loved, and their *greatest problem* indecision. Their *greatest vulnerability* is to flattery. *The Libra motto*: Share and share alike.

☆ FRIENDSHIP, LOVE AND MARRIAGE

Friendship It can be great fun to share a friendship with a Libran: they certainly know how to enjoy themselves, and there are excellent chances of your spending happy, entertaining times together. They are also very good at encouraging us to relax and have fun, being generous, and likely to spend a lot of money on pleasure. They enjoy seeing others having fun, and sharing it themselves.

Any friend of a Libran may, however, find it necessary to be very firm. For instance, if you suggest a night out, the Libran might not want to decide what to do, or even contribute much to the discussion. So take it upon yourself to make the arrangements, perhaps even going as far as to say, 'On such-and-such a date we *will* go here and do this!' If you leave it to Libra to make a final decision and book the tickets, you may still be in a state of indecision when the date arrives.

Librans love sharing their interests with like-minded friends, and if you have a hobby in common, you will spend a lot of time swopping techniques, tools or machines, and generally discussing how you approach various problems.

This zodiac group can be quite demanding, however, and you should be aware that from time to time you will hear a grumble about your Libran's other friends: a common complaint is 'After all I've done for her, and now look at the way she treats me!' And don't think this won't be said of you, to someone else, for Librans expect constant

gratitude, and often find it very difficult to accept the fact that some other zodiac types are less outwardly expressive than themselves.

Love The skies only become clear, bright sunny blue for a Libran when he or she falls in love. And they do this easily and often! They so long to share their lives with a partner that they take flattery as a declaration of true feelings; that way disaster lies, and they should develop a certain scepticism where personal relations are concerned in order to build up resistance to mere flirtation, and recognise the real thing when it comes. It is interesting that members of this group, which has the greatest problem of any of the twelve where decision-making is concerned, will often rush into emotional relationships without due care and attention, and there is a tendency, for this reason, for them to be more than usually hurt and disillusioned when an affair collapses.

Here we have the true romantics of the zodiac, who will see to it that each developing stage of love is colourful and as luxurious as possible. Libran men, for instance, will present their lovers with beautifully romantic gifts—bouquets of roses, beautiful *lingerie*, and so on, while the women will seize any excuse to lay on big, romantic evenings in comfortable ease, and will spend more than they can afford in setting up memorable occasions with their lovers. In order to get as much as possible out of your relationship with Mr. or Ms. Libra, remember that it must be emotionally in balance, and the rapport between you must be constant.

Marriage The only difficulty Librans are likely to have before committing themselves to a permanent relationship is deciding which partner is most suitable! As we have already said, they tend to rush into marriage because of a deep-rooted, instinctive need to relate deeply to another person. It is true to say that they blossom beautifully once committed, but we must remember that no matter how stable their relationship Librans need to be continually reminded that they are loved, and no matter how much their partners reassure them, they still demand more declarations. Perhaps the least admirable characteristic of the committed Libran is a tendency to rock the boat—consciously or unconsciously to pick quarrels or criticise their partners to the extent that sometimes quite serious outbursts occur. The deep-rooted psychological reason for this is usually nothing to do with the subject of the quarrel itself, which will have been set up purely in order that there is an excuse to kiss and make friends again afterwards—another demand for reaffirmation of the partner's undying love.

This can obviously have fairly disastrous results if it occurs too fre-

quently, and Librans should be aware of the fact that they can wear their partners down by such treatment—and indeed that their continual insistence on reaffirmation of affection can be cloying and destructive.

☆ Parent and Child

Much is said about the Libran's easygoing attitude to life, and we feel that sometimes this characteristic is over-emphasised, especially when it comes to the Libran in his or her role as parent. Yes, they will present an easygoing face to their children, but this is probably only because of their usual state of indecision. When the child asks for something, perhaps permission to go somewhere or do something, the Libran parent may say 'Yes'—but for ulterior motives: they don't want to upset the peace of the household, and cannot be bothered to go into the various arguments against the proposition.

It is true also, that Libran parents will do a great deal for their children—they will certainly spend more than they can afford on them, especially on clothes and out-of-school activities, and they will be very keen for them to be kind and considerate. At their best, Librans teach their children good manners and encourage them to acquire all the social graces; but at times, when important matters are at stake, they will say 'You'll have to ask Daddy/Mummy', thus avoiding once more the necessity to commit themselves.

Libran parents can certainly be great fun, and their children will have happy memories of their childhood, but they will also have experienced a certain amount of annoying frustration as a result of Libran indecisiveness. As they get older, they will learn that it's not too difficult to twist their Libran parent round their little finger.

It is important for parents of Libran children to encourage them from a very early age to be as decisive as possible. When confronted with a decision, they will probably find that the child will say 'What do *you* think, Mummy?' In such a situation, parents should relentlessly pass the buck back to the child, explaining the various possibilities, but trying to exert as little influence as possible, and insisting that the child is the final arbiter.

Certainly Libran children will have plenty of charm, and be keen to please parents, brothers and sisters, and friends. They will also be generous and kind, but often with a tendency to laziness. They must be encouraged to get their energies moving, and if they are attracted to any interest, parents should seize on this as an opportunity to

encourage a really deep involvement. This applies particularly to out-of-school activities, for it is all too easy for Libran children to laze away precious hours staring at television or just day-dreaming. Yet there is a toughness about these children which can be developed to the full by involvement in energetic sport.

☆ CAREER AND SPARE-TIME

From what has been said so far, it will be gathered that loneliness is something abhorrent to all Librans, so a career which puts them in a lonely position is to be avoided—a Libran lighthouse-keeper would not be happy. Unfortunately, when we get to the top of our profession we often find ourselves somewhat cut off from friends and colleagues, and important opportunities which occur for successful Librans should be carefully considered from this point of view before promotion (for instance) is accepted.

In view of the Libran predilection for glamour, many do well in the luxury trades: the fashion industry, hairdressing and beauty therapy, interior decoration and fabric design. All these offer a wonderful outlet for the expression of many Libran talents (in the past, a lot of Librans were successful milliners).

Looking at business more generally, Librans are very successful in small businesses. Usually they are in partnership, of course, for Librans should work with a partner who is good at the practical, financial areas of the business, while they are left free to exert their charm, tact and diplomacy on the customers. They are admirable at making other people feel good, and any profession in which they are able to encourage a partner, friends or colleague towards enhanced well-being will be excellent for them. From this point of view they can make excellent teachers, though they find it difficult to cope with disciplining a rowdy mob of schoolchildren. The diplomatic service is another interesting possibility, offering rewarding challenges (and they will certainly enjoy the social life). They make good agents and go-betweens. Interestingly, we find a high proportion of Librans making the grade in the upper ranks of the armed services: many generals have a Libran sun-sign. When this is the case, the individual is responding to the characteristics and sympathies of their partner-sign in the zodiac, Aries.

Librans are by no means uncompetitive, and can be motivated by quite a strident ambition, if they are emotionally involved in their

work. Under such circumstances, not one jot of Libran laziness or of their 'easy-come, easy-go' tendency will appear.

As with emotional relationships, Librans will be very upset if company politics or petty squabbles break out among colleagues. If they are clever they can act as excellent mediators, and help to restore good relationships; their usual tendency not to take sides will strengthen their own position, for they will detach themselves from the *melée* and use their ability to see every side of a situation. In this way they can act out a very important Libran role—that of peacemaker.

Libran spare-time should be spent in two distinct ways: on the one hand, they should develop a skill which externalises a deep-rooted naturally aggressive tendency—the men, for instance, may do very well at karate, and both sexes will get satisfaction from judo, or perhaps from an energetic competitive game such as tennis or badminton. Women may be happy to learn self-defence techniques. On the other hand, every Libran is basically high in creative ability. Both sexes will probably get a great deal of pleasure from photography, especially if they develop real skill: they will produce exciting, sexy glamour photographs, or beautiful, atmospheric landscapes. Libran women make very good dressmakers, and their intuitive powers, which must not be underrated, will often find realisation in the production of clothes which will be well ahead of current fashion trends.

Generally speaking, these are patient people who will happily spend quite a lot of time working slowly and steadily towards achieving high-quality results, both professionally and privately. It is very good for them to learn to play an instrument of some kind, and they will probably get most pleasure from accompanying other instrumentalists and singers, or perhaps performing either pop or classical music as part of a group. They should always put spare-time aside for gentle conversation and for entertaining their much-loved friends.

☆ FINANCE AND INVESTMENT

Librans love spending money, and need to make as much as possible in order to support a comfortable lifestyle. Many find the money market rather boring, and sometimes their tendency to be indecisive can be fatal—on the stock market, he who hesitates is frequently lost! But though banking and finance can form an important part of their lives, either as a career or engrossing spare-time interest, they should leave practical finance to a trusted adviser.

Having said that, if they can become enthusiastic about the areas in which they are advised to invest, so much the better. The Libran woman with some capital to invest is likely to enjoy the possession of shares in, say, a large cosmetic consortium, while others will find the hotel trade or leisure industry interesting.

As for taking financial risks, from time to time Librans can get excited by money-making schemes. If the person planning the enterprise is someone they know and respect, they will probably be happy to participate. But they should carefully consider the practical aspects of the investment, and resist a tendency to allow themselves to be persuaded, perhaps against their better judgement, just because of their liking for their friend. That can be fatal, especially if the person in question has a lot of charm (maybe he or she will be a Libran, too!).

Going into business for themselves, people of this group will do well to support a project which makes life easier for others, or adds extra colour to their customers' lives. Selling clothes springs to mind, or the beauty trade. Running a car showroom, selling home saunas or exercise machines would also be interesting. But remember the need for partnership in business; the Libran will quite certainly be attracted to some aspects rather than others, and the others should be left to a partner, preferably one who finds them interesting!

It may be that the need for balance in investment is as important to Librans in this sphere of their lives as in others; they must be especially careful not to put all their financial eggs in one basket, for here is a dangerous imbalance for us all, and very much so for the Libran, who could be inclined to favour one area more strongly than another. In business they should attempt to adopt a policy of diversification; they will then gather the benefits of a wide range of investments, and not slip into disaster should one much-cherished company go broke.

Tradition suggests that copper mining would be a good area for investment, since copper is the metal of the sign. Investment trusts are easy to cope with—and here, as the individual's cash is spread around by experts, the hard work is taken out of the attainment of capital growth, and decision-making is limited to the choice of the right trust.

Such good investment habits should be acquired from the earliest possible age, since Librans like to live it up, and tend to spend too much cash on the easy life. So it's an obvious advantage if they can make their money work hard for them.

☆ HEALTH AND EXERCISE

It is important for Librans to use their energy steadily and evenly (again

stressing their need for balance in everything). Many Librans are energetic, and get through an amazing amount of work—and at a nice, steady, almost languid pace which disguises the fact. Their admirable control of their energy is to be envied.

But if they do not exercise (or at the very least do a reasonable amount of walking as they grow older) they may put on weight very easily, and the good looks bestowed upon them by Venus, their ruling planet, will suffer. For similar reasons they must be careful about their intake of sweet, rich food. Many a Libran has a sweet tooth, and finds it difficult to refuse when faced with an expensive box of chocolates or a succulent and exotic *gâteau*. A delight in good wine and the occasional glass of spirits or liqueur is an equal stumbling-block. Indeed, the wining and dining that is often part of their lifestyle can spell physical disaster! Discipline is the only answer—extremely boring and difficult.

The Libran body organ is the kidney, and these should be checked out if any symptoms suggest an upset—continual headaches, for instance. Quite often a minor kidney ailment can be the root cause of the trouble. The glands of Venus are somewhat vulnerable—these are the parathyroids, which play an important part in maintaining the balance of the body liquids. The lumbar regions of the back are also traditionally associated with Libra. Libran women who tend to retain body fluids before menstruation should get some treatment, for this could become a significant problem for them. But perhaps the best thing they can do is make sure they have a very moderate intake of sugar, getting the necessary sweetness from fresh fruit, and giving up sugar in coffee and tea (this is particularly desirable). For good health, the Libran should certainly eschew over-indulgence—and happily, they are rather less vulnerable to this than Taureans—the other Venus-ruled sign. If they ignore these warnings, they must beware of gout (a condition caused by a build-up of uric acid), quite apart from the difficulties we have already mentioned.

Basically, the Libran metabolism is slow; if it can be gently but steadily increased, that will be to the Libran's advantage. Where exercise is concerned, and apart from the sports already mentioned elsewhere, if Librans are to get any pleasure from exercise (and many will decide that they quite simply hate it too much to bother with it!) some icing must accompany the cake. They could, for instance, if they can spare both the cash and the time, join a really good health club, where there is a calm atmosphere, and where work-outs are followed by as much cosseting (in the way of saunas or steam-baths, massages or facials) as possible. They will really need to indulge themselves and their bodies

as a reward for all that toil, sweat and tears. But having joined, don't conclude that the massages and electrical slimming *régimes* can themselves be the solutions to a weight problem: you have to do your part, and that means hard physical work and a sensible diet—there are no easy ways to the body beautiful.

Libra should also try to exercise with like-minded friends; if you can't afford an expensive health club, go jogging or running with a friend. The Libran often has quite a strong competitive spirit, and this can be positively expressed in exercise and sport. The most energetic will do well at squash, and swimming too. All kinds of gentle stretching exercises and rhythmic dancing should be agreeable as will sedate traditional ballroom dancing (Libran women will enjoy making their dresses!) or perhaps ice-dancing. Rowing comes to mind, and golf. Incidentally, it is amusing to watch Librans playing that vicious old game, croquet—here is the gentlest of exercise, but one which will enable them to express their volatile temperament!

☆ HOME ENVIRONMENT

Librans can usually adapt themselves to living almost anywhere—though a run-down area where ugliness or poverty is evident would be less bearable to them than to members of any other zodiac group; and if they have to live in a room without a view, they will probably hang up discreet nets to blot out the blank brick walls which face them, or to obstruct the view of an inquisitive neighbour who lives too close for comfort. A prospect of water—a beautiful calm river or lake, or a lovely garden or park will be particularly pleasing if they have to live in a city; but so would life in a high-rise block above a street of up-market boutiques full of the latest fashions and beauty products! An isolated stretch of country outside their front door, the nearest neighbour miles away, will distress a Libran, however happy they may be with their partner.

The Libran home will be full of comfort and charm. Librans have good taste, and usually manage to express it in pastel colours. They like the sensuous feel of velvets and satins, so we usually find that there are plenty of cushions and curtains in those materials, and very often easy chairs and sofas are similarly upholstered. There will probably be quite large arrangements of cut flowers or flowering plants, and the Libran need for balance and harmony will be likely to make its presence felt in the choice of pictures which will often go in pairs, or at least balance each other from wall to wall. Gracious living and charm will be a common theme: reproductions of Gainsborough's portraits of beautiful women, flower pieces, or perhaps prints of exotic birds will be popular. If there is a collection of anything in the house, it could well be of fashion prints, or perhaps ones showing trades and professions of the past—'The Cries of Old London' for instance. Many Librans love china and porcelain figures, modern and inexpensive or old and precious. The floral theme will often be found in the prints of curtains, though these will not be 'countrified', but sophisticated—rich, full-blown roses, poppies, or whatever will be stylised rather than prettified. You will at once be made to feel comfortable and relaxed, and even if the Libran is very young and impoverished, there will be a feeling of leisurely comfort. Gracious living is important to every Libran, where it can be achieved; without it the Libran will feel unhappy.

The bedroom will be as attractive as the living-room, and even more relaxing. There will not be an overtly sexy atmosphere, but gentle hints that the pleasures of love are not to be neglected will be found in the presence beneath the pillow of the best negligee the Libran woman can afford, and on the dressing-table a collection of colognes and scents for either sex. Deep, comfortable duvets or padded quilts will cover the bed and enhance the decor. The bathroom will be well-stocked, and Librans will leave plenty of toilet-water to choose from, and a variety of sweet-smelling guest soaps. The towels will be spectacular in quality and colour—most Librans have a *penchant* for rich towels.

When it comes to dinner, hopefully Libra will have been sensible, for their own sake, in planning the menu. They thrive best on light rather than heavy food. The meal may be fairly traditional—roast lamb or turkey as the main course, a cold soup (*vichyssoise* or an avocado *mousse*, perhaps) as a starter, and if at all possible, strawberries, raspberries or perhaps a lemon *sorbet* as a dessert. Librans tend to fall back on a *rosé* wine if indecision makes it impossible for them to choose a red or white; but a German Riesling will be popular, too. The table will be beautifully set, the china quite pretty—Harlequin sets are often to be found (another reflection of indecision!), and if the hostess is young, she may well have put together various plates collected at flea-markets, but all with similar colours (an elegant effect is made, without calling for the expenditure of too much hard-earned cash). Librans love cut-glass and crystal, and there will be beautiful glassware if possible (Irish crystal, perhaps). Candles are often on the table, even if there is only a remotely romantic mood in the air.

Background music will be lyrical: Viennese waltzes for the

classically inclined, otherwise numbers from nostalgic 1930s musicals, or perhaps some Andrew Lloyd Webber—though the really assertive young Libran may, on the other hand, go for really hard rock at its most strident.

☆ IMAGE

Clothes There is a certain gentleness about the Libran image. The women often choose light, rather flimsy fabrics in pastel colours, which give an overall 'soft' look. This is usually becoming to them, and when we find them wearing a strictly tailored outfit, they can look less attractive—unless they have cleverly teamed it with a feminine blouse with perhaps full, soft, bishop sleeves or a large bow. When frills are fashionable the Libran woman is in her element. She can very often carry off clear, bright reds or navy blue very well, and this makes a pleasant contrast—especially during the winter season.

Interestingly, in spite of their need for harmony and balance we often find Librans wearing dresses with some kind of assymetric line in skirt or neckline—an evening dress with one bare shoulder. The men veer to the romantic in overall image. If there is an opportunity to dress like the romantic hero, they will take it—simulating a glamorous pop star or Lord Byron himself; they can usually carry anything off. Again, when fashion allows the male shirt, open to the waist, to sport frills and full sleeves, it will be the Libran who will carry off the look with the most complete confidence and panache. But of course they can achieve the look they want in other ways: conventionally dressed, a pink or blue shirt with complementary tie of an exotic design, or maybe an off-beat sweater will be equally interesting, characteristic and appealing to the opposite sex.

Libran hair is fine, and many of this sign need to get their hairdresser to give it extra body. Careful cutting is essential, too, if it is to look good. Because they are not the type to hurry unless they absolutely must, Librans often choose high fashion shoes—it's up to them to decide just how much pride must suffer pain for the sake of the image!

Both men and women tend to favour rather sweet fragrances; certainly traditional feminine scents appeal to the women, and once they have decided which perfume suits them, they rightly stick to it for years—it really does become part of their image. They tend to like lightweight jewellery—fine chains with tiny pendants or earrings. Heavy, chunky pieces, whether real or paste, are somehow unsuitable.

Libra will need to take a lot of things on a day out, but will contrive to keep the necessary hold-all or handbag as light as possible—they hate clutter, even if they need it. Hats and gloves are of above-average importance to members of this sign—the young wear them for fun, older people take them more seriously, and many elderly Libran women still spend a lot on elaborate confections which will be worn even for a simple shopping spree, let alone occasions when VIPs are present.

There's no doubt about it, Librans are among the big spenders where clothes are concerned. They both take them seriously and have fun with them; they are admirable sewers and knitters, and this is a help, especially if money is not very plentiful. The final image is always interesting, usually individual, and occasionally a little over the top—we seldom find a Libran of either sex who dresses boringly or completely conventionally.

Extenders While they hardly need to 'extend' their image, because it is always individual, it is not difficult for the Libran man or woman to do so. Librans will love to wear interesting sun-glasses to give themselves a somewhat enigmatic look; they are not deeply mysterious (they leave that to their zodiac neighbours, the Scorpios) but will hide behind their sun-glasses rather as the eighteenth-century woman hid behind her fan—and used it to flirt with. Sometimes they have a delicate complexion, and many of them will wear a broad-brimmed hat or carry a parasol as they stroll along the summer promenade. There's hardly a Libran woman living who doesn't own a spectacular umbrella, covered in flowers or spots, or trimmed with a frill! A flower in the button-hole will sometimes be sported—a simple rose-bud for the man, a large obviously artificial flower (velvet rose, or perhaps an orchid) for the woman—to cheer up an over-formal suit. If Librans carry a camera it will almost certainly be (a) not too heavy, and (b) easy to use. They know themselves well enough to realise that if they have to fiddle about setting exposures they will change their mind about what they plan to take; they must rely on a simple reflex action when taking pictures.

Cars Creatures of comfort, Librans will not like anything spartan. A nice smooth ride in a car somewhat bigger than is strictly necessary, or than they can really afford, is more like it. It will probably have a number of comfort-enhancing extras, and the chances are that it will be a nice, pale blue—though red is sometimes popular. Automatics may be preferred—easier and less strenuous to drive, and the individual will be wise not to go in for excessive speeding; better to spend

more money in a favourite restaurant, than to hand it over to the oil companies in order to arrive two minutes early.

☆ TRAVEL

'I just can't wait to get there!'

This is a phrase we often hear when our Libran friends are telling us about a coming holiday. They may not be terribly keen to cope with all the arrangements of the journey—much less decide where they are going—but the sheer bliss of the anticipation of two or three weeks 'away from it all' with little or nothing to do is probably their idea of heaven on earth.

In terms of the travelling involved, Librans more than people of any other sign will enjoy the relaxed luxury of cruising—indeed, many will save up for years for the holiday of a lifetime on some wonderfully romantic and glamorous liner. However, more routine package tours and the trauma of rushing to the airport and coping with the luggage will be endured because of the pleasures ahead.

On the whole, Librans enjoy lazy holidays. They will be delighted to spend considerable time deciding which cocktail to have before dinner, and whether they should ask the people in the next suite to join them for it, but apart from that it is fair to say that a little easy sunbathing, swimming and perhaps—if they are ultra-energetic—a round or two of golf or the occasional evening danced away at the disco will be enough physical activity for them to cope with.

It is up to the rest of us to encourage the Librans we know to enjoy cultural activities. They appreciate beautiful buildings, works of art and landscapes, but are frequently simply too lazy to go in search of them, so if you are on holiday with a member of this sign and can drag them away from the sunbathing terrace, you will be doing them a good turn in presenting them with great sights. They will not find it too strenuous to explore the most fashionable boutiques in the neighbourhood, however, or to search out the most interesting restaurants! If they are in a country where it is the custom to barter, they could find this excruciatingly embarrassing, not to say boring; the rest of us, less inhibited, should accompany them on shopping expeditions.

The Libran may be exhausted by heat, but also hates the cold—extremes of climate are unlikely to get their energies going. Somewhere where the temperature is between 70°/75°F. would be ideal, for in such a temperature Librans can wear attractive summer clothes without feeling sticky or crumpled after an hour or two away from the

air-conditioned hotel room. They will enjoy the social life of a winter sports holiday, and if they go on one it is up to them to decide just how active the holiday is going to be, and how much skiing they are actually going to do. There will be no such a problem with the *après-ski* hours, when they will be in their element.

If you have a Libran child who has been making a terrific effort at school, you will be quite justified in allowing him or her to relax and unwind during the holidays. But this is no excuse for allowing them to laze away the time and opt out of exciting experiences which will broaden their horizons and give them the opportunity to come into contact with people whose lifestyle and culture is different from their own. On the whole, Librans are sensitive to atmosphere, and it is this, plus your child's natural intuition, which can be stimulated by excursions away from the resort.

Librans will not find it difficult to discover the best kind of souvenirs available: perhaps they should look for some of the more delicate pots or glassware available in many European countries—Venetian glass is an obvious example. Silks and jades will also attract them if they get to the Far East. But they must be prepared to part with a lot of money, for they will appreciate only the best. Needless to say, they will go wild with excitement and delight in *chic* capital cities such as Paris and New York, and will no doubt fall madly in love not only with attractive members of the opposite sex, but some of the beautiful *couturier* clothes to which they will immediately fly in the best shops. It may be a good thing for partners to look after their credit-cards for them during such outings!

☆ PRESENTS TO PLEASE

Give a Libran a present, and you will be positively showered with thanks. Whatever you give them, it will at once be shown off to anyone else who happens to be by, partly because Libra will be truly delighted, and thoroughly appreciate your thoughtfulness, but also because he or she will be (silently) saying 'Look what *he*'s given me—are *you* going to compete?'

Any beauty product is sure to delight a Libran woman, and if you happen to know her favourite perfume, you really cannot go wrong, since the chances are that she will not only use the toilet water but will back the fragrance up with matching soap, talc, or whatever. A beautiful head-scarf or some glamorous piece of *lingerie* (if your relationship is a romantic one) will also be very much appreciated, as will the

★ FAVOURITE TO LIBRA ★

★ **LIBRAN COUNTRIES**—include Austria, Upper Egypt, Japan, Tibet, Alsace, China, Burma, Indo-China, some South Pacific islands.

★ **LIBRAN CITIES**—include Vienna, Antwerp, Lisbon, Freiburg, Copenhagen, Frankfurt, Leeds, Nottingham.

★ **TREES**—Libran trees include the ash, the cypress, and all vines.

★ **FLOWERS AND HERBS**—Libran flowers and herbs include those governed by Taurus, excluding the red and pink.

★ **FOODSTUFFS**—Those listed under Taurus, particularly milk and fruit; sugar, starch and strong alcohol are excluded.

★ **CELL SALTS**—Nat. Phos. and Kali Phos.

★ **STONE**—Sapphire.

★ **COLOUR**—Pale blue, green and pink.

unexpected bouquet of flowers, perhaps as a thank you for a good dinner, or a romantic, perhaps historical novel. The men too will appreciate discreet toiletries, and perhaps have a taste for historical biography. Both sexes will have a *penchant* for highly-illustrated escapist books of any kind, which will stimulate their imagination and give them an opportunity to push reality to one side for a while. Libra is a sign which appreciates music, so you won't go far wrong with a record or tape, or perhaps, more safely, a record token.

If you decide to give a present for the home, try not to choose anything too overtly practical—it should have aesthetic charm as well as a practical use—attractive oven-to-table ware, for instance, or an elegant flower vase; or a specially good-quality pair of guest towels?

When choosing a present for young Librans, bear it in mind that nothing could suit a girl more than a beautifully-illustrated edition of a book of traditional fairy stories. Older children will enjoy romantic novels and perhaps science fiction. Libran boys can be stirred into action by stimulating their interest in sport—equipment of any kind will be welcome, but try to encourage them to become good team-members.

Many Librans enjoy bridge, and board games which can be played in a pleasant social atmosphere. A chess club, too, would provide a welcome haven of peaceful companionship. If your individual Libran enjoys evenings of that sort, there is something else to be considered at birthdays and Christmas—chessmen, cards or board games may well be a great success. Perhaps more than any other sign, Librans enjoy on-going presents, so if at any time you cannot find precisely the right thing, think about their individual interests and try to supply something which will please them indefinitely—for instance, a subscription to a magazine (dressmaking, cookery, photography or whatever). Libra will be reminded of you every time it drops through the letter-box.

★ SCORPIO ★

· OCTOBER 24 — NOVEMBER 22 ·

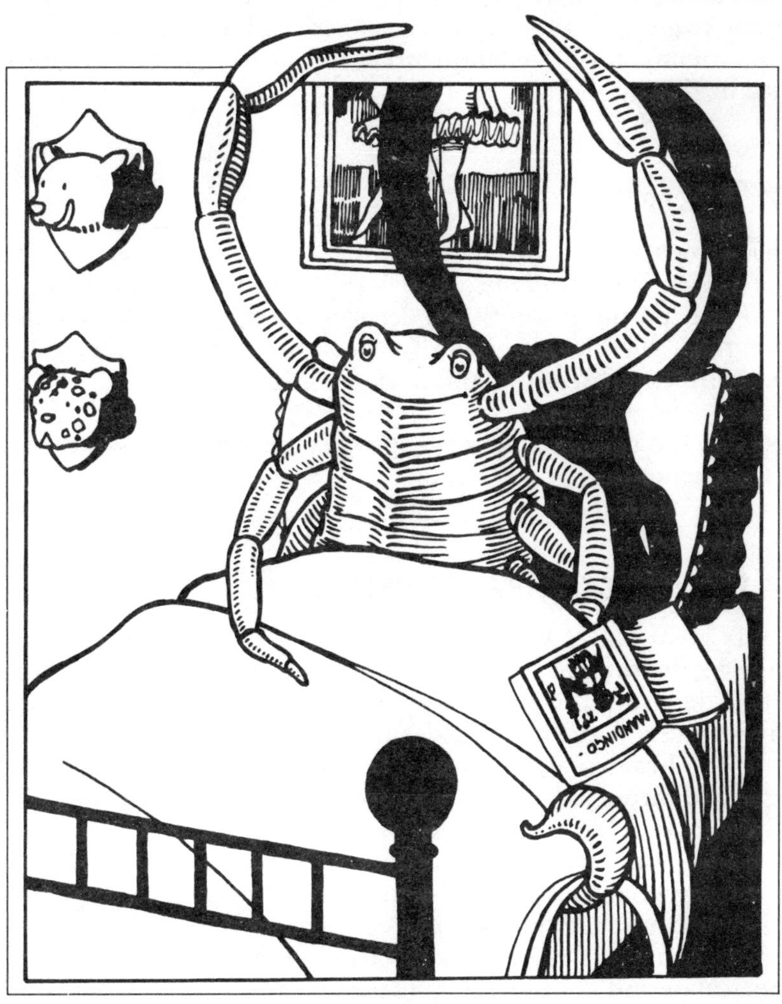

♏

☆ THE MYTH

Orion, the Boeotian hunter and handsomest man alive, made an enemy of Apollo, who overhearing his boast that he would rid the whole earth of wild beasts and monsters, set a monstrous scorpion on him. Failing to penetrate the scorpion's armour with sword or arrows, Orion swam off, whereupon Apollo tricked Artemis into shooting him. Artemis then placed the figure of Orion in the skies, eternally pursued by the scorpion.

☆ THE SIGN

The *ruling planet* of Scorpio, with which it has a special relationship, is Pluto; it is a *fixed*, *feminine*, *water* sign. *Positive traits* include a strong sense of purpose, subtlety, determination, powerful emotional resources, persistance, intensity; *negative traits* include jealousy, stubbornness, obstinacy, secretiveness, suspicion.

Scorpio in a nutshell Energy—physical and emotional; needs positive direction.

☆ GENERAL CHARACTERISTICS

A very great deal is written and said about the sexual proclivities of this sign, but the case is almost always over-stated; what is important is that the Scorpio type has tremendous resources of emotional and physical energy, and these need constant expression if the individual is to live a healthy and fulfilled life. Very often these energies are expressed through sex, but this is not by any means always the case. Scorpios can achieve much, and it is absolutely necessary to their psychological well-being for them to be kept physically active and always to be emotionally involved in whatever is important to them.

Here we have the successful career-person, totally involved in their particular area of work, or the busy housewife keeping her home immaculate and doing everything possible to ensure that her children have a good chance to make as much as possible of their potential. It is when a Scorpio is unfulfilled or has no direction in life that the negative characteristics emerge: they become resentful and jealous, brooding and suspicious, and in extremity, even violent.

A lot of people tend to think that there is something terrifying and sinister about this sign, and indeed many Scorpios who know a little about astrology are apprehensive about admitting their sun-sign. This is entirely unnecessary: in many ways here is the most emotionally strong and physically energetic of all the signs.

Looking at *Scorpios in Fiction* we fix immediately on Ian Fleming's James Bond, physically active not only against his enemies but in bed; Carmen, in Merimée's novel and Bizet's opera, is a typically fiery and passionate Scorpio, while Alexis in the TV series *Dynasty* personifies everyone's idea of the ambitious, scheming, vindictive aspects of the sign.

The Scorpio's *greatest asset* is determination; their *greatest need* is for emotional involvement, positive or negative; and their *greatest problem* is their inability to discuss their problems. Their *greatest vulnerability* is the tendency always to be suspicious, and the *Scorpio Motto*: Still waters run deep.

☆ FRIENDSHIP, LOVE AND MARRIAGE

Friendship Scorpios tie bonds of friendship with great enthusiasm and determination. They are constant friends, provided there is no deeply serious difference of opinion or open quarrel, for this typically causes resentfulness and leads to a serious break.

We can do a lot to bring out the best qualities in our Scorpio friends—by, for instance, sharing a joint interest and helping them to express some of their marvellous energy positively. A shared interest which makes demands on physical energy is an excellent thing, for we can then for instance arrange to meet them at a sports centre, gym or swimming pool; but equally rewarding will be a shared interest in research or perhaps an intellectual or creative subject involving Scorpio's intensity and sense of purpose. In this way the friendship will thrive and between you you will find considerable satisfaction, for you will achieve much, and looking ahead will see yet more to be achieved.

If your Scorpio friends become quiet and moody, do all you can to encourage them to take you into their confidence—it is so easy for members of this sign to bottle problems up and refuse to discuss them. If they do this, their emotions can turn sour, which can lead to the waste of their marvellous energies, and even to their being negatively expressed. Try to do nothing which will cause your Scorpio friends jealousy, for even at this level their most negative behaviour can then emerge.

Love When Scorpios fall in love, they certainly fall deeply and intensely, and will wish to express their feelings with great passion. When we say passion, we don't just mean sexual passion, for their potential torrent of emotion will also be expressed in speech and action. If Scorpio falls in love but the potential partner is unresponsive, he or she can be in deep trouble. Nevertheless, they will pursue the loved one with determination, working out all kinds of ploys to bring them around, and you can expect your Scorpio lover to spend a great deal of money on entertaining you; you will be thoroughly fêted, and your affair will be colourful and memorable.

Most Scorpio affairs are likely to be stormy, with moments of real happiness, for certainly Scorpios have a great capacity for the enjoyment of life; but there will also be moments when difficulties must be faced and resolved, and when, often unjustifiably, Scorpio jealousy will emerge. It is then up to the lover to do his or her best to reassure the Scorpio that their suspicions are unjustified.

It may be difficult to end a relationship with a Scorpio, for they are all-or-nothing people where love is concerned; if a relationship begins to break up, but they are still in love, they will cling on with all their might. Once the tie is broken, however, it can be often extremely difficult to restore it; when an affair is over, it is really over.

Marriage Once Scorpio is absolutely convinced that the time has come for marriage, and that they have fixed on the right partner, they will enter it with enormous determination to succeed. This is often more difficult for them than they anticipate, for however certain they are of their partner's love, jealousy will almost inevitably arise, and may cause a rift. Such rifts are not always the result of sexual jealousy, for it is also true, for instance, that Scorpios need to express their energies in fulfilling interests outside the home—and should their partner have similar needs, jealousy may lift its head. Joint interests are a wonderful insurance against this kind of situation.

Sexual compatibility is, of course, of great importance—probably above-average importance. There should also, however, be a joint desire, and indeed need, for some kind of goal or objective within marriage: this may be the production and bringing up of children, or perhaps the forming of a family business or some other material interest. In any event, some joint activity must be a channel for the enormous Scorpio emotional and energy force, which otherwise may inevitably find a negative outlet.

While Scorpios make very demanding partners, life with them can be enormously rewarding for other zodiac types, for they have the

ability to goad their partners into action and encourage them to make the best of their potential.

☆ PARENT AND CHILD

Scorpio parents will do everything in their power to keep their children's noses to the grindstone, both in and out of school, and involve them in a great variety of interests. They hate to see their children wasting time, and become angry and frustrated if they seem incapable of really enjoying life and getting as much out of it as possible.

They should be a little careful about discipline, for sometimes they can be too demanding, and occasionally too strict; but they are generous parents, and will certainly reward their children for their efforts. They will not be inclined to give way to them, and may give the impression of stubborn intractability. They should strive continually for fairness, and be aware of the fact that strictness can sometimes border on cruelty. The children may well, after all, have a slower metabolism than the Scorpio parents—and a completely different attitude to life; Scorpios perhaps find this more difficult to comprehend than members of some other groups. They should cultivate understanding.

Scorpio parents should try to express their powerful feelings towards their children warmly and affectionately. They will certainly have a very intense relationship with them; but a little lightheartedness won't come amiss. Scorpios have a wonderfully vivid imagination, which can be an enormous asset to a parent; their bedtime stories will inspire their children, who in turn will be encouraged the develop their own imaginations, in a great variety of ways.

No-one who has read so far will be surprised to hear that the Scorpio child will be energetic and need to be kept busy: sport and physical exercise should, for instance, be a notable part of their lives. But it may be that a Scorpio child will fall into a quiet, introspective mood from time to time. If possible a parent should try to find out the reason, for it may be a sign that energy is turning inward rather than being positively expressed. The Scorpio mind is not easy to penetrate, however. It may be that such quiet periods will eventually be impressively expressed in a previously unsuspected creative ability, or the development of a plan involving intense study and research; in which case, young Scorpio is working out all the details in depth before making a commitment. That, of course, is fine, but parents must decide whether it is the case, or whether the child is simply slipping into a negative mood, unable

perhaps to think of a way of expressing strong energies and emotions.

Scorpios need strict discipline, and will thrive on a fairly predictable and constant routine. This gives them a sense of security, which is of enormous importance to them. They will not mind school discipline, but it is important for them (there and in the outside world) to understand the reasons for the rules by which they are invited to live.

☆ CAREER AND SPARE-TIME

Scorpios must be emotionally involved in whatever career they choose to follow. It is often the case that some interest to which they were passionately devoted as children or young people, becomes the basis for their career. They do not find it difficult to study, and will be extremely thorough when they have to learn a technique or study the structure of a business. They may not be able to do so as quickly as some others, but once facts have been absorbed, they are very rarely forgotten, and remain at their fingertips. They know that their best work is not done by hurrying or cutting corners; if they are not thoroughly in command of whatever knowledge they need in a particular occupation, they will feel insecure; they like to be sure that their every action is supported by a fund of tried and tested knowledge. For a Scorpio simply to have to trail off to the office and spend time working at a routine and uninteresting job is to invite boredom and frustration; so whatever career is chosen, it should have a very special significance.

There is one exception to the rule, however—almost every Scorpio has a good business sense, and can achieve great inner satisfaction from the process of making money, however this may be done. So even if the career itself is in a field which does not naturally attract the Scorpio's interest, the process of turning it into money-making concern will fascinate them. The Scorpio ability to work hard is, of course, an enormous advantage, however it is expressed; energy poured into a career should result in their being noticed by their employers, and with any luck in promotion and added responsibility. Scorpios can cope with tough conditions, and whether the work is physically or mentally taxing, their abundant natural resources will stand them in good stead. Those who reach positions of power and responsibility react to employees much as the Scorpio parent does to children (see above).

Professions that often prove rewarding to Scorpios naturally include big business, banking, insurance; but mining too is interesting to them, as is engineering, and the wine trade. A fair number of them

become eminent surgeons and psychiastrists, and indeed any work in which depth research is concerned will prove satisfying.

The Scorpio imagination can of course be expressed creatively, though pinning these characters down to a specific art form is difficult. Many have a talent for singing, astrologically related to their partner-sign in the zodiac, Taurus. The armed forces can also provide a rewarding profession, the Army and Navy being particularly popular. Scorpio's sleuth-like qualities (they love digging for detail) sometimes lead them to police and detective work; others may turn to crime, though we do not necessarily suggest this as a full-time career.

Leisure hours should be as rewarding and fulfilling as the time spent at work; even if Scorpio is not involved in a career—working perhaps as a housewife or mother—there should always be some absorbing interest to mop up the spare physical and intellectual energy (of which there is bound to be some). Exercise is important for everyone, but essential to Scorpios. Many young men and women of this sign will enjoy aggressive sports (see *Sport and Exercise*), and certainly some kind of physical activity should come into their scheme of things, whatever their age or sex. Intellectual energy may be expressed in some subject which demands research or at all events real study: their natural detective-like qualities will thus be rewardingly expressed. Spare-time hobbies which require hours of quiet concentration will be popular, and many Scorpios enjoy reading all kinds of crime and detective fiction, and rather weird occult, mystery or SF stories (the ghost stories of M. R. James make ideal Scorpio reading). If they feel inclined to write fiction themselves, they should perhaps turn their vivid imaginations loose in that particular field. As members of a water sign, they will probably enjoy fishing and sailing, but motor-cycle and car racing and rallying will attract most Scorpios, even if only as spectators. One might also suggest that sexual flirtation and conquest are enjoyed by Scorpios to the extent that they could almost be called a hobby!

☆ FINANCE AND INVESTMENT

It is fair to say that members of this sign should follow their intuition where finance is concerned; their excellent business sense and natural shrewdness and caution seldom let them down.

Most Scorpios are particularly interested in this sphere of their lives, and not only because they, like everyone else, need to make enough money to live comfortably. They will also get special pleasure from

making money, and making it work for them when they have acquired it. Many of them will study the money market with great concentration, using their imagination creatively and investing shrewdly. They are enthusiastic about investment, and while they may appear to take risks, they will only do so after they have gone into every aspect of the concern into which they are thinking of putting money, and use their natural shrewdness to minimise the possible risk. While every investment has an element of risk, Scorpio will see to it that this is carefully calculated.

Scorpios make very good business partners, especially for someone out-going and with a liking for personal contact with possible clients. Scorpio common sense, best exercised after quiet, solitary thought rather than in committee, so to speak, can be put to work in advising the partner, for it is very difficult to catch a Scorpio out. They have a useful and unique way of manipulating the books in order to get the best out of the finance available to them.

The secretive element which is found in most sun-sign Scorpios sometimes forces them into the trap of concealing their income from their partners; this is not conducive to a good partnership, and it is important that a Scorpio should strive to be open with the partner in this area, as in all others. Differences over money, after all, are one of the chief causes of quarrels between committed couples.

Tradition suggests that Scorpio areas of investment include mining—especially for oil and coal, heavy engineering, and armaments. Shipping lines provide another possible source of profit, as does the wine trade and the catering industry. Fishing, too, is an area into which money may be invested. Participation in the organisation of 'heavy' sports such as boxing, football, wrestling, may offer chances for financial participation.

Scorpios who find it unacceptable to invest in stocks and shares should look at the safer approach of investing in long-term assurance policies, putting in sums at regular intervals; the risk is as small as any investment risk can be, and the investor gets inner satisfaction from the regular statements showing a steady increase in the sum which will eventually be paid to them on completion of the policy.

Scorpios will get pleasure from investing in a collection of some kind; laying-down good wines is one example, provided you are confident of being able to resist the temptation to drink your investment, or at least to drink it prematurely.

☆ HEALTH AND EXERCISE

Much has already been said about the very high energy-level of Scorpios. They can achieve much in their day-to-day life as a result of using this positively; and they also need plenty of physical exercise, which must be related to their age and individual capabilities.

Whether they are young or old, at least one of their interests should make considerable demands on their physical energy: for the young, for instance, we cannot too highly recommend heavy team-games. Many also enjoy boxing and the martial arts. These are particularly good for them, since they allow expression of aggression and a somewhat violent streak which is best expressed in a controlled and even aesthetic manner. Of course they also tend to produce strained or torn muscles, bruises and other minor (or in unlucky cases, more major) injuries. All possible care should be exercised. All forms of water sports are excellent, and swimming can be enjoyed by Scorpios of any age-group. Many are excellent at high-diving and under-water swimming.

While not employing very much physical energy, snooker is a sport greatly enjoyed by many of this group, demanding, as it does, keenness of eye, physical control, and a certain degree of deviousness.

All these interests are necessary in order that the Scorpio body and mind do not have an opportunity even to begin to stagnate. Scorpio illnesses seem often to originate with some kind of blockage (psychological or physical), and free exercise of mind and body inhibit this. The blockage can be a physical constipation, and it is important that any Scorpio with this problem (rarely as serious as it is sometimes thought to be) does not rely on violent purging. Consult a doctor, if the difficulty persists. Scorpios engaged in a sedentary career, and who for some reason do not take a lot of exercise, should be particularly aware of the possibility of haemorrhoids; even the most minor symptom should be taken seriously. Varicose veins can similarly be a problem, especially if the person concerned has to stand for considerable periods of time.

The genitals are the Scorpio body area, and can be susceptible. The gonads are the Scorpio glands, also connected with the reproductive system. Again, consult a doctor rather than ignoring any problem or trying to treat it yourself. There may be minor throat ailments; a cold will almost inevitably start there, and there may be a temporary loss of voice.

Scorpios who are in rude health may tend to ignore minor symptoms, or feel disinclined to discuss them with anyone; it is quite as important for them as for anyone else to have regular medical check-ups, especially as they grow older. It is essential for them to remember, too, that emotional and psychological problems, if not openly discussed either with a partner, a sympathetic friend, or a professional counsellor, can have quite a serious effect on physical as well as emotional well-being. Any worry or apprehension connected with a particular problem really should be taken to some confidant, and discussed in detail.

Because they have a vivid imagination, Scorpios are sometimes plagued by frightening dreams and nightmares; their great energy can even inhibit sleep altogether. They must learn to face up to their dream monsters and come to terms with them, accepting that whatever happens in their dreams is a message from themselves to themselves, probably focusing on a deep-rooted psychological problem which is in need of resolution. This may be related to their sexual expression and needs. Again, ideally it should be discussed with someone else. Sleeplessness may mean that sufficient physical energy is not being used up by constructive exercise.

Because of Scorpios' sheer enjoyment of life, and of good food and wine in particular, many tend to put on weight. It is not easy for them to moderate their diet, and sometimes when they discover that they are over-weight they go in for a severe crash diet, losing several pounds, only to put them back on again in a monster celebration. A balance between the good life and boring restriction is advisable; they should be encouraged to keep to it, and praised when they manage to do so.

☆ HOME ENVIRONMENT

The ideal Scorpio home would lie on the banks of a beautiful, still lake, though a pleasant compromise would be some kind of water-garden or even a well. Water, at all events, should be somewhere nearby.

Because they like to live a full, varied and rich life, Scorpios are perhaps natural city-dwellers—though they need a certain amount of privacy, and are very good at making alterations to a house or flat in order to secure it. They must be able to cut themselves off from the outside world, and quite often they will have a private study to which they can retire, and where they can either be reasonably quiet or listen uninterrupted to their favourite kind of music.

The house itself will be well furnished. The degree of opulence will of course be relative; but quality is always important to a Scorpio, and we often find comfortable furniture upholstered in leather. The general effect of the decor can be rather heavy, and even slightly claustrophobic; but it will at the very least be striking and dramatic. Scorpios use dark, rich colours in their schemes of decoration, and black is often popular. The lighting will be directional and sometimes seductively subdued—Scorpios use dimmers to great effect. Flowers used in the house will be exotic; sometimes we find oriental blooms when they are available, and Scorpios do seem particularly to enjoy the flower of their sign, the geranium. There may be some unusual decorative feature, too—a vase of peacock feathers, for instance, a small stuffed creature, or perhaps a 'soft sculpture'.

Scorpio's choice of pictures may favour rather aggressive and energetic abstracts, bull-fighting pictures; Gauguin's paintings may be popular, with their particular form of exotic beauty—as will surreal paintings and imaginative, slightly strange naturalistic paintings or prints. Posters of hard-rock groups will suit younger Scorpios. If the Scorpio is interested in the occult, or in oriental religions, there will probably be some evidence of this about the place.

A Scorpio bedroom will probably live up to the sign's sexy reputation, and be very much what one might expect, the scene being set for love, sex and relaxation, probably in that order. The colours will be subdued, but don't be surprised to find sheets or duvet-covers in dark red, navy-blue or black cotton or satin. Lights too will be dim, and there will be no shortage of mirrors. There will be innumerable fragrances, and the labels will probably have erotic implications. The theme will be continued in the bathroom, where a wealthy Scorpio will enjoy a large double-bath or jacuzzi. Colours will again be dark, especially in choice of luxurious towels.

There is unlikely to be anything too spartan about the Scorpio home, and we will definitely be well entertained when invited there—we can look forward to dinner with justifiable anticipation. The table-settings will perhaps be a little heavy in appearance: if the china has a pattern, it will be bold, flowing and probably traditional—there may well be a certain amount of gold in the design, which may have an Indian or Middle East influence. Scorpios themselves live life to the full, and are particularly lavish when providing pleasure for their friends. The food itself will probably be rich, with a main course very possibly cooked in wine, and/or with a creamy sauce; it will probably have been preceded by an interesting cocktail, and perhaps a shell-fish starter. The dessert could include fruit steeped in liqueur, or maybe a particularly decorative and rich *gateau*. The Scorpio will particularly enjoy selecting a quality wine or two for the feast, and you can usually rely on their judgement and taste in these matters—many make a point

of learning quite a lot about wines, and will serve them with real flair and panache.

Throughout the home, the accent will be on sophistication and elegance rather than on anything 'folksy' or ethnic. As to the taste in music, it will certainly make an impression on the visitor—many Scorpios enjoy hard rock, and others revel in the rich sonorities of Richard Strauss, the more romantic early Stravinsky scores—*Firebird* and *Petrushka*—and the musicals of Kurt Weill.

☆ IMAGE

Clothes The Scorpio image is always interesting, but does rather tend to be dominated by dark colours, even when these are not particularly fashionable. However, Scorpios generally know how to make the most of themselves, and are not too inhibited when it comes to emphasising their good points!

Recent fashion trends, though sympathetic to the Scorpio predilection for dark colours, have not been too kind to the Scorpio who wishes to show off his or her body to full advantage; at such times it will be as well for them to ignore fashion as determinedly as they can in the interests of looking and feeling good.

The famous sexiness of the sign is usually as apparent in Scorpio clothes as in the decoration of their bedrooms; they often particularly enjoy wearing very tight jeans, leather trousers and necklines which tend to stop only at the navel. Make-up is also a strong fashion element with this sign, and young Scorpios can go over the top when experimenting—there is a sense in which the punk image is almost typically Scorpio, for a Scorpio will exploit almost excessively the personal image in which he or she feels most comfortable.

Texture is important to most Scorpios, who will love the smooth feel of pure silk and satin, which will feature strongly in their wardrobes, and not only in negligees. Velvet too will be popular. The feel of wool may not be so agreeable to them; we suggest that very soft mohair, or cashmere if financially possible, should be used for the kind of garment which calls for it; any sharp or prickly texture will be disliked.

Once a Scorpio has learned to *use* fashion, he or she can be extremely smart and elegant; even if the lifestyle is on the whole conventional, a clever use of accessories will give their clothes originality without breaking any taboos of their background, class or income bracket.

Scorpios often have abundant and very strong hair, which can usually be easily styled, and will respond well to good cutting; they will often tint it very cleverly and subtly, and the elderly Scorpio with a shock of silver-grey hair will look just as handsome and appealing as younger brothers and sisters, or even grandchildren. But it must also be said that when one thinks of the typical Scorpio, the image of the punk rocker with hair styled, cut and coloured in the most outrageous way (and with great care) is really not far away.

Large pieces of jewellery can be very successfully worn by Scorpios, and opals—the Scorpio stone—seem almost to take on a different dimension of depth when worn by someone of this sign. The Scorpio metal is iron or steel. Steel jewellery is not unknown, but we suggest that they look again at silver.

Extenders Beautiful, black, real leather handbags and briefcases will be very popular with Scorpios of both sexes. All kinds of leather belts will be popular too, as will high-quality shoes and boots (both sexes like wearing boots, and will often spend a lot of money on them). Fragrances will contribute a very special aura; Scorpios tend to chose 'heavy' ones with a high musk or spice content. The men of the sign must be a little careful here, for sometimes their choice of fragrance can be rather sweeter than they realise, or than really suits their image. It is advisable for them to get their girlfriends' opinions on the matter.

The Scorpio's camera equipment will not be complete without a telephoto lens: once he or she acquires one, photography will take on a very special meaning, since many of the Scorpio characteristics will be expressed in photographing all sorts of detail in interesting close-up.

Whether or not their eyes are specially sensitive, Scorpios usually turn out in sun-glasses the moment the light brightens even a little. They enjoy giving themselves a slight air of mystery, and also feel able to observe other people minutely without giving their curiosity away, and without making eye-contact, which can tend to make them feel vulnerable. For rather the same reason, if hats are worn, they usually have a large brim which effectively shades the eyes; Scorpio women wearing hats will hope to project not only an air of mystery, but the air of the *femme fatale*.

Cars Scorpios need a tough, reliable car which will not lack the counterpart of their own almost excessive energy, and be able to reproduce their own swift acceleration when needed. Their car will be smart and rather more spectacular than they can actually afford; they will buy an up-market model which will help them in their pursuit of

possible lovers. They are clever at souping-up their cars and adding accessories, and it is not unknown for a Scorpio to install dark-glass windows in a modest mini.

☆ TRAVEL

The caricature Scorpio might almost typically be shown at a sunny resort, the woman in the smartest and most revealing of bikinis, the man, shirt open to the waist, sporting a medallion and holding a cocktail as he ogles her.

But this *is* a caricature, any many a Scorpio will take travelling very seriously, doing an enormous amount of preliminary groundwork, and spending much time exploring the destination minutely and from every possible angle. The hotel will be as luxurious as can possibly be afforded: the ideal will be a five-star palace with gymnasia, saunas, heated indoor and outdoor swimming-pools, and certainly with first-class restaurants and cocktail bars.

Few people travel by sea these days, so it is unrealistic to recommend this most attractive of Scorpio forms of transport, except to say that they will certainly enjoy even a brief trip on a car ferry!

An element of the exotic is important to the Scorpio traveller, so not only will they be in search of new and unusual destinations, but the actual travel itself should have an unexpected element: *en route* for the Far East, they should book on the airline of the country concerned, so that they can get a taste of its style—and food and drink—from the very start. And they should not hesitate to plunge right into the life of the area, exploring the *souks*, the red light districts, the small villages, moorlands, or whatever, rather than remaining supine on the tourist beach (though that is unlikely, anyway).

As far as foreign travel is concerned, it is always a good thing to look at the list of places traditionally associated with your sun-sign; in the case of Scorpio, it seems particularly true that these make good holiday destinations, providing that air of the exotic which Scorpios like—Morocco is a case in point. Scorpios will be fascinated by the mystery of the Indian sub-continent, and of Egypt, the odd mixture of east and west which meet in Singapore and Hong Kong, and by the underlying intensity of the Japanese national character. Nearer home, there are the more remote parts of Spain and Italy which offer their own mysterious atmospheres.

Happily, in view of all this, Scorpios are tough enough to cope with Egypt in high summer or Finland in winter. In really hot weather they

tend to dehydrate rather more readily than most, so should drink more before they set out on an excursion, and carry some water with them, if possible, and certainly salt tablets. Many Scorpios take the sun badly, and should be cautious about exposure. They will love the sensuous look of a good tan, but because their skin can be sensitive, they should exercise their natural patience at the beginning of a holiday, and be very free with high-barrier sun-lotions.

Perhaps the most important thing to remember about taking a Scorpio child on holiday is to stimulate its creative imagination. With a natural yen for the mysterious, a Scorpio will certainly appreciate excursions to caves and underground seas, and will enjoy visiting museums of fossils, displays of arms and armour and even ancient instruments of torture! If you can contrive to stay in a converted castle, like some Spanish *paradors* or the little towers of parts of Greece, this will be wonderfully popular. Nearer home, Madame Tussaud's—including, please, the Chamber of Horrors—will attract any small Scorpio; he or she would also delight in a week or even more spent in a tent on the shores of Loch Ness waiting for a sight of the celebrated monster. Any holiday which will help improve a much-loved skill—a sport, perhaps—will be welcomed.

Make sure young Scorpio has his or her own simple camera with which to record any journey, and if they enjoy drawing or painting, encourage that, too.

In general, both children and adults tend to fall with enthusiasm on every foreign dish set before them, sometimes with untoward results. They will generally be adventurous with food in any event, and their systems will be used to the occasional shock; but in some foreign countries the standard of hygiene leaves something to be desired—so care should be exercised, and a medicine-pack should always be on hand.

☆ PRESENTS TO PLEASE

For both Scorpio men and women, you are really unlikely to go far wrong with a present of wine: apart from a personal liking for sweet or dry wines or for, say, sherry rather than gin, it would be a rare Scorpio who would be other than delighted to receive either a bottle or a case.

Fragrances also make a splendid gift for either sex. In general, these should be rather musky, with a somewhat heavy scent. A splash-on toilet water, a body lotion or massage oil would also go down well; indeed, almost anything for the dressing-table.

Scorpio often has an interest in photography, and luxurious coffee-

★ FAVOURITE TO SCORPIO ★

★ **SCORPIO COUNTRIES**—include Bavaria, Morocco, Norway, Syria, the Transvaal, Korea, Uruguay.

★ **SCORPIO CITIES**—include New Orleans, Washington D.C., Baltimore, Cincinnati, Milwaukee, St John's (Newfoundland), Liverpool, Dover, Hull, Halifax, Stockport, Newcastle-upon-Tyne, Fez, Valencia.

★ **TREES**—Scorpio trees include all bushy trees, and the blackthorn.

★ **FLOWERS AND HERBS**—Scorpio flowers and herbs include those listed for Aries, in particular dark red flowers, such as geraniums.

★ **FOODSTUFFS**—Those listed under Aries (see page 17).

★ **CELL SALTS**—Calc. Sulph., Nat. Sulph.

★ **STONE**—The opal.

★ **COLOUR**—Dark red, maroon.

table books of photographs will usually be enjoyed—whether they are glamour photographs, or the landscape or townscape pictures of such photographers as Rolof Beny. As for books for reading, good crime fiction is always popular, as are books on the occult, fairly racy books of one sort of another—from the memoirs of a famous courtesan to modern romantic fiction with a good amount of bodice-ripping.

Attractive *lingerie* will please a Scorpio woman; for men (but women, too) sports equipment will go down very well, but, of course, discover your Scorpio's sporting talents first!

For the home, wine-glasses or a decanter; a handsome lamp, a spotlight, or a reproduction oil lamp might fit well into the Scorpio living-room. A small, pretty soap-dish for the bathroom, or some other bathroom accessory; presents for the bedroom are best left to the Scorpio's lover, who will be perfectly capable of making out his or her own list.

For the desk-bound Scorpio, give something to decorate that desk—a letter-opener, a perpetual calendar, a ruler or scissors, a leather note-pad . . . No doubt a lover would be agreeably pleased with some silk underclothes from his partner; but a more restrained gift might be a fine leather belt or wallet. A father, perhaps, giving a special present to a Scorpio son or daughter, might think of some shares (see p. 134 for those that would be specially interesting) or an investment of some other kind.

A special occasion calls for a special night out: a cocktail at an exotic cocktail bar, dinner at an intimate restaurant where the food is of the highest quality and where some slightly unusual dishes will be found on the menu, with the rest of the evening spent dancing off the calories at a disco. A really memorable occasion would be completed by a night away from home at a really good hotel. It is always worth remembering that for a Scorpio, an event is as important as a more material present, for they love looking back on occasions of this sort, and will treasure them.

⋆ SAGITTARIUS ⋆

· NOVEMBER 23 — DECEMBER 21 ·

☆ THE MYTH

The original Sagittarian centaur, shooting his celestial arrow, was Crotus, who lived on Mount Helicon with his beloved foster-sisters, the Muses. The arrow placed in his hands in the night sky by Zeus was the one used by Hercules to kill the griffon-vulture that tore at the entrails of Prometheus. Because nothing is known of Crotus, other centaurs have often usurped his place in astrology books—most notably the learned King Cheiron, son of Ixion, King of the Lapiths.

☆ THE SIGN

The *ruling planet* of Sagittarius, with which it has a special relationship, is *Jupiter*, and it is a *mutable*, *masculine*, *fire* sign. *Positive traits* include enthusiasm, open-mindedness, versatility, a philosophical outlook, adaptability, sincerity, frankness, good judgement, love of freedom and scrupulousness. *Negative traits* include boisterousness, restlessness, carelessness, exaggeration, extremism, blind optimism, irresponsibility, tactlessness and capriciousness.

Sagittarius in a nutshell The need for challenge and an unconfined lifestyle is paramount.

☆ GENERAL CHARACTERISTICS

If Sagittarians seem to learn more from their mistakes than the inhabitants of other signs, this may well be because they make more of them! While growing up, their love of the unconventional may lead them into moments of social embarrassment; they will tend to be careless, too, embracing risks with an enthusiasm which adds little (for instance) to the comfort of their passengers, while they are driving a much-loved elderly sports car.

An apparent preoccupation with risks and a love of sport and the great outdoors may tend to give the wrong impression of Sagittarians as raving extroverts. In fact, they almost always have a latent attraction to philosophical and intellectual pursuits which should be as important to them as the more physical and daring things of life; it's just that they tend to work towards an interior life through more physical and exciting activities. This progress usually takes place quite naturally as they grow older; the Sagittarian man who insists on playing heavy team games when he is ten years too old for them, and never turns the page of a book, is an undeveloped Sagittarian, and usually rather a bore.

It is important that every Sagittarian controls his or her versatility, otherwise their feeling that they can be good at everything may lead them into a confusing pattern of half-finished projects. Certainly they should be able to look back each year on twelve months during which they have achieved many objectives, completed many varied projects and tasks; but the important word is *completed*, and Sagittarians should beware the temptation to take on too much at once. If they do, they'll find themselves looking back on work either uncompleted or ill-completed, and become extremely restless at the thought of how much better they could have done it.

Sagittarians in fiction could certainly include Rosalind in Shakespeare's *As You Like It*, with her independent, witty feminism; Phileas Fogg, who went *Around the World in 80 Days* had the Sagittarian wanderlust (and Sagittarians are the great gamblers of the zodiac), while Henry Higgins in Shaw's *Pygmalion* (later *My Fair Lady*) showed a tendency to exaggerate, a determined independence and carelessness of evenyone's feelings but his own—typical of some Sagittarians.

Sagittarians' *greatest asset* is enthusiasm; their *greatest need* is for challenge, and *greatest problem* restlessness. The *greatest vulnerability* is blind optimism, and the *Sagittarian Motto* is 'The grass is always greener over the hedge.'

☆ FRIENDSHIP, LOVE AND MARRIAGE

Friendship There's no doubt about it, having Sagittarian friends is great fun. They will encourage you to make the most of your potential, and the chances of being bored in their company are almost nil. You will find that even if you have no interests at all in common with your individual Sagittarian, you will be swept along, almost without knowing it, by his or her natural enthusiasm for a pet subject, and will soon become astonishingly involved.

Sometimes it is up to less energetic types to calm a Sagittarian down a little, and to help him or her to start to think seriously and deeply about all kinds of issues. In this way Sagittarius will begin to develop all kinds of interesting potential which will lead to a broadening of

their intellectual capacity, which is usually considerable. Within every Sagittarian there is an element of the eternal student and the wise philosopher.

You will find that there are two distinct ways in which you can help this interesting zodiac type. If he or she is very much involved in sport and the outdoor life, then it will be good to encourage them in quieter, more introspective and intellectual interests. If, on the other hand, they are always involved in intellectual challenges and demanding study projects, it will be good for them to burn up physical energy through sport and exercise, keeping a necessary balance.

Love Sagittarians are passionate and will have little difficulty in expressing their warm feelings and keeping the flame of love burning once they have kindled it in a partner.

Sometimes they seem not to take their relationships too seriously, and indeed their inherent versatility is often expressed in this sphere of their lives. They like partners who share common interests, and this can be an excellent starting-point for a new romance. A common Sagittarian opening gambit is: 'Can I take you to the big match on Saturday,' or 'Do you know anything about Medieval Latin lyrics—absolutely fascinating!' And the way that Sagittarius describes them makes them sound that way.

You will need plenty of energy to keep up with your Sagittarian lover, but don't be hurt or surprised if he or she is a little offhand at times—this is just their bright and breezy style of expression. The affair will probably have a somewhat casual side, and often those of this sign are not very good at making arrangements in advance—so you may well need to be ready to go to the ends of the earth at a moment's notice. They love surprises, so arrange some sudden excitements for them, too. All this will be great fun, but perhaps a little disconcerting for someone who enjoys a steady routine and a regulated lifestyle.

The Sagittarian lover is not at all possessive, and in most cases will be most upset if accused of jealousy.

Marriage It is important that Sagittarians and their partners both realise that a relationship which savours of the claustrophobic is something with which they cannot cope. Living a life where there is no challenge, but simply a dreary round of routine tasks such as house cleaning will not suit them at all, and jealous scenes are anathema. Restlessness will set in, and the individual Sagittarian will break out of his or her prison in a sudden and perhaps drastic way.

It is important, then, that they find partners who will spark off their interest and fall in line with their natural enthusiasm. In this way the many fine Sagittarian qualities will emerge, and both the Sagittarian and the partner will not only develop a truly rewarding lifestyle, but come to realise that there is never a dull moment in it!

Shared intellectual interests are as important as sexual compatibility. It is also a good thing if the Sagittarian and his or her partner are on a par with one another as far as intellectual development is concerned; if by chance this is not so, it can cause problems, especially if the disparity is in a subject that the Sagittarian finds difficult to grasp. Should this occur a wise partner will appeal to their Sagittarian's love of challenge and thus motivate greater achievement, so that there will be a levelling-off within the relationship. Much can be achieved through mutual challenge.

☆ PARENT AND CHILD

In many ways, Sagittarians make ideal parents. Children respond marvellously well to their natural enthusiasm and zest for life—and if they don't, it is a challenge in itself for the Sagittarian parent to find out why, and to discover a totally new approach which will motivate the child.

Once Sagittarians have decided to start a family, this in itself will be an important and fascinating experience for them. The Sagittarian mother will have to face up to certain problems, however, and these should be carefully considered before the decision is made. While she (and Sagittarian fathers) will be fascinated by her children's development, and will want to start teaching them to read at a very early age, she must accept the fact that there will come a time when toddlers' conversation and limited behaviour will quite simply bore her; she must arrange to have a few hours every week when she can follow her own interests totally away from the demands of her children. If this is not done, boredom will lead to restlessness, and she will be a less good mother than she would wish.

Sometimes, in their enthusiasm, Sagittarians can become a little too demanding of their children—not in the way of the members of some signs, who insist on strict discipline, but because the Sagittarian will get bored and annoyed if their children are not taking advantage of the opportunities presented to them.

Sagittarian children need to be taught the difference between positive enthusiasm and over-boisterousness. Put a suggestion to them and they may start leaping about with excitement—which may or may not be a good thing! It is important that parents discover, at an early age, where their children's interests lie: they will certainly *have* interests, and these should be positively encouraged. Remember, if possible, to alternate a more intellectually demanding hobby with a more physical one. This will be ideal, preventing the young Sagittarian from becoming too obsessed by one aspect of life. If a young Sagittarian girl, for instance, wants to go to ballet class, it will be good for her to be given books on the history of the dance and on all areas of the subject; this, running parallel with the physical exercise involved, will develop her reading skills, and also her natural breadth of vision.

At school youngsters will only keep the rules really enthusiastically if the reasons behind them are sensible ones: it is always important to appeal to their strong sense of logic when telling them what they should not do. Members of this sign have great creative potential, and often a talent for languages; both should of course be encouraged as early as possible.

☆ CAREER AND SPARE-TIME

Whatever career a Sagittarian finally decides to adopt—and we find them in all walks of life—it is important that they should be able to see very clearly each step that lies ahead of them.

When making a decision about a career, they should remember that they find it extremely difficult to cope with claustrophobic working conditions, and are never really happy with too predictable a daily routine. For Sagittarians to be at their best, they must be allowed to do things their own way: in other words they should be given as much freedom of expression as is practically possible. A job that involves travel is excellent, especially if the person concerned is working for a large multi-national company—getting away from the office will help them to convince themselves that they are not just a small cog in an enormous machine.

The Sagittarian breadth of vision and adventurous spirit are areas of the personality which should be expressed in the career if at all possible. And it must be remembered that they are very good at planning on broad, sweeping lines, but not good at coping with detail. So it is an excellent idea to involve them in the early stages of a project, when the concept is first mooted: they grasp the overall conception quickly and well. It is important they they recognise this quality, but equally important that they learn that they are generally useless at dotting i's and crossing t's. Let them leave this to other zodiac types (perhaps Virgoans!) who enjoy working in detail. Getting bogged down in detail, the Sagittarian will tend to take short cuts, and make silly, time-consuming mistakes.

As with Ariens (another fire sign) we find many Sagittarians making the grade in professional sport—though this is sometimes over-stated by astrological writers. If Sagittarian determination is turned that way, however, the chances of success are considerable. Travel has already been mentioned, and this can be combined with a natural flair for languages. They also make enthusiastic salespeople. There are many successful Sagittarian publishers and teachers, though the latter find greater satisfaction when working at college or university level with older students, than in teaching young children. The law and the church are traditionally associated with this sign, and it is true that many are successful in those professions.

The Sagittarian need for continual challenge is as important in spare-time interests as at work. If by chance the individual does not have a challenging job, then the need for challenge should be satisfied after work. The best counter to a dull job is some horrendously demanding study project which will lead to a qualification, and to a possible new career away from the rut in which they find themselves.

Contrast and variety are important in spare-time interests, too. So if daily work is physically demanding, the hobby should make demands on the mental capacity; and *vice versa.* The Sagittarian adventurous spirit should be remembered as well—it is certainly lurking inside all members of this positive and lively sign, and will be expressed at its most fulfilling through travel. If real travel is impossible, the reading of adventurous travel books will be much enjoyed.

Here is the hunter of the zodiac, and while most Sagittarians do not, these days, go tearing through forests in pursuit of big game, the instinct is a strong one, and is sublimated in the hunting down of bargains—antiques, second-hand washing machines, items in the sales. It is a time-consuming aspect of Sagittarian lives, for this sign loves restoring and repairing what they have found.

Avid members of evening classes and further education courses, Sagittarians will always reply to an enquiry about their lives: 'Oh, I'm studying . . .'—anything from modern Greek to the classical guitar. Just because they are so versatile, they can, like their zodiac partners, the Geminis, be somewhat superficial in their attitudes. They will get little inner satisfaction from a small amount of knowledge; they must experiment, but will be most rewarded by involvement in many areas of one particular subject.

☆ FINANCE AND INVESTMENT

There will of course be members of this sign who will be fascinated by making money, and this in itself will be a considerable challenge for them. However, there will be many others who will find it excruciatingly boring.

When a Sagittarian invests he or she will do so with enthusiasm for the product into which money is being invested. Generally speaking, they may tend to get very carried away with the idea, so if an inventive friend comes to them with a good idea—or someone involved in high finance makes an inspiring suggestion—it is all too easy for them to be carried away, and perhaps put too many financial eggs into one basket. They need to be very careful, partly because they are basically such nice people, always willing to help when and where they can. Needless to say, if there is something for them at the end of the affair, that's fine. They need to be in control of their risk-taking tendency, part of every Sagittarian character.

It is often the case that a natural gambling instinct emerges in a Sagittarian, especially if he or she has any spare cash (and sometimes if they haven't). This can be fun—the Sagittarian gambling instinct is a strong one, and provides a counter to a dull lifestyle, or if difficult problems need an antidote. Heavy gambling can then take place, and the habit can even become an addiction. And it is not only the casino which can grab them, or the occasional gamble on a sporting event; card games, bingo, mah jong, or even a gamble on a simple incident ('I bet A crosses the road before B') can lead to trouble, and every Sagittarian should be aware of the fact.

Sagittarians who go into business for themselves may not want to involve themselves with a partner whose main eye is on finance. They'll be more likely to want to handle every aspect of the business themselves. They may well be versatile enough to cope, but bearing in mind their general dislike of detail and inability to cope well with it, there may be trouble when they have to work on their tax returns. In that situation, they really should pass the accounts over to a partner, or at least employ an excellent accountant, while they display their natural exuberance and keenness to the clients. Remembering that they are good at selling, Sagittarians can certainly get good commission if working for someone else—and indeed make quite a lot of money.

Sagittarians who are investing would be wise to use a broker or their bank, thus avoiding careless mistakes or unnecessarily chancy gambles. Traditional areas of Sagittarian investment include publishing, the Press and other media, the luxury trades, the gas industry and tin—and any area of life where learning is involved.

☆ HEALTH AND EXERCISE

If Sagittarians do not get regular exercise, their whole system stagnates, and they become restless to the point at which they are difficult to live with.

They need to discover what kind of exercise best suits them, and then make sure it becomes a part of their everyday life—we hesitate to say 'routine', for Sagittarians hate anything which is rigidly restrictive. This is a major difficulty where exercise is concerned, for it can be extremely boring, involving the repetition of certain physical actions at the same time every day.

Ideally, a Sagittarian who can possibly afford it should join a good gymnasium or health club, where they can pursue one routine of exercises until they begin to feel bored, and then change to another; where there are a number of exercise machines on which to work; and where there is also a group of fellow members against whom they can compete—consciously or unconsciously—and with whom they can talk and relax after the session.

As for Sagittarian sports, they should probably change with the changing seasons, thus offering a certain amount of variety: tennis or swimming in summer, football or hockey in winter, for instance.

The Sagittarian body area covers the hips and thighs, so these are in one way or another vulnerable—perhaps most obviously in that they can collect unwanted fat; regular exercise and a reasonable diet are the only way to keep this problem in proportion. Elderly Sagittarians may find that the hip-joints are the first in which they begin to feel a certain stiffness. Once more, good exercise is the answer.

The Sagittarian organ is the liver, and members of this sign certainly enjoy their food and drink—so the liver may from time to time be overloaded, and a certain amount of liverishness can be the result of over-indulgence! It is a good idea to encourage them to restain themselves somewhat, though this will not be easy. Neither are they very good at dieting. But if a strict diet becomes necessary, it is just about possible to appeal to their liking for challenge.

There is also a strong emphasis on the pituitary gland, the so-called 'master gland' that regulates hormone production and governs physical growth.

Because Sagittarians like adventure, they sometimes take unneces-

sary risks, and for that reason tend to be accident-prone. (This is especially true on the roads, both when driving and as pedestrians.) Younger Sagittarians in particular should be made aware of this, for as children they can be vulnerable. Older members of the sign are not very eager to modify their exercise routines as they grow older, and can sometimes damage themselves (often without realising it). It is not always easy for them to be sufficiently careful. They are 'whole-hoggers', and hate to do things by half-measures; but common sense should prevail.

Members of this sign should include energy-producing high-protein food in their diet, which develops the brain-cells as well as the muscles; heavy demands will probably be made on both! If the Sagittarian has a sweet tooth it ought to be curbed, for though sugar produces energy it also produces surplus weight, and as we have seen, these people can be prone to this.

Bearing in mind the pacy lifestyle of most Sagittarians, especially the younger ones, they should be very careful not to eat too much junk food. They should make sure that they put some time aside for creative shopping and cooking, and for proper meals. Otherwise that lifestyle will suffer badly. Citrus fruits, especially grapefruit, and all fruits containing plenty of vitamin C are particularly good for members of this sign.

Sagittarian well-being will only be maintained if the lifestyle is in all senses comfortable to the individual. If depression catches up with them they should look to their living conditions, or their personal relationships; either or both may be too claustrophobic, and it will be this that will be causing the mental state which is having a detrimental effect on their physical well-being.

☆ HOME ENVIRONMENT

Given a free choice, a sun-sign Sagittarian—though he or she may have to live in the middle of a town—would probably choose at the very least to live near a park or open ground of some sort. They do not thrive in one of a row of terraced houses facing an identical row across a narrow street, each tethered to its neighbour, for a Sagittarian needs something interesting to look at through the window—ideally, an open stretch of land, preferably with rolling hills which offer several focal points of interest.

The house itself should have an unclaustrophobic atmosphere—the modern fashion for 'doing up' tiny mews houses will not appeal to a

Sagittarian; open-plan living, with an accent on space and large windows is much more in their line. Even when space is at a premium, the Sagittarian will want to create an uncluttered area—not always easy, given their tendency to have books like some people have mice.

The ideal home will have a warm and comfortable glow to it, but 'Goodness, how tidy!' is not the phrase likely to leap to your lips as you enter the Sagittarian house, with its hall full of elderly duffle-coats, wellies, hats and college scarves hanging from every peg. Nor is your first impression of their living-room likely to be one of great elegance. Yes, there may be handsome books about—but they'll be well-used, and are likely to have been put back hurriedly, upside down and in the wrong place on one of the many shelves.

The Sagittarian being, as we have said, the hunter of the zodiac, hunts for bargains rather than big game, and their houses betray the fact, being stuffed with interesting trophies carried off from sales—in the village hall or at Sotheby's, depending on individual circumstances! Remember, a bargain is a bargain to a Sagittarian. That enormous armchair from a gentleman's club may be far too big for the room, but it *was* only fifteen pounds, and how comfortable it is! The desk will be worth looking at—and count upon it, even if there doesn't seem to be one, there will at least be a table or flat surface of some kind at which the Sagittarian can settle down to study. And isn't that a globe of the world propping up the index-volume of the *Encyclopaedia Britannica*? Up on the shelves with the books will probably be team photographs, a trophy from a school race, relics of youth and perhaps athletic ability.

The Sagittarian kitchen may be no place for you, if cooking's a keen hobby—there is likely to be as much chaos there as anywhere else in the house. This isn't of course to say that they don't turn out a good meal. They are likely to use plenty of spices, and the sound, solid fare you'll enjoy at a Sagittarian home will include good, rich casseroles—perhaps involving hare, rabbit, pheasant or other game—with plenty of pulses to thicken them up. They may start the meal with grilled grapefruit, for they like to awaken the palate with something sharp and tart. But you may get artichoke soup, for all bulb vegetables are associated with Sagittarius. The sweet may involve currants or sultanas, and there may be a *penchant* for full red Spanish wines.

The table will probably be set with rather chunky tableware—oven-to-table dishes are specially attractive—and dark blue may figure somewhere; the plates may be pictorial (a view to look at when you've cleared your plate!). Glasses will be big and firm and dependable, perhaps a trifle clumsy.

A peep into the bedroom will probably reveal at least a king-size bed—Sagittarians can be very restless sleepers; and that splash of colour must surely be a Spanish Casa Pupo bedspread? The pile of bedside books may have been knocked over by the family terrier, perhaps on his way to bed in the same room. Many Sagittarians will favour an intelligent, bright, vivacious dog as a pet.

See if you can spot a landscape painting, perhaps by Constable, or a Turner seascape—a reproduction of one of Stubb's horse paintings, or perhaps something connected with the age of Elizabeth I. Sagittarian taste in music will include Berlioz or Brahms, the open-air sound of Aaron Copland or Vaughan Williams, country and western songs or guitar music, and perhaps there will be a guitar itself in the Sagittarian home.

☆ IMAGE

Clothes Of all the twelve signs, Sagittarius presents the most casual image. This may be because of an interesting psychological identification with youth and student days; we usually find this sign tends to hang on to its student image much longer than any other, so that years after they have left college or university we find many Sagittarians still wearing their college colours or even a blazer.

It is essential for this type to feel very comfortable in their clothes, especially when, because the situation demands it, they have to dress more formally than they would on an everyday occasion. Many will bend the rules of dress when they follow a conventional career, and sometimes get into trouble—for instance, wearing a sweater when a formal shirt and tie would be more acceptable. Interestingly, one of the give-away indications of this sun-sign is the wearing of polo-necked sweaters; both sexes seem to adore them.

Whatever background or career they have or follow, it is advisable for Sagittarians to be able to put on their clothes in the morning when they get up, and forget about them for the rest of the day. This is psychologically important, for if they are coping with restrictive clothes, in particular tight skirts, they will feel claustrophobic, and as the reader will be now have gathered, this is something they cannot tolerate. Many Sagittarians enjoy wearing dark blue, and when it is fashionable, purple. This is the colour of their sign, and does seem to suit them particularly well.

When it comes to formal evening wear, the Sagittarian—especially the men—will do their darnedest to get out of it; but we suggest that the women of the sign should look for some attractive separates in, say, pure silk—the outfit should include a nice, soft, full skirt, so that even on this kind of occasion the Sagittarian will not be inhibited by her outfit. Both sexes usually have quite a shock of exuberant hair—sometimes quite difficult to control. Best if it can simply be brushed into an interesting shape or style, because again they will not want to feel constricted by a complex hairstyle continually in need of repair.

High fashion shoes should, needless to say, be chosen with particular care—the occasion will be ruined if Sagittarian feet are uncomfortable.

These days, the very best kind of outfits for people of this sign are probably tracksuits and jumpsuits, for here fashion (sometimes quite high fashion) and comfort go well together, and to ring the changes our Sagittarian friends can indulge in a variety of training shoes in matching colours. One Sagittarian male we know will only go out without a hat when the summer temperature is at its height; but this is for practical reasons. However, Sagittarians often also choose hats just for the fun of it.

Extenders Although Sagittarians need to feel free and uncluttered, we seldom meet one in the street who isn't carrying a large bag crammed with books, magazines, sports equipment or something else entirely necessary to their self-expression. Uncharacteristically, they are often personally heavy-laden! The older generation will frequently carry a large handbag containing all sorts of things—like magic, they can produce chocolates and toffee bars for adoring grandchildren, or all manner of curios.

A Sagittarian investing in a camera should think seriously of buying a wide-angle lens—almost at once he or she will want to photograph some gorgeous landscape or building, only to be disappointed that they 'can't get it all in'.

Belts will only be worn for practical reasons, and jewellery will be chosen for the simplicity of its design, and maybe sometimes for its texture—many Sagittarians will be seen playing with a heavy piece of amber, or a pendant of some other kind, getting sensual pleasure from its touch.

On the whole, spicy but very fresh perfumes will be preferred—something invigorating and 'healthy'. Generally speaking, the men are not very much in favour of after-shave lotions or colognes, but if they do use them they will be anything but sweet. Many Sagittarian men will experiment at some time in their lives with a beard, which often suits them extremely well.

Cars An elderly but fast sports car may well be the first choice of a young Sagittarian who has just passed his driving test. It will probably move pretty fast, but it will hardly be a luxurious ride. Later on, when the individual has collected a family or perhaps wants to make some adventurous journey with friends, a Land-rover or estate-car is often chosen, simply because it's tough enough to cope with difficult road conditions, which somehow Sagittarians seem often to have to face.

☆ TRAVEL

Of all twelve signs of the zodiac, this is the one which is most closely related to travel. Most Sagittarians adore this, however it may occur, and long for an excuse to go off to the travel agent's to purchase airline or railway tickets. They certainly enjoy travelling as much as arriving at their destination.

Because they are by nature independent, they will plead with their parents from an early age to be allowed to take school trips, or even to be more adventurous and go off on their own or with a friend or a small group. Physically, they cope extremely well with changing climates and conditions, though sometimes (and especially when they are very young) they tend to get so fascinated with the changing landscape and customs of the country they are travelling in that they become careless with their possessions, and in coping with the practical side of life.

Once they become used to travelling, it is quite good for adult Sagittarians to start to plan their own journeys and to work out routes for themselves. Yet they need a lot of support from their partners, who must see to it that they are not taking any short-cuts, either in the planning of the trip or the journey itself; the chances are that in their enthusiasm they will find themselves halfway up a mountain unable to move either way, or at the end of an unfinished stretch of motorway.

Sagittarians also need to be aware of the fact that they may tend to be over-ambitious in their journeys, always wanting to see what is over the horizon, and ending up much further afield than they originally intended. This may be good fun for a Sagittarian, but can be exhausting and trying for everyone else. Their ideal holiday will indeed be ambitious, but carefully monitored—a round-the-world trip is presumably at the top of every Sagittarian list. At least they should be able to express their sense of adventure, particularly in exploring unusual places. They will tolerate primitive conditions for the sake of travel, and many will go on taking camping or caravan holidays at an

age when the rest of us would prefer to relax in a comfortable and elegant hotel. In spite of this, the Sagittarian will certainly be eager to have a good hearty meal every day, and will probably be prepared to spend quite a lot of money on it.

Parents of Sagittarian children must be prepared for them to become slightly restless if they are on holiday in a place where there isn't a great deal to do. Because these children will probably be very lively, it goes without saying that their parents will need a rest, and should encourage the young to use their imaginations, and also to find out as much as possible about the new environment. Here, for instance, is a marvellous way for them to show off a knowledge of the local language, which they may have learnt before they leave home. At least they should have a suitable phrase-book of their own, so that they can communicate with the local children.

Many Sagittarians will of course enjoy the sun, and will often seek it in winter; but equally, because they are, on the whole, outdoor types we find that if they are on holiday in the winter they will be making the most of the ski-slopes. Winter sports are certainly very good for them, and the exhilarating thrill of improving their technique will do much to ward off the dreariness of winter, as well as being a marvellous form of exercise. They should be careful not to be too daring, and attempt exploits outside their range. Pony trekking will also be popular, and when the Sagittarian decides to settle down at a more or less conventional holiday resort, he or she should make certain that it has good sports facilities, and that there is an ample supply of books by their favourite authors—all this in order to avoid boredom and resulting restlessness. It is far better for people of this sign to get to know local forms of transport, and use them, rather than simply going around in a tourist bus. In this way they will benefit from really meeting the local people, and their imaginations will be stimulated by the atmosphere, the sounds, the sights, the smells. Travel should be an important ambition for every Sagittarian.

☆ PRESENTS TO PLEASE

It is not difficult to choose a present which will please a Sagittarian. Even if this happens to be something which relates to an experience they would rather forget, they will find a way of making use of it and benefiting from it.

They will be very pleased with an original book on a place or a topic in which they are interested. If the Sagittarian is creative, he or she will

★ FAVOURITE TO SAGITTARIUS ★

★ **SAGITTARIAN COUNTRIES**—include Spain, Arabia, Hungary, Australia, Yugoslavia.

★ **SAGITTARIAN CITIES**—include Toledo (in both Spain and Ohio, U.S.A.), Avignon, Toronto, Naples, Stuttgart, Budapest, Cologne, Nottingham, Bradford, Sheffield.

★ **TREES**—The lime, birch, mulberry, chestnut, ash, oak.

★ **FLOWERS AND HERBS**—include balm, bilberry, borage, cinnamon, dandelion, dock, mosses, pinks, sage, thistles.

★ **FOODSTUFFS**—Asparagus, tomatoes, onions, leeks, celery.

★ **CELL SALTS**—Silica and Kali Mur.

★ **STONE**—Topaz.

★ **COLOUR**—Dark blues, royal purple.

happily receive some basic materials of their art or craft—their imagination will immediately take off, and they will think of a number of ways of using them before the wrapping paper has reached the floor.

Because they like to enjoy life, some of the most welcome gifts you can give will be related to their experiences—for instance, if you can discover something your Sagittarian friends haven't done before, and introduce them to it, they will feel that their experience of life has been deepened, and will be grateful for the fact. Don't hesitate to throw them into the deep end of any experience: you could, for instance, take a Sagittarian opera buff to a wrestling match or *vice versa*!

The gift of a sweater, preferably with a polo-neck (see *Image*) or a jolly knitted scarf or woolly hat, will also be acceptable, as will some kind of sports equipment. But basically you cannot go wrong provided, in the first instance, you ask yourself what is going to present your friend with a challenge; in that way you will be bound to please them.

If you are going to stay in a Sagittarian home, you might like to give them a framed antique map, preferably of their area, or of some other stretch of country known to them. They will certainly find somewhere to hang it the moment they have unwrapped it. A large reproduction poster of a 1920's or 1930's liner, car or railway-engine would be equally welcome, as perhaps would a colourful reproduction of a landscape in southern France—a Dufy, perhaps.

Before giving a Sagittarian child a present, it will probably be as well to find out their favourite subjects. While the last thing to do is to give them boring textbooks, there may be some aspect of a school subject which is enthrallingly treated by a non-academic writer, and which will fascinate them in their free time. The heroes and heroines of history will interest them; so will stories of travel and exploration—indeed, an ideal present for a young Sagittarian just starting to read would be stories of children who live in other lands—and incidentally, an adult would delight in a subscription to *The National Geographic Magazine*! Young Sagittarians will enjoy playing with soft toy animals more than anything else.

CAPRICORN

· DECEMBER 22 — JANUARY 20 ·

☆ THE MYTH

The fish-tailed goat, the symbol of Capricorn, represents Ea, 'antelope of the underground sea' as he was called in Sumeria, where he was god of supreme wisdom, 'he whom nothing escapes'. He emerged from his watery home to teach men the true values of civilisation, and is notable for never being known to be angry. In ancient texts he is often shown as a man wearing a fish-shaped cloak, the head over his head, the tail covering his heels. In earliest times he was a water-god; it was the great astrologer Ptolemy who made Capricorn an earth sign.

☆ THE SIGN

The *ruling planet* of Capricorn, with which it has a special relationship, is Saturn; it is a *cardinal, feminine, earth* sign. *Positive traits* include ambition, aspiration, a good sense of humour, prudence, discipline, patience, determination, caution; *negative traits* include meanness, pessimism, over-conventionality, grumbling, wet-blanketing.

Capricorn in a nutshell Ambition will be methodically calculated, and patiently achieved.

☆ GENERAL CHARACTERISTICS

It is common knowledge that Capricorns fall into two distinct groups: some set their goals very high and strive after them with singleminded purpose, eventually reaching the top of the hill; others will nurse similarly high aspirations, but their outlook and attitude, chiefly because of a lack of self-confidence, often prevent them from getting to the top. The latter will claim that they have lacked opportunity or educational facilities, or that some heavy burden has prevented them from striding confidently towards their goal.

Interestingly, it is often the case that one group falls into the pattern of the other, so that even the most successful members of the sign will have surprisingly frequent periods of grumbling. It does no harm to moan about problems, but it should be recognised that this can slow Capricornian progress simply because of the boredom it inflicts on colleagues and friends. The marvellous off-beat Capricornian sense of

humour generally does a great deal to mitigate this state of affairs—it is usually extremely dry, and sometimes older men of the sign will laugh with the corners of their mouths turned down. Using their sense of humour in day-to-day life will stand Capricornians in good stead.

In early years, they are not always terribly self-confident, and confidence should be developed; they are reliable and disciplined, but should try not to become slaves to conformity.

Perhaps the quintessential *Capricornian in fiction* is Soames Forsyte in Galsworth's *The Forsyte Saga*, whose ambition and possessiveness unbalances his life to the extent that his personal relationships are cold and stultified. Shakespeare's Malvolio is another good example; in more modern times, Charlie Brown's friend Lucy, grumbling and moaning and trying to re-make the world in her own mould, is doubtless a Capricorn.

The Capricornian's *greatest asset* is a powerful driving force; their *greatest need* is for personal achievement, and their *greatest problem* their incessant grumbling. Their *greatest vulnerability* is to social climbing. *The Capricorn motto*: Onward ever, backward never.

☆ FRIENDSHIP, LOVE AND MARRIAGE

Friendship It is possible to have a lot of fun with a Capricorn friend; shared interests will be pursued with enormous enthusiasm. But don't be surprised if, from time to time, when you meet your Capricorn friend, there is absolutely nothing right with their world, their job and their terrible boss (who is over-demanding and for whom they can do absolutely nothing right).

This view of life is part of their personality, and must, willy-nilly, be part of your friendship, for you must allow them to get their grumbles off their chest. Once they have had their moan, encourage them to enjoy themselves—you can usually appeal to their sense of humour, and very soon will find that they are playing the role of what some astrologers call 'the giddy mountain goat', having released themselves from the inhibitions which plagued them while they were tethered to their problems down in the valley!

It is good to appeal to their strong ambition. Having achieved one thing together, why not suggest that you move on to another, even more demanding project or interest? In this way you will thoroughly enjoy your friendship, for you will both get satisfaction from the mutual interest.

When you arrange to meet a Capricorn, their sense of pride will join with their natural reliability to make them on time and will ensure that the hours you spend together will pass according to plan. They are extremely loyal and faithful, and your friendship should last for years, provided their ambition and tendency to social climbing do not outstrip their feelings of loyalty to you.

Love When Capricorns fall in love, they fall deeply. But before allowing themselves a free expression of their emotions, they will rationalise their feelings and make quite sure of their ground, for committing themselves puts them in a vulnerable position, and it is difficult for them to cope with uncertainty and the fear of rejection. Because of this cautious approach, they often give the impression that they are cold and uncaring, and certainly this can be a barrier.

Capricornian lovers will want to impress their partners, but will sometimes spend less on them than they can afford! The courted ones should recognise that meanness with money together with a cool initial approach is part of the Capricorn psychological make-up; once the individual has relaxed into the relationship, lively, fun-loving qualities will be expressed more openly, and there will be much pleasure together. Nevertheless, a certain caution will be present throughout every state of a developing romance. This again is part of the Capricorn make-up, and does not mean that the individual cannot love deeply and very sincerely.

Sometimes it is necessary for their partners to help Capricorns to relax, especially if the individual has had a rather strict upbringing; while in many ways this may have been good for them, it can tend to reinforce their somewhat prim and proper attitude to life, and in particular to restrict a free expression of emotions.

Marriage Once committed to marriage, the individual Capricorn will take it very seriously and will become a true and stable partner. But because they are ambitious, there will sometimes be a conflict between career demands and the amount of time they spend enjoying their marriage and children. It is sadly also true that they can contrive a romance, and a marriage, solely for the purpose of advancing their career. The boss's daughter is never entirely safe from his Capricornian employee. Moreover, in order to achieve an ultimate objective or to hang on to it once it has been achieved, the businessman or woman will tend to bring a bulging briefcase of papers to go through during the course of the evening, when he or she should be relaxing. Or they will stay on and work late in lonely offices. This is something about

which their partners should be very firm, and they themselves should recognise the dangers. While they are eager to provide the very best of material comforts for the home, and the finest of educations for their children, they may miss out on a great deal of pleasure, sometimes to the degree that they hardly know their children, because of their exclusive preoccupation with their career. It is up to individual Capricorns seriously to question themselves about this; it can break up a marriage.

Involvement in partners' and children's interests should be cultivated at an early stage, and when the partner drops a hint that the Capricorn should relax more and have some good, honest, simple fun for once, the hint should definitely be taken! When the Capricorn sense of humour comes to the surface, the partner will realise that the battle is won.

☆ PARENT AND CHILD

The Capricorn parent can be a great deal of fun, but there are many points to be considered before they take up the role.

The Capricorn women must accept the fact that if she has been in a successful career the joint income will drop considerably if she is at home raising the baby, and that if she returns to her job prematurely she may not be expressing her maternal instincts sufficiently strongly. (For she will be ambitious to be a good mother too.) The Capricorn man must be prepared to spend time with his children, and not become a distant and unapproachable father. He can find the role a difficult one, and when accused of being distant will reject the suggestion.

Both father and mother are very keen indeed for their children to make as much of themselves as possible, and will drive them into becoming involved in many activities both in and out of school. All-round, the Capricorn parent must try to relax, have fun, and fall in line with what the rest of the family suggests—if necessary breaking his or her own disciplined routine to do so. It is only thus that the family will become a happy, relaxed, contented unit. Sometimes, Capricorn parents will behave rather selfishly where the children are concerned; they will wish them to be at home for dinner at a specific time, or there on the spot ready for the regular visit to grandfather or grandmother; they find it difficult to be sympathetic to the youngsters' individual interests.

It is often forgotten that unconventional parents can have a child who is more conventional than they! This is sometimes the case when

the child is a sun-sign Capricorn, whose loyalty and sense of pride are admirable, but who should be teased, from time to time, especially if they become a little up-tight and pompous. Should young Capricorn start to grumble, appeal to the natural sense of humour—in that way they can begin to laugh at themselves.

These children will certainly be keen to get to the top of the class, but it is no good trying to force the pace with them; steady progress and gradual attainment is their best way forward. They should always be encouraged to relax and have fun; their many fine qualities must not be belittled, but if they are too serious they may later become compulsive workaholics with no time for real pleasure in life.

Many Capricornian children have very deep, warm feelings which will probably tend to be hidden; it is up to parents to reach these and develop them, so that they may flow freely. They will be popular at school, coping well with school rules. They should be encouraged as much as possible to enjoy the outdoor life: rock-climbing, geology, and the appreciation of beautiful buildings will be a source of inspiration to them. Most sun-sign Capricorn children should be encouraged to read as much as possible from a very early age, and any musical talent should be fully exploited.

☆ CAREER AND SPARE-TIME

A sense of security is on the whole important to this zodiac type. On the other hand they have this tremendous, driving ambition. Capricorns will be unlikely, however, to take uncalculated risks just in order to move nearer their eventual objectives; and indeed they should resist the temptation, for if the risk proves a bad one the damage to their sense of pride and self-confidence will be incalculable.

They cope well with regular hours, for routine fits in well with a disciplined lifestyle, giving them a sense of security. Many do extremely well in banking and all forms of big business, while others will become prominent estate agents or property managers. Those who enjoy the outdoor life often find a rewarding niche in agriculture, while others cope very well with living and working under spartan and difficult conditions. There is in a sense an attraction to adventure, but only if it is likely to lead to some satisfying and rewarding goal.

Of all zodiac signs, Capricorn is the one that can best cope with a lonely top position: for instance, many headmasters and headmistresses of large schools and colleges have Capricornian sun-signs. We find others as chairmen or managing directors of large companies or

groups of companies. If they veer to the medical profession they can become prominent dental surgeons, osteopaths or bone specialists. If they start their own business they usually do very well indeed, since 'going it alone' is part of their psychological motivation. The successful self-made man is in many ways essentially Capricorn, and indeed they should think very carefully before committing themselves to a business partnership which involves close collaboration, because in some cases (perhaps due to the ambition in Capricorn) there can be personal problems. So, more than with any other zodiac sign, the formation of such a partnership should be considered in very great depth. The chances are that any member of this sign would be prudent and cautious enough to do this anyway!

Sensitivity to colleagues' needs and suggestions is something that Capricorns should develop, whatever profession they decide to enter. There is a tendency for them to stride on regardless, and while they know that it is right to rely on themselves, they could be lacking in that team-spirit which can promote fine results. If they learn to work as a member of a team—which can mean a certain amount of ribbing from colleagues—and allow free rein to their own delightful sense of humour, they will become extremely popular, and will no doubt reach their much-treasured objectives all the sooner with the help of the people with whom they work.

The big question about Capricorn spare-time is, do they have any? They are so involved with their objectives in life that hobbies and spare-time interests are often relatively unimportant to them. Nevertheless, they will sometimes be canny enough to learn a skill which will support their career. The young executive, for instance, will become adept at golf just because the game so often offers the opportunity of combining social intercourse with career advancement. Many will enjoy attending certain social gatherings for the same reason. No doubt they will often get considerable pleasure from going to concerts or the races—but this will be all the keener if they can talk about these, afterwards, with senior colleagues; and of course if they are seen there by someone who matters in the development of their career, even better! Many indeed will make a positive hobby of social climbing.

The Capricornian element, *earth*, often finds interesting expression in the choice of Capricorn hobbies, where they exist. It is good for them to work with natural materials, for instance: such crafts as weaving, knitting, crochet will appeal, together with sculpture and pottery; these are all excellent forms of self-expression. Capricornians make excellent gardeners; geology and geography are interesting studies for them. Capricorn is a sign also closely connected with music; its appre-

ciation and performance is something worth serious consideration. Favourite reading will include the classics, or long family sagas.

☆ FINANCE AND INVESTMENT

Capricornians are generally eager to invest, and will probably do so from quite an early age. As children they may well put pocket money carefully aside, and not be at all keen to take it out of the bank even for such important occasions as holidays and Christmas.

Members of this sign are often of a pessimistic nature, and their reason for being 'careful' with money stems from a consideration for the proverbial rainy day, and for protecting themselves from possible financial wet weather. Many keep immaculate account-books, not only in business but for household expenditure too. They are very clever with money; they can make a little go a long way when they must, and similarly they will invest it wisely and cautiously when setting it aside. Because they tend to dislike financial risk-taking, it is probably better for them to put their money in building societies, or at least gilt-edged securities. If the individual is working in a financial institution—in banking, perhaps, or insurance—he or she will make very good use of the instinct they will develop for investment, and should be able to get a good return for their money.

The clever purchase and sale of stocks and shares will undoubtedly prove rewarding once the Capricorn is confident in judgement, and brave enough to take the necessary risks.

Traditional areas of investment for Capricornians include heavy industry, agriculture, insurance and any big business, the china clay industry.

Many Capricorns truly appreciate beautiful furniture and antiques, and as they become more prosperous will enjoy collecting *objects d'art*. They will sometimes invest in an 'old master' portrait of someone who will become, for them, an 'ancestor', to be hung in a prominent position on their walls. In general, the collecting urge, which is strong and rewarding, seems to stem from their polar sign, Cancer, and we suggest that if readers are thinking of starting a collection of some kind, they should consider some specific interest of theirs (perhaps something unusual) and base the collection on that, or if they are sufficiently wealthy consider collecting antique silver; they will certainly get a great deal of aesthetic pleasure from this (and should *use* the silver they collect), and while it is not as stunning an investment as it was a decade or so ago, it is still a valuable commodity. Curios of all

kinds, especially 'fairings', might be fun, as will glassware, marquetry or miniature furniture. Those with tastes in contemporary work might like to commission young potters to make individual pieces for them—there might be some financial risk if they are thinking of the matter as an investment; but there would certainly be considerable pleasure as well. Capricornians are traditionalists who love quality, and if they remember this they won't go far wrong, whether they are buying for pleasure or profit.

☆ HEALTH AND EXERCISE

'Keep moving!' should be the Capricorn motto where health is concerned, for the major problem is likely to be a stiffening of the joints as the years go by. The knees and shins are the traditional Capricornian body areas, and these tend to be vulnerable, and when there is an involvement in sport will tend to collect cuts and bruises, or, even more serious, knee injuries (this, and cartilage problems, can occur also while working-out at the gym or at home).

The skin is also related to this sign; it is often finely textured and rather sensitive, and the individual Capricorn should take special care of it, and be prepared to spend quite a lot on moisturising creams. The teeth and bones may need special attention, too, and should not be neglected. We cannot urge them too strongly to have regular dental check-ups. Traditionally, the skeleton is also related to Capricorn, and the reader will find many references to 'teeth, skin and bones' under this sign. Exercise is essential to keep the joints in good working order, for it should be borne in mind that many Capricorns must spend a lot of their working lives sitting behind desks. Those who live an outdoor life, working perhaps in agriculture, or who use physical energy a lot, are less likely to 'seize up' or suffer from rheumatic conditions, but all Capricorns should continue sporting interests for as long as possible, in the interest of maintaining physical mobility.

It is often the case that Capricornians do not seem to mind the cold, and indeed when we go into their homes we can find them a little chilly. But this is something that is in fact rather dangerous for them, for the cold can bring on all kinds of rheumatic pain. In view of the connection between this sign and the skeletal system, it is surely common sense to live in a very warm atmosphere, thus avoiding the onset of such problems. They will undoubtedly wear nice, warm clothes when out of doors in cold weather, and will probably enjoy wearing heavy sweaters in the house; but a chilly atmosphere is some-

thing they should avoid if they are going to keep mobile to the end of their lives.

Saturn, the ruling planet of Capricorn, is connected with the gall-bladder and spleen—but also with the skin, teeth and bones. There is also an association with the anterior lobe of the pituitary, which regulates the sex glands and bone and muscle structure.

We have said that it is of special importance for Capricorn to maintain their mobility and to take regular exercise. Jogging is excellent for them, for they don't mind being alone, and whatever environment they live in, they will probably enjoy getting out into the neighbourhood and examining the passing scenery as they wend their way through it. This is also a very inexpensive form of exercise, and provided they buy good quality running shoes which will cope with the varying road surfaces, they will do very well. Many an ambitious Capricorn will take part in the nearest marathon run. When they get older they should perhaps slow down to a walking pace, and walking can be enjoyed at any age, especially if they become enthusiastic members of a rambling club.

Many Capricornians make superb athletes, doing spectacularly well at high-jump and long-jump. All kinds of mountaineering and rock-climbing will be popular and rewarding, and the excitement of canoeing down fast-moving rivers—'shooting the rapids'—will be worth thinking about. We have already mentioned golf as an excellent Capricornian game by which the social and business interests can be furthered! Really serious Capricornian keep-fitters will probably acquire their own exercise machines and work away at cycling, rowing or jogging, as and when time permits. They might also consider walking up the stairs to their office, instead of taking the lift. Being disciplined in lifestyle, if they decide to become involved in regular exercise and spend hard-earned money on a subscription to a health club, or on exercise aids, they will certainly not be inclined to give it up. Boredom is not something likely to impede their progress.

☆ HOME ENVIRONMENT

With increasing family fortune, the chances are that Capricorns will move house rather more frequently than people of many other zodiac signs. We will see them starting off their relationships—or even before they have formed a permanent one—buying a small flat or house in an unfashionable area of the town, and before we know where we are they'll have graduated to something bigger and a little grander. And so

they progress until they are living in the most prestigious area of their town, and supporting an impressive and expensive, if still cautious, lifestyle.

Many Capricornians prefer living in the country but have to live in a city because of their choice of profession. This is a tendency which seems to be shared by all the *earth* signs, but Capricorns who have really 'arrived' will live in some delightfully wooded suburb, perhaps a fair distance from their work, happily parking their large car at the station to catch the 8.30 train every morning, and returning in the evening in time for a large dinner to be eaten at an impeccably-set dinner-table.

The house itself may be a genuine period piece, or in the Georgian style, but it will certainly be impressive. If the Capricorn is young, it will be sparsely furnished, but as the household gets larger the quality of the furnishings will improve, and in general it will be part of every Capricorn's ambition to own an elegant, well-furnished, attractive home.

There will probably be a feeling of space as we enter the house; the living-room will be somewhat conventional where the choice of carpet, furniture and curtains are concerned. There will be few gimmicks, and equally few trendy or eccentric items on show. The decoration and will include some pieces specifically bought as an investment (see *Finance and Investment*), and these will be proudly displayed— you may even be regaled with tales of how your Capricorn friend acquired some of the possessions.

Unless you yourself do not mind a fairly low living temperature, you may be rather dismayed by the lack of physical warmth, the first time you spend an evening with a Capricorn. The room temperature may well be rather lower than is comfortable—so wear an extra garment or two! Neatness and tidiness will be characteristic, and sometimes the rooms will even be over-formal in appearance—which does not mean to say that they will not be comfortable or original and interesting. The Capricorn's taste in music may also make its presence felt—there may be a piano or some other musical instrument in the room. The classics will be popular; or traditional jazz or ethnic music. Early music played on original instruments may be an interest.

Leather upholstery and pure wool rugs and hangings are often popular; generally, there are few frills or fussy trimmings. Capricorns are not at all keen on these. In addition to the 'ancestors', a tapestry or wool hanging may decorate the walls, or perhaps an interesting seascape.

The Capricorn dining-room will either be very basic, the plain wood

table being set with pottery and raffia table-mats, or be superbly set on classical lines—white linen, traditional porcelain china, silver cutlery, cut-glass. The meal will probably be hearty, and the individual Capricorn will no doubt want to impress you with his or her cooking skills and knowledge of wine. Fish is often served, and lamb and red meat dishes are popular. The dessert will probably not be very sweet; it may include some stewed or preserved fruit. There may be an ambitious cheese board, and you will be unlikely to go away feeling hungry. Fellow guests may be chosen as much for their likelihood to impress the company as because of any personal charm.

Other rooms in the house will be in either the distinctly basic ethnic taste, or follow the formal, classical, traditional values. Look out of the windows, and you are likely to see a garden which will be interesting and pleasing to the eye, whatever its size—though a view of several hundred acres tended by a dozen gardeners may well be the fantasy in every Capricornian mind.

☆ IMAGE

Clothes The Capricorn image is, in general, a conventional one. Capricorns like to spend quite a lot on their clothes, especially if they wish to impress someone in authority. Many young people will buy their first formal suit when they have to attend their first important interview.

On the whole, dark colours suit them best, and there are very few Capricorn women who feel that their wardrobe is complete without the classic 'little black dress'. The male equivalent is probably a neat pin-striped suit. There is no need for Capricorns to look at all dreary or boring in these somewhat formal clothes; they soon learn that it is possible to create a restrained but dramatic effect by the addition of some interesting jewellery or other accessory.

Irrespective of their figure, the women usually have very good legs, and these are frequently enhanced by interesting tights and elegant shoes. When shorter skirts are in fashion, they can wear them far more effectively and with greater confidence than many other zodiac types. As far as high fashion is concerned, they will tend to be conservative and to go for classic styles which are unlikely to date quickly. Sometimes they tend to buy clothes and not to wear them for some time, waiting for the right occasion on which to blossom forth.

Although many young Capricorns will not favour an entirely formal look, they too will have a certain conservatism in their image, and

indeed this is good for them, for restraint rather rather than razzle-dazzle is the most effective way of promoting their personality. Even the giddiest mountain goat on a night out with friends will attract most attention when dressed with a certain modesty and discretion.

It is often interesting to steal a glance at the male Capricorn's tie: this often reveals membership of some more or less exclusive club or society, or an ardent supporter of a charity. (Here is a good conversation-point.)

We often find Capricorns wearing pleasant shades of pale grey and dark green; they can enjoy an interesting contrast in their image if in the summer they wear white or the very palest shades of green. It is good for them to wear fabrics made from natural materials; in many respects they will be more comfortable in them, and because Capricorn is an earth sign the very texture of wool, pure cotton and linen will flatter them.

Capricorns are not over-concerned about their hair, and the simplest, most practical of cuts will suit them. Country-living Capricorns will probably have a selection of practical caps and hats for every occasion, and when an occasion demands the wearing of a hat they will be disinclined to spend a fortune on it. Needless to say, the typical 'city gent' image is completed by a bowler, and those who are in the sort of profession which encourages one will be very happy to conform.

Extenders As far as image-extenders are concerned, quality will rule the day. Capricorns buying a briefcase or a real leather handbag will expect it to last for years, and will see that it does. If there turns out to be the slightest flaw, it will be back to the shop before you can turn round. The same applies to shoes, and anything ultra-fashionable or too outlandish will probably be ignored. It is essential for all Capricorns to have one or two pairs of really stout walking shoes, for almost inevitably the time will come when they will wish to take a long country hike across the hills, or even the mountains, and they must be prepared!

The choice of fragrances will veer towards traditional scents which may have been around for a century or more; certainly there will be no liking for overpowering perfumes which dominate a whole atmosphere. Unfortunately, the metal of Capricorn is lead, which has not played an important part in the history of jewellery! Forget about it, and turn your attention to silver, especially antique pieces, or perhaps the work of a young, up-and-coming designer who produces interesting and unusual work.

It is probably true to say that a Capricorn would not like to advertise the fact that he or she is a tourist, so the smaller the camera the better. Here again, permanence and durability are important criteria.

Cars That sleek, black, elegant vehicle, whether it is a Mini or a Bentley, will surely belong to a Capricorn. For discretion and conventionality will rule: for instance, while many wealthy members of the sign will spend a great deal on their car, they may feel that a Rolls-Royce would be too ostentatious, and will opt for something equally prestigious but less obvious. To think of a Capricorn in anything but a black car is absurd!

☆ TRAVEL

Travel brochures will be studied, agents consulted and meticulous arrangements made for the annual Capricorn holiday. Most important, the trip will be budgeted down to the last coin of local currency, and hopefully the trip will run entirely according to plan.

It seems that two very contrasting sorts of holiday will appeal to this zodiac sign: there will be those who enjoy educational and informative tours and excursions complete with daily lectures; others will be happier striding off into a remote area of the world, complete with rucksack, camping equipment, water-purification tablets and supplies of emergency food.

Capricorns take their travelling very seriously, and will enjoy their trips in retrospect. In some ways they may be rather apprehensive about travel; it is best for them, when they are young, to start their travel experiences fairly near home, or at least in a country whose language they know quite well.

The ideal resort for a Capricorn will certainly be one which has an unspoiled beach within easy reach of some wonderful mountain scenery, for Capricorns love the mountains and also enjoy being near water. Lakes are popular, for this reason; the English Lake District in particular, but also the Swiss lakes, spring to mind. They will be happiest travelling overland, and the journey itself will be rich in experience—the changing landscape not least among them.

Capricorns tend to wilt in a very hot climate, and it may be that it is humidity that defeats them. If they are somewhere hot where the air is dry they will probably survive very well; they can cope with cold weather better than many others, so holidays in far northern or

southern latitudes will certainly suit them. Indeed, many are at their best taking winter skiing holidays, or at least staying in a bracing climate perhaps on very high ground. Many Capricornians may feel much healthier in a cold climate than in a very hot one, and when they are in the sun, they need to take a good supply of protective skin-creams—their skin does not always respond kindly to sun.

Bearing in mind their love of quality and need to get value for money, they will probably not want to stay at the newest, smartest hotel in town, but rather favour one which has either been personally recommended, or has built up a sound reputation for service and reliability. They would hate to think that they are paying through the nose for something as ephemeral as fashion. But no expense will be spared for polite, considerate service and quality food.

Talking of food, members of this sign should think twice before embarking on exotic local dishes; because a tendency to worry can catch up with them while they are travelling, their digestion—especially when away from the security of their own home—can be somewhat vulnerable.

The Capricorn child on holiday must be allowed to develop self-confidence gradually; initially, he or she may be rather shy and apprehensive about mixing with other children, and somewhat wary of local children and hotel staff. Obviously this is a good thing in some ways; but young Capricorn will learn far more if he or she is encouraged to be just a little more adventurous. They should be encouraged to make a collection of small shells, stones, minute pieces of coral, and so on. (We say small because we are thinking of the extra luggage weight on the way home!) On holiday, appeal to the young Capricorns' natural sense of ambition. Set them some task to achieve before the holiday is over: to swim an extra length of the pool, ride a pony, learn a new game—something of that sort. This will add to their self-confidence, and give them a sense of pride and achievement—and something to talk about when they get home.

Finally, if you are at all uncertain of what the weather is going to be like, it will be as well to find a long and exciting book to read if rain strikes. All being well, however, Capricorns will enjoy exploring local buildings of note: cathedrals, temples, amphitheatres—marvelling at the achievements of past generations, and seeing how past traditions are being used in the present. A good generalisation about Capricorns is that is is the achievements of man on which they love to focus, whether they are on holiday or at home.

☆ PRESENTS TO PLEASE

It would be too cruel to say that you should never think of giving a Capricornian a present because you could never afford it! But the main thing is to make sure that however small your present is, it is of good quality. Capricorns are *not* amused by trendy, fashionable presents or by *kitsch*.

Happily there are two areas in which you cannot go wrong: music and books. Obviously you should discover your individual Capricorn's taste in either; but having done that, you can delight them by tapes or a record album, the latest prize-winning novel or collection of photographs of a country they love.

Many Capricorn women will be delighted with a quality headscarf or box of pure linen handkerchiefs; a really handsome tie will equally delight a man—but so would quality desk-furniture: letter-opener, leather-bound diary—but all good traditional stuff; no 'executive toys'. Apart from anything else, there would be no time to play with them! A silver picture-frame would go down well; so would a decorative fossil, beautifully mounted.

Presents for the home—wedding presents for instance—might include table linen (either ethnic or traditional); glassware, some fine crystal perhaps, or plain modern glass; something made of leather? A dinner guest bringing the traditional bottle of wine should make sure it is a good, or at least an original one. The hostess would appreciate a potted plant, perhaps a variegated ivy.

Bearing in mind the fact that Capricorns are the bookworms of the zodiac, you will be popular if you give the children books of adventure and exploration or historical fiction. We must accept the fact that many youngsters of this sign tend to be loners, and will probably create their individual world, and be quite happy within it. Do not root them out unnecessarily; but try to encourage them to develop a few really rewarding ties of friendship, perhaps by presenting them with some interesting game which can be played by a limited number of people. This will help them to improve their powers of communication, which will be important to them later in life. Sports equipment will also be popular, especially good running shoes, track suits and nice, warm sweaters to wear in the open air on chilly days.

Many Capricorns have a strong scientific and/or mathematical bent, so do not be apprehensive about presenting children of the sign with chemistry sets, pocket calculators and computers, at a really early age.

Remember that sometimes people of this sign seem a little inhibited in expressing their very real pleasure on receiving a present which

★ FAVOURITE TO CAPRICORN ★

★ **CAPRICORN COUNTRIES**—include India, Mexico, Macedonia, Thrace, Albania, Saxony, Bulgaria, Lithuania, the coastal strip of Yugoslavia, Afghanistan, Orkney and Shetland.

★ **CAPRICORN CITIES**—include Oxford, Ghent, Delhi, Mexico City, Port Said, Brussels, Constanta, Mecklenburg. The administrative centres of all capital cities are traditionally ruled by Capricorn.

★ **TREES**—Capricorn trees include the pine, yew, willow, elm, aspen and poplar.

★ **FLOWERS AND HERBS**—Capricorn flowers and herbs include amaranthus, belladonna, comfrey, hemlock, henbane, medlar, onion, pansy, quince, rye, wolfsbane.

★ **FOODSTUFFS**—Meat is a prime Capricornian food; malt foods are favoured, and starchy foods are popular.

★ **CELL SALTS**—Calc. Phos., Calc. Fluor.

★ **STONE**—Turquoise or amythyst.

★ **COLOUR**—Black, grey, dark brown and dark green.

delights them. The single phrase they utter will be really sincere, however, and there will be no need to feel that the gift is unappreciated.

AQUARIUS

· JANUARY 21 — FEBRUARY 18 ·

☆ THE MYTH

The original Aquarian figure was that of an Egyptian god pouring water from a flagon, and presiding over the source of the Nile. For the Greeks it became that of Ganymede, son of King Tros of Troy, the most beautiful youth alive, and therefore chosen by the gods to be Zeus' cup-bearer. Zeus abducted the boy and made him immortal, setting his figure in the sky, smiling as he dispenses nectar to the father of heaven.

☆ THE SIGN

The *ruling planet* of Aquarius, with which it has a special relationship, is Uranus; it is a *fixed*, *masculine*, *air* sign. *Positive traits* include humanity, independence, friendliness, originality, loyalty, idealism, intellectuality; *negative traits* include unpredictability, eccentricity, contrariness, stubbornness, tactlessness, perversity, a tendency to be fixed in opinions.

Aquarius in a nutshell The need for independence and an individual lifestyle can be taken to extremes.

☆ GENERAL CHARACTERISTICS

One of the most positive characteristics that invariably surfaces in Aquarians is a positive friendliness; they always seem to be where the need arises, ready to help others at a moment's notice. This is not because they are emotionally moved to do so, but because they realise that when practical help is necessary they are able to give it straightforwardly and unreservedly.

It is true to say that in many respects Aquarians are very private people who will in some way develop a lifestyle unique to them. In spite of their overwhelming friendliness and helpfulness, many will fight shy of a permanent emotional relationship because of the necessary sacrifice of that lifestyle, and to a certain extent of their much-treasured independence.

Sometimes other people feel that it is quite difficult to get really close to Aquarians, and if this seems to be the case the situation must simply be accepted: Aquarians frequently lack both the desire and the capacity to be as close to others as others may wish them to be.

They are positive and optimistic in outlook, and will often be leaders of their generation, expressing opinions which are ahead of their time. But it can be the case that once they have formed those opinions they will find it quite difficult to reassess them as years go by, so that as they get older they may tend to lag behind the opinion of their contemporaries.

Dr Who is perhaps the most popular modern *Aquarian in Fiction*—though perhaps something of a caricature, with his 'mad scientist' image. Dickens' eccentric Miss Haversham (in *David Copperfield*) is another prominent member of this sign; Murial Spark's Jean Brodie is a quintessential Aquarian—almost too perfect an example, and Shaw's Major Barbara another.

Aquarians' *greatest asset* is their humanitarianism; their *greatest need* is for independence, and *greatest problem* their remoteness. Their *greatest vulnerability* lies in their unpredictability. *The Aquarian Motto*: Hear no evil, see no evil, speak no evil.

☆ FRIENDSHIP, LOVE AND MARRIAGE

Friendship Friendship with an Aquarian is something to be treasured—and respected. They are extremely faithful friends, and once a bond has been established it is a bond for life. There will be times when you may not see your friend for a long while, but the chances are that when you meet up again it will be as though you only saw each other yesterday, for you will immediately pick up where you left off.

In need of help, you will often find that it is an Aquarian friend who will be first to the rescue—expecting nothing in return, for going to the rescue of a friend is logical and obvious, when it is necessary. This is an enviable and splendid trait, but Aquarians should be aware that it can go too far, for some people will take advantage of it, and overwork the Aquarian capacity for real friendship.

Aquarians are wonderfully sociable, in spite of the area of their personality which insists on a certain privacy. They enjoy being members of groups or societies, have a vast number of acquaintances and are extremely stimulating company. Life will never be dull when you are with them—even if you occasionally find it irritating, or even worrying, that you cannot be as close to them, emotionally, as you may wish. This personal detachment must be respected. Be grateful for an unpredictable but continually interesting and stimulating friend; these

qualities will more than compensate for a certain 'distance' they will always maintain.

Love The Aquarian power of attraction is considerable, but it is often said that it can be compared to a magnetic force which can equally attract and repel. It takes the form of a certain glamour, almost like that of a film-star, but as with a star and the public, there is an unspoken injunction to 'keep your distance'.

When Aquarius falls in love the fall is a heavy one, and there will be no holding back; an exciting, rewarding and fulfilling partnership should follow. An Aquarian, however, does seem usually to require something out of the ordinary in a personal relationship, and this can sometimes show itself in a somewhat unusual choice of partner—from another ethnic group, perhaps.

However confident you are of the devotion of your Aquarian lover, remember that this is an air sign, and its inhabitants do not always find it easy to display emotion; one statement of devotion seems to them to be perfectly adequate, and it is not easy for them to repeat their declarations of love. Characteristic contrariness can often emerge in this sphere, however, and many will be extremely romantic.

Aquarians tempted to give a relationship the atmosphere of a romantic novel should ask themselves whether they are getting out of touch with reality—this can happen, and when it does it can be more of a problem for them than for many other zodiac types, for any sacrifice of independence will be regretted in the end.

Marriage Married Aquarians must remember that sacrifices will have to be made—not only of their independence but of the very individual lifestyle that they have probably built up. Their whole way of life is often linked to a deep-rooted psychological desire to protect themselves in some way from other people, and this can be a cover-up for a lack of ability to relate in total depth to another individual.

Needless to say, this can cause serious problems within a marriage, since the Aquarian may well not be able to communicate with his or her partner as freely as is necessary to sustain a long-term relationship. This, of course, is not the case for every individual Aquarian, but it is certainly a possibility, and it is as well for both partners to recognise that the Aquarian will definitely need some independence within the marriage, which will work best when the Aquarian is also emotionally involved in a rewarding career.

Those sharing an emotional relationship with an Aquarian can experience great joy, for they are kind and considerate people whose

ability to help their partners to achieve individual as well as joint objectives is very worthwhile, and should be treasured. If the Aquarian can add, from time to time, a touch of true glamour and romance, this will revitalise the relationship and help make it even more worthwhile. The need to suppress unpredictability and stubbornness is something which must be recognised by an Aquarian husband or wife.

☆ PARENT AND CHILD

Aquarians will always encourage their children to think for themselves—and will also be very good at not foisting their own opinions on their offspring. Once the children have sorted out their attitude to life, the Aquarian will be happy to rest assured that they will be as independent and self-sufficient as themselves.

The parents will want to give their children plenty of free expression, and perhaps many will bring them up rather unconventionally. But it is important for Aquarians to remember that they may give birth to a child who will thrive in a more conventional atmosphere than the one *they* prefer, and will be happiest at a school with a rigid discipline and an ordered routine—which would certainly not have suited the Aquarian! The trap of a parent assuming that a child will see life in precisely the same way as him or herself is perhaps more dangerous here than for other signs.

Aquarians are keen to be very fair to their children, and will listen carefully to their point of view. Sometimes, however, they can lack warmth and spontaneous affection, and recoil from physical contact and open expression of emotion. Perhaps one of the finest Aquarian parental qualities is honesty: they are unlikely to fob their children off with excuses or irrational fictions, and always come straight to the point; the children should therefore be very much aware of right and wrong.

Aquarian children may prove 'different' in some respects from brothers and sisters, and while this tendency should not be unduly pandered to, they should be allowed to express their originality freely and creatively. Bearing in mind the fact that they are humanitarian, it will be good for them to involve themselves, after school hours, in some form of humanitarian work. Parents should watch out for unpredictable and perhaps stubborn tendencies, which can be stumbling-blocks to progress in later life. The child will do well at school provided he or she is not stifled or restricted by being forced into a repressive routine, or made to obey rules which seem to them to

be illogical. They will probably do well in scientific subjects, English, and any area of study that involves the deep past or the distant future. Parents must expect their Aquarian children to make somewhat uneven educational progress: some years they will leap forward, responding well to the curriculum, and during others they will fall back somewhat—probably due to incompatibility with those who are teaching them.

Out of school, music, drama, skating and the less 'heavy' sports will probably prove most enjoyable for them. It will be a very good thing for them to take an active part in the upbringing of younger brothers and sisters. Here they will be expressing their natural kindness, and also developing inner warmth and a positive expression of their emotions—something that will stand them in good stead later in life.

☆ CAREER AND SPARE-TIME

The ideal career for someone with an Aquarian sun-sign will include a strong element of human contact, and in some way be connected with their caring attitude to their fellows. They will, for instance, make excellent social workers, using their kind, cheerful qualities, but being able to detach themselves from the illness or tragedies of others sufficiently to be able to be really helpful.

Many Aquarians have a scientific bent, and will find a niche working in the development of communications techniques, in television or in any area in which inventiveness and originality of approach are called for. We also find a great many people of this sign working as radiographers, in the air force or for airlines, and at the United Nations and its associate bodies—here again, their humanitarian qualities receive full expression.

Aquarians need to be given their head, and allowed to get on with their work without the chatter or intervention of colleagues or people who question their motives and cramp their style. If this is not the case, they will be extremely angry and very stubborn, and simply walk out of their job. This does not mean, however, that they are incapable of working with colleagues. Indeed, they can do much to encourage team-spirit, provided they themselves are allowed a certain amount of freedom of expression.

Many Aquarians will use their creativity in a scientific way, thus becoming the inventors of the zodiac. Sheer brilliance often emerges in members of this sign, as does a certain zany quality which some people tend to shrug off as eccentricity. They may be right to do so, but it is always as well to give the individual Aquarian the benefit of the doubt!

They are quite capable of working alone, provided they are genuinely involved in and enthusiastic about what they are doing. If the work is dull, they will get on with it, yes; but their minds will be elsewhere.

The Aquarian sense of drama is often in evidence in their careers, and when this is the case they can become extremely successful: in the fashion trade, the theatre and any area which calls for flair, a certain brilliance of approach, and the kind of originality which will catch the eye and imagination of the public.

It is quite good for members of this sign to become involved in the ecology movement, especially where the earth's resources are concerned. This can be a real source of inspiration for them, and, from modest beginnings they can do much to put the world's problems to rights. Working on behalf of trade unions, and for people in trouble is also likely to be dear to them.

An Aquarian's spare-time will be spent in a great variety of ways. We find them attending a lecture society one evening, going off to rehearse with their local drama group the next, on a charity committee the following evening, and so on. Somehow, they manage to fit in many varied interests—and still have time in plenty for their friends—especialy those in need of help.

They usually enjoy entertaining, and will often produce superb meals out of almost nothing. They seem to pick up quite a lot of the more glamorous, dramatic side of their partner-sign in the zodiac, Leo; so there is invariably something lavish about their style of entertainment, and sometimes about the way in which they spend their spare time in general. They will, for instance, enjoy going to first nights at the theatre, film premieres and big concerts, and will attract attention not only because of their dynamic personality but because they display a very glamorous image.

If the individual Aquarian is wealthy, he or she may enjoy learning to fly, or will have one or two hobbies which are really original: sky-diving, ballooning, perhaps mountaineering. In spite of all their varied interests, it is quite good for Aquarians to keep a certain amount of spare time entirely free of commitments, not only because it is necessary for them to unwind, but because they enjoy doing things on the spur of the moment; if they are totally committed, this great pleasure is defeated.

☆ FINANCE AND INVESTMENT

Very few Aquarians will want to spend much time considering where

and how to invest any capital they may have. A simple deposit account at a bank or building society will be quite adequate for them, and they will feel that the return they get for their money is about right; the idea of making a large fortune out of the labour of other people will, on the whole, be repellent to them.

When not entirely lacking in the gambling instinct, they can tend to go overboard in one spectacular gamble which will probably not pay off. The tendency to put all their eggs in one basket has ended badly for many an Aquarian. It is their liking for the glamorous life which can sometimes betray them into, for instance, investing heavily in a play or a film, and not covering themselves adequately. Best for them to cool it, and look long and steadily at any proposition put to them.

In domestic affairs, Aquarians can sometimes be rather secretive about their income; if in partnership with someone who is also working, there should be a firm agreement about who pays which bills—but also general flexibility, for in the Aquarian's preoccupation with many things which seem more important to them than money, they may not be aware of (say) the rising cost of living, and take it amiss when it is pointed out to them that they are no longer in touch with reality on the matter!

Similarly, in business Aquarians will not primarily be preoccupied with finance: the world of ideas is the world in which they live, and they may come up with a brilliant scheme. The accent will surely be on 'brilliant'; but whether it will be as financially as successful as they hope is another matter. So it will be a good idea to get the support and advice of someone who will look at their idea critically and objectively, and who will have a practical business sense which can be brought to bear on the scheme, to shape it up in accordance with conventional business practices. At such times Aquarius must not become stubborn, clinging to the original conception through hell, high water, and possibly eventual bankruptcy. They should be flexible and listen to advice. They can then do extremely well.

Aquarians will have little enough spare time, but may want to use some of it by helping to set up a business with someone else to raise funds for a favourite charity. This too is best done in partnership, with Aquarian flair and originality combined with the business and financial acumen of—say—a Capricornian.

An Aquarian really thinking of serious investment might look at television or radio companies, companies manufacturing scientific instruments, airlines, the communications industry in general, the chemical industry, and any form of scientific research into products which will improve general living standards.

☆ HEALTH AND EXERCISE

It is essential for Aquarians to be aware that their circulation is extremely vulnerable. If it deteriorates, their whole system can suffer, and problems such as varicose veins and hardening of the arteries can catch up with them. While they often thrive in cold weather, it is at such times that the problem can arise. So they should always have plenty of warm clothing available in case of a cold spell, especially to keep their legs warm!

The traditional Aquarian body area is the ankles, and it is amazing how many of them, when involved in sport, in dancing or exercise programmes, stumble and twist, strain or even fracture their ankles. Many Aquarian women love to wear high-heeled shoes, and are then even more likely than usual to injure this sensitive area.

We often see the relationship with the polar sign, Leo, in Aquarians' health: Leo rules the spine and heart, and many Aquarians suffer—even more than in general—from backache; the relationship between the heart and the circulation is an obvious one. The ruling planet of the sign, Uranus, is also connected with the circulatory system; but in addition the gonads are associated with the planet—and so is the pineal body, sometimes known as 'the third eye'.

Aquarius is high on the list of signs which respond well to, and take an active interest in, holistic medicine. Aquarians will be fascinated by the various techniques and disciplines which are increasingly accepted in medicine—many of them will have been using these for a number of years, and thoroughly benefiting from the experience. Although this is a scientifically-orientated sign, many Aquarians will not be too happy about taking courses of medicinal drugs, even antibiotics. If they can set about curing an illness by any other means, they will be happy to do so. It seems that they respond particularly well to chiropractice, acupuncture and acupressure and aromatherapy. Aquarius has much to do with the so-far-unmeasured flow of positive energies from the body—astrologers have suggested that Aquarius pours from his vessel not just water or wine, or even nectar, but energies which conventional modern medicine tends to ignore. Aquarians certainly have a great deal of sympathy with this point of view.

As with the inhabitants of the neighbouring sign in the zodiac, Capricorn, it is very important for Aquarians to keep moving. Both zodiac types are extremely prone to rheumatic and arthritic conditions (from an astrological point of view this relates to the tradition that before the discovery of Uranus in the eighteenth century, the planet Saturn once ruled both these signs). With this in mind, Aquarians

should specialise in the kind of exercise that will not only keep their circulation in good order, but also prevent stiffening of the joints. Aerobics, all kinds of dance movement, or swimming should form part of their exercise regime and their day-to-day fitness. When young, they often do well in athletics, but if they are encouraged to become members of a team they must remember that they are the individualists of the zodiac, and may have to work a little harder than most if they are to become a fully integrated team member.

Light food, without too much rich sauce is best for an Aquarian—which is sad, because they tend to like rather rich, heavy dishes. If they put on weight and decide that they must diet, those of this sun-sign can go about it rather erratically, and may not be very good at maintaining a reduced intake of food. This will need application, and when they have achieved their target weight loss they should resist the temptation to celebrate with a meal of such dimensions that most of the weight goes straight back on again.

If anyone requires, these days, to be reminded of the benefits to society of the Blood Donor organisations, Aquarians should not be among them, for their strong humanitarian qualities will underline the duty to give blood. As it happens, the association of the sign with the circulatory system also suggests that it will be particularly worthwhile for them to do this regularly. No self-respecting Aquarian will travel without a card donating his or her body and its organs for transplantation, to save the lives of others.

☆ HOME ENVIRONMENT

Aquarians are not too fussy about where they live; they can cope equally well in town or country, in a crowded suburb or a quite village—and they have a knack of organising their social life according to their environment. They like an interesting view, but because they are the individualists of their zodiac it is quite difficult to generalise about this, or indeed anything else that is Aquarian!

Even if their home is a small one, Aquarians like a feeling of space, and have a happy knack of achieving this. Many enjoy living in a somewhat clinical home environment; they will decorate their rooms in white or in pastel colours, and there will be an overall clarity and an un-cluttered effect. Textures will be enjoyed, and interestingly and unusually blended. A shaggy woollen rug will make a satisfactory base for a smart reclining or rocking chair, perhaps with a chromium frame and white leather upholstery.

There will be patterns, and objects of interest, but these will be used and displayed in out-of-the-way corners, rather than too obviously. There is often a hint of vanity in the Aquarian personality, so we generally find that there are plenty of mirrors, not only giving a feeling of space, but satisfying the Aquarian instinct to steal a glance at themselves from time to time.

Sometimes Aquarian homes veer towards the futuristic in decor; sometimes their characteristic eccentricity will make its presence felt in some interesting and unusual piece of furniture or work or art. There may be a collection of modern art prints, for instance, or unusual curios. Because Aquarians are often inventive, they will enjoy owning unusual mobiles or the latest executive toy. But they will be quite ready to get rid of these the moment they are bored, or when they see something else that attracts their attention. Glassware, in a variety of forms, will also be seen, and most Aquarians enjoy experimenting with various forms of lighting, giving their homes a dramatic look—though they should be a little careful that the lighting does not become overdirectional and uncomfortable.

Like their neighbouring zodiac sign, Capricorn, some Aquarians prefer living in a slightly cooler atmosphere than many other people, and it is as well to bear this in mind if you are invited to their home on a chilly day!

The bedroom and bathroom will not lack glamour: we may well find an extensive collection of toilet waters, perfumes and cosmetics there, and there could even be a hint of Hollywood razzle-dazzle: extra lighting for the dressing-table, for instance, and maybe the bed-covers will be in luxurious satin. But don't expect the atmosphere to be heavily seductive—it will more likely be pleasantly charming, and your host or hostess will probably have spent quite a lot on making it accord completely with their taste.

The dining-table will be attractively set, and that too could be made of glass, and only covered when strictly necessary. The china will probably be plain white porcelain, perhaps with a silver rim; or you could find that there is a hint of pale turquoise, which is very much the colour of the sign. The glasses will probably have cost rather more than the household can actually afford, and will either be beautiful cut-glass or more modern in design, depending on the taste of their owner.

It is good for Aquarians to eat rather light food, so perhaps white meat or fish will be on the menu, along with some interesting salads, and a dessert which might include meringue or ice-cream or a citrus fruit *soufflé*. The wine may well be a very dry white, and if Aquarius is

in a truly festive mood, and feeling generous, your chances of champagne will be good.

Cool, modern jazz will be popular if the Aquarian's taste goes that way; on the other hand Bach, so elegant, poised and assured, is often popular with Aquarians. Similarly, they will like delicate, perfectly-formed plants and flowers, often going for Japanese flower-arrangements, and not choosing the heavier, more romantic traditional vases of lush roses.

☆ IMAGE

Clothes Young Aquarians will probably be among the fashion leaders of their generation. They will regularly buy fashion magazines, and interpret the ideas in their own way; many have a happy knack of being able to predict coming trends.

As they get older, however, they tend to become less adaptable, and will often cling on to an image which they created when they were young, and which they feel is particularly 'them'; this reluctance to move with the times can be a real drawback, for their clothes tend to make them look older than they need. They should try to be adventurous, experimenting with new styles in order to prevent this premature aging. Aquarians can nevertheless look extremely glamorous, especially on occasions which call for evening clothes or when they are able to wear something really unusual (which they perhaps bought while travelling abroad).

The colour of the sign, pale turquoise, really does suit them extremely well; but they can look equally good in other pastel colours. Rough textures tend on the whole not to suit them; they look their best in the smoother materials—satin or silky textures.

Aquarians must learn to control their eccentricity; it can of course add real interest to their image, but can spell disaster if allowed to go over the top.

Many Aquarians have rather fine hair which does not always adapt well to bulky, *bouffon* styles. A sleek style is easier to cope with, and more effective. It should be remembered that a dated hairstyle will not look good—another area where the individual Aquarian should be careful, reassessing and re-styling from time to time. If a hat is necessary, or simply enjoyable, Aquarians can come up with some fairly extraordinary confections, which will either add excitement and interest or let down the whole effect. Take advice from friends, and try not

to be too stubborn when they come up with a really interesting suggestion.

Many members of this sign will spend a lot of money on their shoes. They will certainly enjoy fashionable ones, and the women will look particularly good in high heels or evening shoes trimmed with *diamanté* buckles. Indeed, sparkle and glitter is very attractive to any Aquarian, to the extent to which they can overdo it especially during the winter party season!

Getting a young Aquarian girl to wear school uniform will be an irksome process for the parent and child alike: she will do everything possible to alter it in some subtle way so as to express her individuality and originality. Should she go on to a career which demands comformity—as an air steward, for instance—she will have to conform, but if she can she will always find a tiny way in which to break the rule of uniform dress; and this does not apply exclusively to female Aquarians—there is an element of truth for the men, too, who will find their own way around any rule demanding dull or uniform dress.

Extenders As soon as young Aquarians are aware of fashion at all, they will have a marvellous time going around department stores and boutiques looking for colourful, zany, way-out handbags, bangles and all kinds of accessories to bedeck themselves. With increasing age, developing taste, and greater selectivity their choice will settle down, but nevertheless we will, from time to time, see an interesting piece of jewellery, some unusual belt or maybe an antique evening bag which has attracted the attention of our Aquarian friend.

They should not allow a conflict between the necessity to conform and their need to be unconventional to cramp their style when choosing any kind of image-extender: it is here that they should be able to create a really unique look. The women, for instance, might wear a chain and pendant, but on close examination the pendant could turn out to be a locket containing a lover's photograph, or maybe a perfume bottle containing their favourite fragrance. This will be very light, with overtones of the fresh air; but at the same time it will be unusual and create an aura attracting attention and curiosity rather than exuding heavy sensuality.

The metal of the sign is uranium, so we can only advise that they forget it! Platinum, it seems, makes a superb substitute. Any Aquarian camera should have a good flash unit; there are *no* lighting conditions in which an Aquarian will not want to take a picture!

Cars When an Aquarian starts a love affair with a car, it will be for

life. Many Aquarians remain devoted to ancient, much-restored Minis, or other cars well over twenty years old, which are polished, re-sprayed and restored—a real extension of the Aquarian image. Many Aquarians have dreams of owning a vintage car, which could be their idea of heaven. At the other end of the spectrum, some spend a fortune on the latest, most glamorous and up-to-date vehicle to hit the market.

☆ TRAVEL

Generally speaking, Aquarians enjoy flying—partly because this is one of the three air signs of the zodiac, and as they take off from their home airport, they will feel that indeed the sky's the limit.

They may tend to plan somewhat eccentric holidays in unusual places, off the beaten track. The connection between the sun-sign and the distant past often attracts them to places with a very long history, which fascinates them; unusual archaeological sites will interest them, too, and they might do well to investigate the chances of actually joining an archaeological dig.

In contrast to this, there will be times when an Aquarian will want to catch up with the latest scientific development, and will try to find places of interest which can further their knowledge and enthusiasm for this. It will be extremely surprising if an Aquarian is not among the first people to book a seat on a space-vehicle! When comets or eclipses are only visible from certain places in the world, they will tend to chase off in hot pursuit.

They are not, however, averse to living it up, and we find them spending a fortune in the world's best hotels, lying glamorously on beaches and sun-terraces, and frequenting the best bars after dark. They will be tempted to sample the more unusual local dishes, and while it would be silly to discourage this, it should be remembered that heavy food isn't too good for them, and that a sudden over-enthusiastic encounter with *couscous* might have a disastrous effect on the rest of the holiday.

Because they are extremely individual, they will often like to plan their own holidays, thus defeating the attempts of other people to herd them on to package tours. They are not at all keen on doing what everyone else is doing, and when they have to visit some temple, cathedral or site with a party, they will break away whenever possible, exploring it on their own.

Although Aquarians can cope with most climates, they particularly enjoy winter holidays; the sight of the sun glinting on snow will be

especially invigorating, as will the exercise provided by skating or skiing, inevitably backed up by generous hours of *aprés-ski* activity. Their complexions are rather pale (whatever their ethnic group), and their skin can be sensitive; Caucasian Aquarians under sun and wind can suddenly resemble beetroots, so heavy barrier creams should be packed if the climate calls for them.

Because of their deep-rooted humanitarian instincts, many Aquarians will want to see for themselves parts of the suffering Third World, and will be spurred on to additional efforts to help out. Many are interested in comparative religion, and will find visits to—say—Jerusalem, Mecca or the banks of the Ganges particularly rewarding.

A certain perversity may become apparent when parents tell their Aquarian children where they are going on holiday: ten to one the young Aquarian will want to go somewhere completely different! To avoid arguments, it will be as well to show the child plenty of photographs of the country to be visited, and to make sure that he or she is thoroughly involved in the plans from the earliest possible stage. In this way their natural enthusiasm will be sparked off, and they will learn a great deal from their trip—they are very good at asking questions (and indeed at listening to the answers).

Encourage your Aquarian child to save up rather more pocket money for the holiday than he or she may need; they are almost sure to find some really unusual and perhaps wildly odd souvenir that they will just *have* to bring home. Hopefully, you'll be able to get it on the plane without having to pay too much for excess baggage.

If your young Aquarian is deeply involved in a specific art form, one of the nicest holiday opportunities is the discovery of how local people similarly express themselves—local musical instruments, the regional dances, and so on. It is also very good for Aquarian children to make contact with their contemporaries in other countries. Understanding between nations is quintessentially Aquarian.

☆ PRESENTS TO PLEASE

Originality is the hallmark when choosing a gift for an Aquarian. This can present difficulties, but there are a few basic guidelines. They like pure, geometric lines, things that shine and glitter, and love very clear objects such as glass ornaments or vases.

If you want an attractive present for an Aquarian woman, you might look for a very modern piece of costume jewellery, perhaps made of acrylic or crystal, or a piece of original glassware for her

★ FAVOURITE TO AQUARIUS ★

★ **AQUARIAN COUNTRIES**—include the U.S.S.R., Poland, Sweden, Ethiopia, Israel, Syria, Iran.

★ **AQUARIAN CITIES**—include Bremen, Hamburg, Moscow.

★ **TREES**—Fruit trees are governed by Aquarius.

★ **FLOWERS AND HERBS**—Aquarian flowers and herbs are those shared with Taurus and Capricorn.

★ **FOODSTUFFS**—Foods that appeal to Taureans also generally appeal to Aquarians.

★ **CELL SALTS**—Nat. Mur. and Mag. Phos.

★ **STONE**—The Aquarian stones are amethyst and aquamarine.

★ **COLOUR**—Electric blue.

dressing table—if it has an iridescent pattern or a slightly smoky appearance, you cannot go wrong. Toilet waters or bathroom cosmetics (provided the fragrance is light) will certainly be appreciated by both sexes. A subscription to a fashionable magazine might be popular, and it won't be too difficult to discover which one will be most suitable. Many older Aquarians are fascinated by what the younger generation is getting up to, so don't be surprised if they drop a hint that they would like a magazine actually aimed at a much younger readership!

Some of the nicest presents an Aquarian can receive are those which will extend their field of experience—for instance, if you want to give them a very speical treat, and they have never flown in a helicopter or a hot air balloon, this would be ideal, especially if it is a surprise. You might also draw their attention to some new, interesting hobby. Aquarians have open minds about their spare-time interests, and if you know one who has just retired you could do a lot for them if, by means of a gift, you can introduce them to something new and different.

A truly lovely wedding present for an Aquarian would be a modern decanter and matching glasses, or perhaps a glass salad-bowl and salad-servers. Or if you only *just* know the person concerned, remember that they love clear, perspex salt-and-pepper grinders!

If you are going to dinner and your hostess is an Aquarian, you will not fail to please her if you present her with an orchid—the flower of the sign which, as it lasts for many weeks, will remind her of you and the happy evening you spent together.

It should not be too difficult to choose a more personal gift for either sex—they certainly like quality, especially as they mature in years, so you might consider choosing some item made in pure silk, in a plain pale or clear colour, or some simple table-linen which is nicely made and has a minimum of fussy decoration. Heavily embroidered items with many bright colours will be less likely to appeal.

A gift of wine will be welcome, but probably the individual Aquarian would prefer a half-bottle of dry, quality champagne, to a litre of plonk. As you give it to them, explain that they should open it in one of their quieter moments, and think of you!

★ PISCES ★

· FEBRUARY 19 — MARCH 21 ·

☆ THE MYTH

In Babylonian mythology the goddesses Anunitum and Simmah, representing the Tigris and Euphrates rivers, were the two fishes of Pisces, swimming in opposite directions with a cord joining their mouths. Later, in Greek mythology, it was Aphrodite and her son Eros who turned themselves into fish to escape the wrath of the monster Typhon; Zeus commemorated the event by placing the constellation in the skies.

☆ THE SIGN

The *ruling planet* of Pisces, with which it has a special relationship, is *Neptune*, and it is a *mutable*, *feminine*, *water* sign. *Positive traits* include kindness, charity, creativity, intuition, imagination, self-sacrifice. *Negative traits* include deceptiveness, disillusion, lack of self-confidence, evasiveness, nebulousness, general weakness of character.

Pisces in a nutshell Self-confidence must be acquired if individual potential is to be realised.

☆ GENERAL CHARACTERISTICS

Pisceans are among the kindest, most charitable and self-sacrificing of all twelve signs. Sometimes they will set aside the development of their own careers in order to look after their young families, or other people. They are often very creative and clever, but it is quite difficult to convince them that their talents are worth bothering about.

They can live life in their own dream world, and sometimes as a result get totally out of touch with reality; they are often not very practical, and need quite a lot of help when it comes to the organisation of their lives or showing off the results of their labours.

They will often be swayed too much by emotion and intuition, and need to recognise the fact that their imagination will take over at the least provocation, and that as a result they can worry about nothing. They must at all costs avoid slipping into self-deception, because they tend to think that in deceiving themselves and others they are finding an easy way out of difficult situations. This can be disastrous, for their lives become webbed with complications.

They will be at their best when expressing their creative potential in some way, but it usually takes a stronger personality to encourage them to do so, and to live a really fulfilling and rewarding life. Pisces is often called 'the poet of the zodiac', but while many are interested in poetry it is really a psychological description, for they need a certain amount of poetry in their lives. The symbol of the sign is two fishes swimming in opposite directions, but connected by a cord between their mouths. Pisceans are often inclined, when they want to take one action, perversely to take the other.

Cinderella is perhaps the archetypal *Piscean in fiction*—the skivvy, working hard for her stepmother and ungrateful sisters, unable to believe that she is worth saving from a life of drudgery, but delighted with the poetic flourish of the pumpkin coach and its horses; Long John Silver, in Stevenson's *Treasure Island*, has the overweening sentimentality of Pisces, but also bottomless charm and capacity for deceit, and an artfulness which is rarely lacking in members of this sign.

The Piscean's *greatest asset* is sympathy for others; their *greatest need* for encouragement. Their *greatest problem* is their lack of self-confidence, and their *greatest vulnerability* not being able or willing to face reality. The *Piscean Motto*: 'Whatever will be, will be.'

☆ FRIENDSHIP, LOVE AND MARRIAGE

Friendship If you have a Piscean friend their kindness and generosity will overwhelm you at times, but it will be up to you to give them every possible encouragement to make the most of their very fine qualities. You will find it extremely difficult to convince them that they are really good at what they are doing, and all too often you will have to do battle to make them face up to the fact that they really can achieve a very great deal, either in their career or in private hobbies and interests.

For instance, if your Piscean friend makes beautiful things, they will think nothing of them; but the chances are that you may know another person who would be in a position to sell them, thus enabling Pisces to make quite a lot of extra cash. They may well be reluctant to let you deal with whatever they have made, but you will be doing them a favour if you insist: while the cash will of course be acceptable, the psychological boost and the inner strength it will give them will be far more important.

Pisceans generally fall in line fairly easily with other people's wishes when it comes to outings, but there will be times when you could be quite annoyed, not only because Pisces is disorganised but because of a certain amount of shyness, which can seem like bloody-mindedness, and which may hold them back on social occasions when others are present who really could interest them.

Love Pisceans have a very high level of emotion which they are all too willing to express generously towards their lovers. They make very sensual and rewarding partners, and will sometimes overwhelm a lover with kindness and affection. If they use this powerful force positively, it will obviously be a marvellous and enviable one; but sometimes, especially when their imagination is working overtime, many Pisceans unfortunately resort to emotional scenes.

A relationship with a Piscean will be a memorable one, because it will be at the very least, highly romantic and in many ways remarkable. There will be no lack of expression of emotion, and their great thoughtfulness will add a whole dimension and a great deal of colour. However, when they fall in love it is very easy for Pisceans to see their partners through rose-coloured spectacles—facing up to the reality of a partner's faults is difficult for them, so that sometimes they will commit themselves to a relationship ignoring areas in which they and their partners could clash.

Pisceans are passionate but not overtly or forcefully so; while there will be moments when you will both reach the heights, for most of your time together you will have a simple, straightforward but charming and delightful life. You may have cause to tease your Piscean lover about sentimentality, but don't forget that a little of this quality does no harm.

Marriage As Pisceans make romantic lovers, they also make tender and caring partners. Once committed to a permanent relationship they will work hard and energetically to make it 'take'. They will be extremely intuitive when it comes to assessing what their partners really think or need, and are well able to keep one step ahead in the relationship—often to the point at which they will say something which the other is just beginning to formulate!

It is up to Pisceans' partners to encourage them to be practical and decisive, since sometimes they will tend to pass the buck, not wanting to worry too much about the consequences of their actions—or about financial decisions or other aspects of their lives which needs a practical decision.

If things go wrong, they can become extremely evasive, vague and deceptive, so it is again up to their partners to recognise that they will take an easy way out of a tricky situation if it presents itself. Their reason for doing this is often that they do not wish to hurt their partner; but it is much better to aim always to be straightforward and uncomplicated, since one small complication often leads to another, and before they know where they are they have spun a web of intrigue from which it will be very difficult to release themselves.

Shared interests and good communication are essential in all permanent relationships, and particularly so when a Piscean is one of the partners.

☆ PARENT AND CHILD

Piscean parents can be a little too easy-going with their children, but will do everything possible to develop their potential. This will certainly take precedence over their own interests and inclinations, and it is almost as though the child will become their *alter ego*, especially if the youngster is artistic or has any interest to which he or she is totally dedicated.

At once, then, Pisceans will remember their own childhood, and perhaps a secret longing which was not fulfilled; the level of encouragement they give the child will be well above average, and even if the parent is poor, enough money will be scraped together to allow the child to have proper training. Unfortunately it is all too easy for clever young children to twist their parents around their fingers, and Pisceans are a prime candidate for this; they must be aware that it can happen.

As to more practical matters, Piscean parents must also appreciate the fact that in the eyes of their children they can be quite infuriating at times, their evasiveness and sometimes even well-intentioned kindness putting their children in an invidious position, not knowing where they stand where morals are concerned, or how to cope with difficult situations.

Piscean parents are at their best when making their children aware of the beauties of nature and art, and encouraging them to be sensitive to the needs of others, especially in circumstances of suffering.

It is absolutely essential to encourage a Piscean child to be straightforward and honest. This may not be as easy as with children of some other signs, for you may well find that young Pisces, in order not to hurt or upset you, will tend from a very early age to tell a few minor untruths. This really needs a lot of gentle but very firm correction, for

it is in the child's own interest to have a potentially negative trait under control.

There is usually a strong creative streak in youngsters of this sign, so do encourage them to draw and take photographs—give them a cheap camera as soon as they are able to use it. Their imagination can be fostered in all kinds of ways, and if they are at all scientific they should be encouraged towards those areas of science which allow a free expression of this quality.

They may appear to be a little lazy at school; this is probably because they are living in their own dream world, identifying with characters and creatures from fairy stories and mythology. This is all right to some extent, but can lead to suffering when harsh reality catches up with them. They should be made aware that this can be the case. Try to guard them against school bullies, or teachers insensitive to their finer imaginative qualities. They will make good progress provided they develop straightforwardness and do everything possible to increase their powers of concentration.

☆ CAREER AND SPARE-TIME

Assuming that Pisces has developed self-confidence and recognises the fact that the practical, materialistic areas of life must be coped with, he or she will be in a good position to make a mark on the world—and in a variety of ways.

Many follow professions which allow them scope to work in some way 'behind the scenes', with other people actually showing off the end-product. We find Pisceans as wonderful nurses, and in various other branches of the medical profession; there is a strong traditional link, too, between Pisces and the Church. Some have a real vocation for the priesthood, and many become lay-preachers. Taken to an extreme, it is not uncommon for a Piscean to withdraw completely from society, and become a monk or nun. But the caring professions in general are well represented within this sign.

It is interesting that the theatre is also well represented among typical Piscean professions. This may usually be a medium for people who 'show off' and want to take centre stage; but when a Piscean becomes an actor or dancer, they are in many ways hiding behind a public persona, for in interpreting a role they are taking on the character in the play or ballet, and it is this element of disguise that is psychologically fulfilling for them. Many make superb comedians,

impersonators and mimics. They may turn to the fashion trade or the cosmetic industry, and counselling will also attract them.

We must not forget the fact that this, like Gemini and Sagittarius, is a *dual* zodiac sign. Sometimes we discover Pisceans who follow more than one career simultaneously—diversification is the spice of life to them. Basically they are versatile, and provided that versatility is controlled they can achieve much. If they make their career in business, they will be shrewd and clever, but in general it will be the influence of other signs and planets in their birth-chart (the map of the sky for the precise time and place of their birth) that will underpin a conventional career.

As Pisces rules the feet it is worth the individual working in the shoe trade, considering taking up shoe-design (if they are creative), chiropody, or reflexology.

If at all possible, Pisceans should try to involve themselves in a career which has variety and reasonably flexible working hours. While they may find security in a predictable job, it may be that they could also find this somewhat claustrophobic and stifling. They certainly need direction, which they can take extremely well, and must be shrewd enough to learn how their superiors cope with authority and decision-making; in due course, if they are good at what they do (which will probably be the case) they will be likely to have the opportunity for promotion.

Pisceans really must be encouraged to use their spare-time to develop their enormous potential; when they feel the merest glimmer of interest in a subject, they should give themselves the opportunity to develop a skill, and their friends and partners must if necessary nag them out of the excuses they will set up in order to avoid this. They will be quite likely to say that they 'haven't the time', that their children exhaust them, or that in any case they really wouldn't be very good at it . . . Such excuses, however true or untrue, should not be allowed to prevail—Pisceans produce them because they lack the self-confidence simply to dive into some new project.

It is particularly good, psychologically, for Pisceans to attend some kind of dance or movement class. Yoga is excellent, as is any spare-time commitment which will help them centre their personality and develop inner strength. All kinds of creative craft-work are to be recommended; flower-arranging—they do wonders with dried flowers and grasses; caring for small pets, and fishing. Pisceans are often avid readers, and great appreciators of poetry in particular. The latter is yet another art-form which should be encouraged if an aptitude is shown for it. Being involved in a group such as a charity, or a movement such as that for nuclear disarmament, will also be interesting and worthwhile, for these are the peacemakers of the zodiac.

☆ FINANCE AND INVESTMENT

Thinking of the main characteristics—strengths and weaknesses—of this sign, we are strongly tempted to say, when it comes to finance and investment, simply 'Don't!' *Don't* have anything to do with the management of your own money, *don't* take financial risks, *don't* be tempted by the glib tongues of those who try to tell you they have a good, quick tip or money-making scheme.

Pisceans can, on the whole, be very gullible and easily parted from their money, and unless they fall into that rare category of people who are tremendously shrewd and artful, and who because of their background and training have a quick eye for an investment, we would strongly advise them to seek professional help from bank managers and accountants when dealing with long-term commitments, and from more practical friends or partners before making any important purchase or working out a budget for their living expenses.

This does not mean to say that there are no wealthy Pisceans! Quite the reverse, in fact; but it is often the case that those of this sign who have made the grade financially have done so through their ability to 'produce the goods'—through creativity and practical effort, and not because of cool, calculating financial prowess. And it is common for such successful Pisceans to be backed up by a bevy of advisors.

Pisceans must learn to recognise the fact that others will realise that they are 'an easy touch', and that should a friend approach them with a money-making scheme, particularly perhaps if they like the individual concerned, they may allow personal feelings to overwhelm caution. However, that having been said, they are unlikely to take much notice of our friendly warnings! They usually have to learn the hard way in such situations. Their tendency to feel sorry for people will sometimes allow them to lend money to friends or even near-strangers against their better judgement. Alas, they don't always get it back. At such times they should allow their charitable nature a different kind of expression. It will be much better to give the person in need a small sum than to lend them a larger amount which may never be returned.

It is obvious that Pisceans should plump for the simplest possible forms of investment when they have any spare cash. This is particularly good for them, for if they can be brave enough to tuck it out of the way, it will work for them, and they will be less likely to fritter it away on pleasing inessentials. Building Society or National Savings bonds are a particularly good idea; if they wish to be a little more adventurous, the fishing industry, shipping lines, private medicine or pharmaceuticals and footwear manufacturing are suitable areas for investment. Women might consider buying stock in department stores or the cosmetic industry.

But the key-word is CAUTION.

☆ HEALTH AND EXERCISE

The Piscean system, on the whole, is a somewhat sensitive one; perhaps because more than they realise, Pisceans are unconsciously affected by atmosphere and the reactions of others. Although they may shrug off an unkind word, or some small injustice, it is often the case that these can have a negative *physical* effect, and as a result they can get headaches, suffer from slight digestive problems, or simply feel that they are 'not very well'.

The Piscean body area is the feet. Pisceans either have particularly beautiful feet, and can wear fashion shoes with impunity, or exactly the reverse. They can suffer from bunions, blisters and so on, and can never get shoes to fit them. This being so, we often find them going barefoot or even in inclement weather wearing exercise sandals perhaps with thick socks to keep out the cold.

Their ruling planet, Neptune, is related to the general nervous system, and in particular the thalamus—a structure in the brain that plays a vital part in transmitting stimuli to and from the sensory organs—hence the sensitivity of their whole beings to prevailing conditions and atmospheres.

It cannot be too strongly emphasised that Pisceans are prone to respond negatively to medically-administered drugs. They should watch their reactions to antibiotics, in particular, and even aspirin may have a negative effect. Interestingly, many will fight shy of using drugs altogether, and if they feel this way they might look at the possibilities offered by homoeopathy and alternative medicine.

When the Piscean experiences a period of stress, he or she is most vulnerable where drugs are concerned; under such conditions their natural caution will vanish, and a tendency to escapism is likely to emerge, so that they may attempt to find release through alcohol, cigarettes and hallucinatory drugs. This can spell even greater danger for them than for members of other signs, since their tendency towards addiction is stronger. We cannot too strongly urge them to bear this in

mind, and encourage readers with Pisceans friends to be aware of the danger, particularly when the Piscean's life goes wrong, or there are difficult problems to face.

One of the best antidotes to Piscean problems and a way to inner contentment is through a study of yoga. The physical side of the discipline will be superb exercise for them, and yoga will also help them to centre themselves, psychologically, so that when they are under stress they will be far less likely to slip into any form of negative escapism.

Pisceans usually most enjoy rhythmical, steady and non-competitive sport and exercise. Those with energy to spare will perhaps be sympathetic to the elegance of fencing or the speed of squash or tennis. They generally make excellent swimmers (and this, as the most comprehensive form of exercise, is fully recommended). Dance classes, and ice-skating, might also be considered. Those who have classical ballet classes as children should be encouraged to carry on with them as long as possible.

Although we do not necessarily think of Pisces as being a particularly accident-prone sign, they tend to be at risk when helping others. For instance, if they see someone drowning they may all too readily throw off their clothes and dive in without considering whether their swimming skill, let alone their life-saving technique, is strong enough to cope with the situation. It is on occasions such as these that they are at risk. Rather differently, they should be specially careful when driving, because of their distinct tendency to day-dream. If they are in a car by themselves, they may well drift off into their own delicious private world, waking up to find that they have not been conscious of the road for several miles.

In order for Pisceans to keep healthy they should be thoroughly aware of the sensitivity of their system, and strengthen this as much as possible through exercise; if they can link creative forms of expression with the growth of physical energy they will achieve a double purpose. Any skill which develops powers of concentration—mind over matter—will be good for them. Aim at sure-footed balance, mental and physical.

☆ HOME ENVIRONMENT

Pisceans like to live on a coast, or at least near water; if there is a large willow-tree or perhaps a feathery silver birch overhanging the house, this will be pleasing. Sometimes they will create a delightful environment in a very poor district of an inner city area; in doing so they will

get to know local people and be in a position to help them—a way in which they can express their kindness and charity.

A Piscean home will always be a very interesting place to visit. It may not necessarily be very smart or fashionable, it may not even be very tidy, but the prevailing atmosphere will be one of ease and there will always be something attractive in the way of decoration, objects or paintings which will merit attention and study. If your Piscean friends have children, expect to see their little boots lined up in the hall, and their paintings tacked to the walls and cupboard doors.

You will be welcomed most warmly, and probably your Piscean friend will be full of apologies for one thing and another, and most concerned about your welfare. Try to get your host or hostess to relax, and reassure them that all is well, because then they too will enjoy the results of their efforts to entertain you, and these will have been considerable.

The home will probably give the impression of rambling space, even if it is quite small. It may be somewhat cluttered, but the clutter itself will be interesting. We are likely to find many beautiful books, for instance: poetry, collections of photographs, art books. There may be something refreshing and relaxing to look at, such as a lovely group of plants, a floral arrangement, or perhaps a small tank of tropical fish.

The floor may be sanded and polished, with contrasting shaggy rugs upon it; and you are likely to sink into deep cushions on an elderly settee. Pisceans often love to sit on the floor, and will certainly encourage you to use the best piece of furniture while they squat on a rug or a large bean-bag.

When Pisceans choose a wallpaper they will tend to centre on something which will add a depth of perspective to their home: this might be a somewhat meandering floral design or perhaps may include trees of various sizes. The wall itself will then seem less of a barrier than it actually is. Light-weight nylon or bead curtains or perhaps shutters of cane will often act as room-dividers; Pisces can then pull them across when dinner is over, disguising the chaos of a dining-table of used dishes. Velvet may be a prominent upholstery fabric, and the colours used will be pale pastels, green and grey being popular. Sometimes these are directly in contrast with very dark blue—one of the colours of the sign—or even a touch of exotic purple, dark red or black.

While the Piscean kitchen is likely to have a good washing-machine, maybe a dish-washer and all the modern appliances the individual can afford, it may well be extremely chaotic, not only because Pisces is in the throes of preparing a meal, but because they like to live in what to them is order and what to everyone else is chaos! They think they know where they put everything, but because of their tendency to flap it is quite likely to be somewhere totally different. Here is a type who will buy a cake-tin and keep a selection of spices in it.

You will certainly enjoy a good meal with a Piscean: they like to eat well, counting this among the sensual pleasures of life, and indeed look upon cooking as an art. The food will be quite rich, and there may be some exotic or unusual dish on the menu. Light wines will be enjoyed, perhaps the Austrian range, possibly slightly sweet. The dessert may well be a sweet, delicious pudding with a rich chocolate sauce, perhaps one of the reasons why Pisceans tend to put on weight rather easily! We know many Pisceans who choose very delicate, pretty china. In contrast, others will go for studio pottery, or for unusual design. The glassware may be translucent rather than transparant, and sometimes the cutlery can have strikingly original handles in wood or mother-of-pearl.

In the background, you may hear modern romantic ballads, the lyrics of which tell sad stories of love and loss! More classically, Chopin and the major Tchaikovsky ballet scores will be popular. On the walls will often be romantic landscapes—Corot may be a major choice—seascapes and river scenes; there may also be some early ikons, or religious paintings.

Relaxed comfort rather than elegance will reign in the bedroom. Bathrobes, kimonos, pairs of pretty slippers will be in evidence, as will a pile of extremely varied bedside books ranging from the erotic to the poetic and even the practical. Certainly a Bible or prayerbook will also be somewhere about, if your Piscean friend is of a religious disposition. In that case, there may also be a niche holding a statue of the Madonna, a patron saint, or perhaps a Buddhist or Hindu god, which apart from anything else will help the Piscean to relax, or aid meditation. It is here that Pisces will find the very necessary seclusion which must form a part of their lives.

If there is a garden, it will almost certainly have a lily-pond with some goldfish; maybe it will sport a fountain. There will probably be a nice collection of ferns or plants with a feathery foliage, and indeed if there is no garden it is this kind of plant that will find favour in the house: Pisceans are usually pretty good at plants, and will own more than most people.

☆ IMAGE

Clothes Pisceans look marvellous, whether dressed in rags or

inhabiting the latest Paris model. The women are brilliant at making an interesting effect: they will take a length of fabric and either fashion it quickly into an unusual garment, or drape it around themselves and by dint of clever folding and pinning give the impression of being an excitingly dressed woman of fashion.

But they must be careful. Rather like their water-sign sisters, the Cancerians, they can mar their image by slight carelessness. If they have made the garment themselves, tacks, pins or an unfinished hem will too often be on view to critical eyes.

Pisceans look their best in soft fabrics such as wool and pure silk crêpe, or maybe translucent ones such as georgette. Sometimes they favour an ethnic look, and this suits them well. Generally they will give the impression of dressing in a slightly unusual and original way. They are not usually slaves of fashion, unless their lifestyle demands it.

Many Piscean men own an elderly, much-loved velvet jacket. Certainly the texture of velvet is extremely flattering, giving them a slightly poetic look.

You can usually recognise a Piscean by their feet. Glance down, and they may be standing with feet crossed—a decided representation of the fish's tail. Their shoes may break down as a result and become shapeless rather earlier than might be expected, so don't be surprised if you meet an interestingly well-dressed Piscean with rather scruffy footwear. We have already pointed out that they either have a lot of trouble with their feet, or none at all; and they should choose their shoes accordingly. At all events, shoes are of above-average importance.

Hats are not particularly important to Piscean—like some other groups, they can take them or leave them alone—they may sport a fur-fabric hat in the coldest weather. Velvet berets suit the women well, and they might consider wearing one on a formal occasion.

Piscean eyes are a striking feature; they usually look as though they are ready to burst into tears—of joy, as much as of sorrow. This, of course, is related to the ever-present abundant emotion of the sign. Most Piscean women are consciously or unconsciously aware of the dynamic attraction they can express with their eyes, and will be very clever when experimenting with eye make-up. Ranges of colours that have an iridescent gleam are particularly popular. So we get a whole spectrum of colour, not unlike the beauty of fish-scales, enhancing the Piscean look.

Needless to say, Pisceans should have a good supply of beach-wear in their wardrobes—their liking for the sea and swimming will make this necessary. They should also make sure they have a good, thick beach-robe or towel, since their skin seems to collect more water than that of most other signs, and they tend to make their towels very wet indeed.

Extenders Perhaps the most important image-extender in which a Piscean can invest is a good camera—*ciné*, video or still. In many ways photography is very much a Piscean hobby, and it really is a very good idea for those of this sign to keep a camera at the ready when they are travelling, and to have a miniature camera in their handbag or the glove compartment of their car.

Pisces' handbags and briefcases should certainly be capacious; like members of some other signs, Pisceans need and indeed seem to collect a lot of 'necessities' which must be carried about with them. We venture to suggest that they invest in an 'organiser' handbag, so that they can put their necessities in compartments especially designed for them. But this may only work in theory, and not in practice, for the chances are that Pisces will use the compartments for anything but their intended purpose, so that the whole bag becomes even more cluttered than a conventional one. Shiny surfaces such as patent leathers and perhaps metallic finishes will be popular, and provided Pisceans are reasonably discreet in their choice of accessories, these will look well.

The metal of the sign is, sadly, tin; but what about looking at titanium? This gives off the whole colour range of the spectrum, and is particularly attractive to Piscean taste. Moonstones look marvellous on members of this sign.

Cars It is as well for Pisceans to aim to own a car which will give them a nice, smooth ride. While this is a water sign, they can more than many other zodiac types suffer from travel-sickness and especially if they are drivers who have to be passengers they may tend to worry a little too much about the quality of the driving. A car with a metallic finish—in, perhaps, silver-grey, pale blue or green—will be thought ideally attractive.

☆ TRAVEL

Because this is a water sign, it is likely that Pisceans will in some way want to be near water when on holiday. A seaside resort is an obvious answer, especially if it is somewhere quietly relaxing with a romantic atmosphere and in beautiful surroundings. But many Pisceans will

particularly enjoy a holiday on a river-boat or perhaps exploring inland waterways and canals.

A nostalgic trip down the Mississippi, or a magical cruise down the Rhine (with visits to the fairy-tale castles) would certainly stir the Piscean poetic imagination.

They will enjoy both cruising and camping, and often travel without a particularly rigid itinerary, since wandering aimlessly from place to place, either in a car, on a cycle or by boat, will give them a great deal of inner satisfaction and help restore them from the rigours of their day-to-day working lives. More than the average, Pisceans really do need to cut out and get away from it all, and should aim to do so whenever possible.

Here are members of a sign who will want to taste local delicacies; but sometimes their digestion is more sensitive than they realise, so (like many other zodiac types) they need to take their most effective remedies with them when they are abroad, whether visiting a highly civilised or a Third World country. Because they are not terribly good organisers, once Pisceans get to a resort they may well like to seek out the help of a local tour operator or travel agent; but they must be careful, since they will not care to be over-regimented on excursions, especially if they are rushed through places that interest them, only to spend for too long at some other, more commercial, location, completely devoid of interest. Rather a beautiful cathedral or palace, any time, than an underground salt mine. Bearing in mind that they are likely to get pretty foot-sore on long walking expeditions, they should be quite certain that they don't take new walking shoes or sandals with them.

The actual temperature will not worry Pisceans too much; it will be what the weather does to the landscape that will interest them. They will, for instance, like to look at a native village in bright sunshine and then perhaps return to it a few days later to find it under a dust-storm or perhaps surrounded by mist. They will brave the rigours of the local climate for the sake of experience, and that of seeing for themselves just how local people live.

When they are shopping they should search for locally woven or painted lengths of fabric: *batik* or tie-dying will attract them. They can have these made up when they return home.

Piscean children are not too difficult to please or keep amused when on holiday, for wherever their parents take them they will discover their own new world which will extend their individual inner imaginative life. They will inevitably benefit considerably from travel experiences. Parents will find that whether they visit the London Dungeon,

Disneyland or Chartres Cathedral young Pisceans will, at some future date, use their memories in a creative way, perhaps painting a picture, perhaps writing a poem, but certainly using the experience to enlarge their vision of life.

While obviously all parents should watch their young children carefully, Piscean children have a special talent for slipping into a dream state during which they can wander off in any available direction. This can of course be dangerous, and they should be tactfully shown the danger, and carefully watched, especially if they have little knowledge of the local language. Beautiful underground caves with stalactites, and deep forests will be thoroughly enjoyed. Pisceans should never be without a notebook and pencil or sketchbook in which to record their impressions.

Grown-ups and children alike may well be attracted to some expensive souvenir on the first day of their holiday. It will be as well to fight the temptation to buy it on the spot, which could leave them short of ready cash.

☆ PRESENTS TO PLEASE

It is usually not difficult to please a Piscean with a present: they will be delighted by the very fact that you have thought of them at all, and their immediate response will be 'Oh, but you shouldn't have!'

If you are visiting someone of this sign, you might like to present your host or hostess with a delicate potted plant, if you know that they enjoy owning plants. A box of Turkish Delight will be acceptable as an after-dinner treat, as would delicious crystallised fruits.

For a birthday or Christmas present, something made of silk or velvet will be thoroughly acceptable, or a piece of hand-made craftwork or delicate modern pottery. A present which will please many women of this sign would be an exotic pair of velvet or satin bedroom slippers with ostrich-feather trimmings. If we think of their love of the sea, something made of shell will very likely be to their taste—a tray, perhaps, or even a lamp. A piece of mother-of-pearl, too, would be welcome.

Most Pisceans of both sexes enjoy wearing toilet waters, and on the whole they cling to a particular brand. Obviously research is necessary into the taste of your own particular Piscean; but once you have discovered this, you cannot fail with this kind of present.

If you have to give a more important wedding gift or anniversary present, Pisces is one of the signs sympathetic to natural materials, so

★ FAVOURITE TO PISCES ★

★ **PISCEAN COUNTRIES**—include Scandinavia and Portugal, many small Mediterranean islands, and the Sahara.

★ **PISCEAN CITIES**—include Alexandria, Seville, Compostella and Bournemouth.

★ **TREES**—Piscean trees include all those common to the seaside, or with a strong association with water—chiefly the willow.

★ **FLOWERS AND HERBS**—Water-lilies, and those attributed to Cancer and Sagittarius which flower in Piscean colours.

★ **FOODSTUFFS**—Those attributed to Cancer (see page 70).

★ **CELL SALTS**—Ferr. Phos. and Kali. Sulph.

★ **STONE**—Moonstone.

★ **COLOUR**—Soft sea-green.

you won't go far wrong with something made of wood, pure linen, cotton or wool. A beautiful blanket, duvet or quilt might well be popular, as would a set of cushions which fits in with the Piscean scheme of decoration. Like the members of their neighbouring sign, Aquarius, many enjoy the look of translucent glassware, modern glass and mirrors, so here too is ample scope.

To encourage them towards accuracy and precision in cooking, a set of measuring-spoons or traditional kitchen scales (perhaps the old-fashioned kind with a brass bowl and weights) might be a very good idea, and will take the guesswork out of measuring.

Piscean children will love to be given clothes in which to dress up, ballet shoes, and large books of fairy stories with particularly gorgeous illustrations. Older boys may be attracted to fishing, so something to improve their technique and collection of fishing tackle will more than likely be popular—but above all it is the child's abundant imagination that should be encouraged, so some basic play material which can be transformed into almost anything is a good idea. Very young children will particularly benefit from extremely simple toys, which their imagination can make into a car, a railway engine, Cinderella's coach or whatever. A sophisticated model car remains forever only a car.